ISRAEL IN SEARCH OF A WAR
The Sinai Campaign, 1955–1956

Israel in Search of a War

The Sinai Campaign, 1955–1956

———

Motti Golani

Foreword by
Avi Shlaim
St Antony's College
Oxford

sussex
ACADEMIC
PRESS

2 4 6 8 10 9 7 5 3 1

First published 1998 in Great Britain by
SUSSEX ACADEMIC PRESS
Box 2950
Brighton BN2 5SP

and in the United States of America by
SUSSEX ACADEMIC PRESS
c/o International Specialized Book Services, Inc.
5804 N.E. Hassalo St.
Portland, Oregon 97213-3644

British Library Cataloguing in Publication Data
A CIP catalogue record for this book is available from the British Library.

Library of Congress Cataloging-in-Publication Data
Golani, Motti.
Israel in search of a war : the Sinai Campaign, 1955–1956 / Motti Golani.
p.   cm.
Includes bibliographical references and index.
ISBN 1–898723–46–X (h/c : alk. paper). — ISBN 1–898723–47–8 (p/b: alk. paper)
1. Sinai Campaign. 1956.   I. Title.
DS110.5.G634   1998
956.04′4—dc21   97–39710
CIP

Printed by Biddles Ltd, Guildford and King's Lynn
This book is printed on acid-free paper

Contents

Foreword

The conventional wisdom about Israeli foreign policy can be summed up in two Hebrew words: *ein breira* – there is no alternative. This view pictures Israel as the defensive party that resorts to force only because the implacable hostility and active belligerence of her Arab neighbours leave her no other choice. According to this view, Israel's foreign policy is not chosen by her but largely imposed on her by a uniquely harsh and hostile regional environment. All Israel's wars, this view maintains, have been defensive wars, undertaken reluctantly in response to an Arab attack or in the expectation of an imminent Arab attack.

This traditional view could not be easily sustained in relation to Israel's invasion of Lebanon in 1982. Israel enjoyed overwhelming military superiority over all her Arab neighbours and the PLO fighters in southern Lebanon posed no threat to her basic security. Israel went to war not because her existence was threatened but in pursuit of various other objectives such as the defeat of Palestinian nationalism and the creation of a new political order in Lebanon. Menachem Begin, the head of the Likud government that launched this war, almost admitted as much in an address he gave to the IDF Staff Academy soon after the war. In this address Begin divided Israel's wars into two categories: wars of no choice and wars of choice. The 1948 War, the June 1967 War, the 1969–70 War of Attrition between Israel and Egypt, and the October 1973 War were all described as wars of no choice. The Lebanon War of 1982 and the Sinai Campaign of 1956, on the other hand, were described as wars of choice in the sense that they were not imposed on Israel but initiated by her in pursuit of various national objectives. With this admission, unprecedented in the history of the Zionist movement, the national consensus round the notion of *ein breira* began to crumble, thereby creating the space for a critical reexamination of Israel's earlier wars. The declassification of a vast quantity of official documents under the thirty-year rule greatly helped in this process of review and reevaluation.

The last decade saw the publication of several books by revisionist

Israeli historians or 'new' historians as they are sometimes called. Most of this literature focuses on the creation of the State of Israel and on the first Arab–Israeli war. The new historians have challenged many of the claims of the traditional Zionist rendition of events. They challenged the claim that the military balance in 1948 overwhelmingly favoured the Arabs; that the Palestinian refugees left of their own free will; that all the neighbouring Arab countries were united in their determination to prevent the establishment of a Jewish state; and that Arab intransigence was alone responsible for the persistent political deadlock after the guns fell silent.

Motti Golani is a young Israeli historian whose work has focused on the second Arab–Israeli war which is usually called the Suez War in the West and the Sinai Campaign in Israel. His book *Israel in Search of a War: The Sinai Campaign, 1955–1956* is an original and important contribution to the study of Israel's early history. The book has many strengths. It is based on careful and comprehensive research, especially in the Israel State Archives and in the IDF Archive. The arguments and conclusions are supported by strong evidence from primary sources, some of which is used here for the first time. It sheds a great deal of new light not just on the war itself but on related subjects such as civil-military relations in Israel, the policy-making process in defence and foreign affairs, the extraordinary influence exerted by Chief of Staff Moshe Dayan in pushing Israel into war, and the collusion with Britain and France which preceded the attack on Egypt.

Last but no least, Dr Golani shows honesty and courage in following the evidence to its logical conclusion, regardless of how damaging it might be to the official or semi-official Israeli version of this war. As the title of his book suggests, Dr Golani holds that the 1956 war was not imposed on Israel by her enemies but deliberately sought by her. Although the Czech arms deal announced in September 1955 began to tip the military balance in Egypt's favour, the balance was restored by secret arms acquisitions from France and in October 1956 Israel did not face any imminent threat of Egyptian attack or any other serious threat to her basic security. Israel's motives for embarking on this military venture included the consolidation of the alliance with France, territorial expansion, the overthrow of Gamal Abdel Nasser, and the establishment of a new political order in the Middle East. Whatever else it might have been, the Sinai Campaign was not for Israel a war of *ein breira*.

Avi Shlaim
St Antony's College, Oxford

Preface

The Suez Crisis in 1956 was one of the defining events of the Cold War era. Its ramifications, though, go beyond its impact on global inter-bloc relations and extend also to other spheres of crucial importance in historical perspective. It forced France and Britain to come to terms with the fact that the age of classical imperialism had passed forever; generated a dangerous rift in NATO by disrupting the Anglo-French alliance with the United States; and caused the intensification of the Israeli-Egyptian conflict. It is the last point which forms the subject of this book. The road to the crisis and the war – the Suez Crisis and its culmination in the Sinai War – are analysed here from the Israeli perspective.

Israel became involved in the crisis on a completely independent basis. To the Israel of 1956, the motives that induced Britain and France to attack Egypt were of no relevance. Why, then, did Israel agree to assume the role of *provocateur* and provide "yesterday's Powers" with the pretext to attack Egypt?

In an attempt to understand Israel's motives, I examined the dilemmas that confronted Israel from the beginning of 1955 – it was then that David Ben-Gurion, the young state's "founding father", returned from voluntary exile at Kibbutz Sde Boker in the southern desert wilderness. My research led me to conclude that Israel had been "in search of a war" before the onset of the Suez Crisis and without any connection to it. It was not by chance that some in Israel began to entertain the possibility of an Israeli-initiated war upon Ben-Gurion's return to the government. The option of such a war had been raised by the army. Lt. General Moshe Dayan, the Chief of Staff from 1953 to 1958, maintained that Israel's survival was contingent on its defeating Egypt, the leader of the Arab world, in a "second round". A victorious Israel could then enter peace talks from a position of strength. The Israeli army considered the outcome of the "first round" in 1948–1949 (Israel's War of Independence) intolerable, a situation Israel could not live with. Dayan won Ben-Gurion's support for his approach. However, this was not enough. Despite Israel's unsteady security situation, it was not possible to muster a Cabinet majority for the policy espoused by Dayan and Ben-Gurion until the spring of 1956.

The Israeli military wanted a war; but to create a suitable "war coalition" at home the military chiefs needed the support of an external Power that would supply Israel with arms and give it backing in the international arena. France's readiness to provide both elements in return for Israeli support of its struggle against Egyptian President Nasser – whom the French believed was behind the surging revolt in Algeria – gave Israel what it considered the necessary foundation for going to war against Egypt. Like Israel, then, France had a score to settle with Egypt that antedated the Suez Crisis and was in no way connected with it.

The determination of British Prime Minister Anthony Eden to punish Egypt militarily for nationalising the Suez Canal Company in July 1956 gave the French and Israeli planners the international framework they sought. The Suez Crisis, the timing of the war and its conduct – these issues affected only Britain, France and Egypt. Israel involved itself for its own reasons, but under Anglo-French conditions.

This study focuses on the Israeli decision to go to war, on the view from Israel of the run-up to the campaign waged by the tripartite coalition against Egypt and on Israel's political and military collaboration with France and Britain during the war itself. It was my privilege to be the first to unearth a wealth of pertinent archival material, primarily of the Israeli defense establishment, which was the dominant factor in Israel's embarkation on the road to war. I have also made use of much previously unexamined French and British material. I have tried not to defend the Israeli position in every case, but at the same time to be empathetic towards the young state's adversities, although I know that lapses are inevitable. In any event, I have endeavoured to fulfill the historian's obligation to be neutral without pretending to be objective. The Suez Crisis and the Sinai War are simultaneously a historical event and a still-unstaunched wound in Britain and France as well as in Egypt and Israel. The historian is therefore compelled to exercise more than the usual dose of caution.

It is my pleasant duty to thank those who helped me bring this work to completion. I am grateful to my friend and mentor Professor Yoav Gelber from the University of Haifa for the advice and the extensive knowledge which he continues to share with me; to Dr. Mordechai Bar-On, a veteran of the period covered by the book and more recently one of its pre-eminent students, who interweaves testimony and research so adeptly; to Professor Keith Kyle, from the Royal Institute of International Affairs (Chatham House) in London, who guided me expertly through the labyrinth of British policy; and to Professor Avi

Shlaim from the Middle East Centre of St Antony's College, Oxford, for his consistently insightful counsel. My unbounded gratitude to Dr Emanuel Lotem, who translated the book patiently and knowledgeably into English; and my heartfelt thanks to Mr Ralph Mandel from Jerusalem for his skilful editing of the English text and for plying me with astute queries. I owe a special debt of thanks to Anita and Anthony Grahame of Sussex Academic Press in Brighton, England, who saw the book through the press with devotion and forbearance. The Yad Avi Hayishuv Foundation in Jerusalem, the Research Authority of the University of Haifa and the Association for the Heritage of Moshe Sharett, Israel's second Prime Minister, made possible the book's translation. I am grateful to them. Finally, the Center for Judaic Studies at the University of Pennsylvania and its director, Professor David Ruderman, provided me with a flawless research environment in which I was able to complete the manuscript.

My wife Sarki and my daughters Lior and Nizan gave me the necessary balance without which I could not have pursued the study to its conclusion.

Motti Golani
University of Haifa, Israel
June 1997

Israel in Search of a War

The Sinai Campaign, 1955–1956

1

Israel on the Road to War

Black Arrow

During 1954, a serious deterioration occurred in the security situation along Israel's borders, particularly with Egypt. Armed infiltration into Israel, masterminded by the Egyptian Army, was becoming increasingly frequent. At the same time, there was a rise in the number of firing incidents between Israeli and Egyptian troops, especially along the Gaza Strip boundary line.[1]

Israel finally decided that a forceful reaction was called for. The objective chosen – and not by accident – was an Egyptian Army camp, rather than a target of Palestinian infiltrators. On the night of February 28–March 1, the Israel Defence Forces (IDF) conducted a major retaliatory raid, code-named Operation Black Arrow, near the town of Gaza. IDF paratroopers raided a military camp near the Gaza railway station; the Egyptians returned fire, and the ensuing battle got rapidly out of hand. The paratroopers, having accomplished their mission (to destroy the camp), withdrew with 8 fatalities. In this firefight, and in a cut-off ambush laid by the raiders, 38 Egyptian soldiers were killed. Overall, the number of casualties on both sides far exceeded previous IDF operations.

Black Arrow had a major impact on subsequent developments in the Middle East. Yet a distinction should be made between Israel's actual intentions, which were rather limited, and Egyptian and international reaction to the raid, which was far harsher than Israel had anticipated. It was certainly an impressive operation, at least as outside observers saw it. Egyptian casualties were unusually high. Egypt's President Nasser subsequently claimed, on several occasions, that this operation had undermined his faith in Israel's peaceful intentions, hence his approach to the Soviet Union for arms. However, this offhand explanation cannot be taken seriously. Nasser's Egypt had broken off the secret contacts it had maintained with Israel prior to this raid; and similar indirect contacts would resume later on, under various auspices, even after the Czech–Egyptian arms deal (which became public knowledge in September 1955) had been signed. Any attempt by the Egyptian Army to curb infiltration from the Gaza Strip into Israel had long since ceased. War with Israel was never very low on Egypt's agenda, and Nasser had no need for a localised event such as Operation Black Arrow to decide on the arms deal with Czechoslovakia.[2]

By Israel's lights, the Gaza raid was part and parcel of its standing policy of retaliation against any of its neighbours that harboured Palestinian infiltrators; the operation was not deemed by its planners to have any unusual significance. It merited just a few lines in the diaries of both Ben-Gurion and Dayan. Instructing the IDF Spokesman to issue a false statement about the raid, Defence Minister Ben-Gurion sought to explain away the entire operation as a vigorous local reaction by an Israeli patrol to an Egyptian provocation.[3]

The aftershock of Operation Black Arrow, therefore, took Israeli leaders by surprise. They were especially dismayed by the severity of international reaction. Having been excluded from all the various alliances created by the West in the Middle East, Israel felt itself uniquely vulnerable. The situation had become even bleaker since October 1954, when Egypt and Britain signed an agreement for the withdrawal of British troops from the Suez Canal Zone. Since then, Israel had faced the prospect of losing the "British buffer" between itself and mainland Egypt. Added to this were initial reports of the Anglo-American Plan Alpha, in which Israel would be called upon to make major territorial concessions for peace. And now, following the Gaza raid, the international community (a term virtually identical in the Israeli mind at the time with the Western powers) excoriated Israel for its aggressiveness.

That reaction, in turn, had its impact on an internal power struggle within Israel's top leadership, between Ben-Gurion and Prime Minister Moshe Sharett. The two leaders were constantly at odds over the road Israel should take in order to secure peace and guarantee its survival. Whereas Sharett insisted that patience and moderation would eventually bring about Arab acceptance of Israel's existence, the Defence Minister took the position, at least since his return to the government in early 1955, that only another military blow, preferably aimed at Egypt as the leading Arab country, would convince the Arabs that Israel was here to stay, so they might as well make peace.

At the time of the Gaza operation, Ben-Gurion had been back in office for less than a week. He saw no difference between this raid and similar ones he had ordered in the past, and its sharp international repercussions had not been intended. In any event, the real turning point in his perception of the situation, and consequently in his view of how Israel should conduct itself, came shortly afterwards. As of late March 1955, Israel's defence policy underwent a veritable transformation. Although the methods used for retaliation remained basically unchanged, the motive was now completely different: in place of the tit-for-tat approach in an effort to calm the frontier, Israel would attempt to escalate retaliation into war.

The "Insider"

Ben-Gurion's return to the Ministry of Defence, his awkward relationship with the moderate Sharett and the fact that he could rely on the firm support of the Chief of Staff, Lt.-General Moshe Dayan, for his hard-line policy made for a far more vigorous political climate in Israel. Escalation was looking for an excuse to happen, and it presented itself towards the end of March.

On the night of March 24–25, the guests at a marriage ceremony held in a private home in the new immigrants' village of Patish in southern Israel were gathered in one room to celebrate. The room was well-lit. Suddenly, hand-grenades were thrown into the room and shots were fired. One guest, a woman, was killed, and about 20 people were wounded, including several children. The perpetrators' footprints were tracked to the Gaza Strip.

Significantly, the young woman who was killed was not a new immigrant. She was from Kfar Vitkin, a well-established village in central Israel, and had come to Patish as a volunteer, to help the new immigrants adjust to their new country. It was a shocking attack – much more than previous incidents, if we may judge from the reactions of Israel's three major policy makers: Ben-Gurion, Sharett, and Dayan. Beyond the outrage over an attack on innocent civilians celebrating a happy occasion on sovereign Israeli soil, the victim's identity generated an unusually strong reaction among the leadership. Varda Friedman was an "insider", her family belonged to the social stratum that produced Israel's ruling elite, and the group of volunteers of which she was a member had been organised by Dayan himself, whose background in fact was quite similar to her own.

Ben-Gurion's reaction to the Patish incident was quite unusual, for both its "level of reprisal" and its obvious warlike thrust. He proposed, literally, to drive the Egyptians out of the Gaza Strip – in short, to conquer the Gaza Strip. Before presenting this idea to the Prime Minister and the Cabinet, Ben-Gurion had put three questions to the Chief of Staff, which clearly indicated that he was well aware of the proposal's import:

1   How long will it take [the IDF] to conquer the Gaza Strip?
2   Is the IDF ready for war against Egypt?
3   Is the IDF ready for war against all the Arab countries?

Dayan was actively seeking a dynamics of escalation. A strong Israeli reaction to the next few terrorist attacks originating in Egypt could, he felt, bring the two countries to the brink of war.[4]

Did Ben-Gurion and Dayan want to take advantage of the consensus on the need to retaliate for Patish in order to launch a full-scale attack on Egypt, which they regarded as the chief confrontation state? Apparently, they did. By his own testimony, Ben-Gurion wanted to use the occasion to settle a long-standing account with Nasser, which included numerous Egyptian violations of the Israeli-Egyptian armistice agreement of 1949, as well as a blockade which Cairo had imposed on Israeli navigation in the Gulf of Eilat and the Suez Canal.

In contrast to previous occasions, Ben-Gurion's reaction to Patish not only included an order to initiate a military operation, but also specified the target and the objective. Customarily, the military would submit a proposed action to the Minister of Defence. The latter would either approve the plan and forward it to the Prime Minister, or reject it on the spot. Ben-Gurion now took a different route: he himself formulated a proposal by which Israel would initiate the first step in an escalation process intended to culminate in war. The cards were now on the table; the weekly Cabinet meeting which followed the Patish murder was the first since 1948 to seriously address the question of whether Israel had reasonable cause to launch a war.

As Sharett confided to his diary, Ben-Gurion was quite vehement at the meeting, stating that he was not speaking just for the record: he really wanted to persuade his colleagues. Still, he had apparently not worked out the matter fully in his own mind at that juncture – otherwise it is difficult to explain some of the phrases he used, such as "we shall drive them away in disgrace", when fears of British intervention were expressed, or his reply to Sharett's prediction that economic sanctions would be imposed on Israel and the refugee problem aggravated: "We will muddle through." Ben-Gurion understood the import of such questions. Did he shrug them off because he did not bear, at the time, ultimate national responsibility, being "only" Minister of Defence? Whatever the reason, there was one person even more convinced than Ben-Gurion himself of the usefulness of an Israeli-initiated war: Chief of Staff Dayan.[5]

"A Near-Insane Derring-Do"

Two persons brought Ben-Gurion back from semi-retirement to the helm of Israel's defence: Moshe Dayan and Shimon Peres, in their official capacities as Chief of the General Staff and Director-General of the Ministry of Defence, respectively. Both personally loyal to the "Old Man", they also exercised an unusual influence on him and saw eye-to-eye in all matters involving Israel's security. Upon returning to the Ministry of Defence, Ben-Gurion immediately set up a team of three – himself, Dayan and Peres – which he called "the inner staff". Ben-Gurion convened the forum on a weekly basis (usually on Thursdays), inviting others according to the subject at hand. This trio led Israel's quest for "a second round", with Dayan usually in the forefront.[6]

Moshe Dayan, the IDF's fourth Chief of Staff, had an extraordinary influence on the political system to which he was formally accountable. Not even Yigael Yadin, a former Chief of Staff who would become a renowned archaeologist – and a Ben-Gurion favourite – had wielded as much political clout as Dayan did in the mid-1950s as holder of the top military position in the land.

Dayan was hardly an obscure army officer when Ben-Gurion appointed him Chief of Staff on 6 December 1953, one day before his retirement to a remote kibbutz, Sde Boker, in the Negev desert. Dayan's political skills were already manifest in 1949 when, as military commander of Jerusalem, he took a leading role in shaping a series of agreements with Jordan – first in discussions with his opposite number on the spot, later at the armistice negotiations held in Rhodes. As his career progressed – head of Northern Command, then Southern Command, and afterward as Chief of General Staff Branch – the opinionated Dayan never made a secret of his views on matters lying well outside his military brief.

Dayan was born into Mapai, the ruling party at the time, from which the present-day Israeli Labour Party evolved. Both his parents represented Mapai in the Knesset, Israel's parliament; indeed, his father, Shmuel, was a Knesset Member (MK) at the time Moshe became Chief of Staff. Moshe Dayan himself had been elected to represent his party in the Constituent Assembly, the forerunner of the Knesset, before it was decided to bar officers in active service from holding membership in elected political organs. Nevertheless, he took part, though not as a member, in various Mapai deliberations. His hard-line stance on defence affairs was well-known. Hence his appointment by Ben-Gurion as Chief of Staff. On the same day, Ben-Gurion made another calculated move: he appointed Shimon Peres Director-General of the Ministry of Defence. These two "Ben-Gurion youngsters" took it upon themselves to keep the self-exiled Ben-Gurion abreast of political and defence developments.[7]

Dayan, then, was forced on the new Prime Minister, Sharett, who had every reason to regard him as a Ben-Gurion loyalist. Worse, though, was the fact that Sharett both mistrusted and feared Dayan. Sharett saw in the Chief of Staff's hard-line attitude a real threat to Israel's security. Yet dearly as Sharett would have liked to remove Dayan, all he could do was to control his decisions and actions. In any event, he could not bring himself to rescind an appointment made by Ben-Gurion, Israel's founding father.[8]

Time and again, Sharett thwarted Dayan's tough proposals, which he saw as entailing far more than a desire to punish the perpetrators of robbery and murder. Dayan for his part took a dim view of Sharett's attitude; the Prime Minister, he believed, would do "anything to prevent war". His own approach was different: "Anything but compromise Israel's vital interests, even if it means war." If freedom of navigation or the right to use water from the Jordan River for irrigation were vital interests, then they must be insisted upon – and if the Arabs should initiate hostilities as a result, then so be it. Peres took his cue from Dayan, arguing that to place current security uppermost is like "mending one's shirt when one's body is in danger". Their position on the problem of infiltration and retaliation was similar: reprisals must hurt, otherwise they are meaningless – even if there is a danger of escalation to war.[9]

Dayan never spoke about an Israeli-initiated war in so many words before April 1955, but this had always been the real thrust of his entire posture, which was in no way "hysterical", as Sharett tended to describe it. Nor did Dayan favour a tough reaction for its own sake – for him, it was always a means to an end. He possessed, said Ben-Gurion, "a near insane derring-do, tempered by profound tactical and strategic calculation". Dayan made no effort to hide his views from outsiders. As he explained to CIA chief Allan Dulles during a visit to the United States in July–August 1954, Israel had very good reasons to seek war – notably its inconvenient boundaries and the Arab countries' rapid military build-up. Nevertheless, as he hastened to reassure his interlocutor (in accordance with government policy), Israel did not pursue a policy of warmongering. Although true at the time Dayan spoke, this ceased to be the case as 1955 went on.[10] By then, Dayan had become convinced that another all-Arab war against Israel was imminent and that Israel could survive only by initiating war first, at a time of its choosing and on its terms.

No War without an Ally

Dayan knew that as long as Sharett held the reins of government his policy would remain on paper only. Hence his desire for Ben-Gurion to return to government, and the sooner the better. But he would soon find Ben-Gurion, too, reluctant to push a hard-line approach over the brink of war. The "Old Man" needed persuading, but this turned out to be not so difficult. A dynamic of mutual influence developed between these two leaders, with each alternating in taking the lead. In fact, Dayan was fulfilling Ben-Gurion's hidden wishes by pushing forward ideas which the "Old Man" dared not or could not bring to the fore himself.[11]

Dayan had been able to persuade Ben-Gurion to return to government chiefly by arguing that Sharett's "softline" policies were an existential danger to Israel, besides fomenting much discontent in the IDF. According to Dayan, even a peace agreement which would leave Israel in its present circumstances was undesirable. With no control over its water sources, unable to use its southern maritime outlet to the Red Sea, and pressed by hard-to-defend boundaries, Israel must not accept a peace agreement based on the 1949 armistice lines. But neither, under those circumstances, could Israel afford to let the Arabs start another war against it – a "second round", in the parlance of the time.

Thus, Ben-Gurion's willingness to return to government at the end of February 1955 was a clear signal that he concurred with Dayan. However, he conditioned his advocacy of an Israeli-initiated war on Israel's securing an alliance with a foreign power which would support Israel in such a war. Ben-Gurion held that Israel could not bear the burden of war alone, either politically or militarily. In the past, he had reacted with cautious reluctance to the war idea, but he now began actively to seek a "mutual defence pact" (as he insisted on calling it) with the United States.

Linkage between an Israeli-initiated war and an alliance with a foreign power became a firm foundation of Ben-Gurion's foreign policy. Whenever the possibility of such a war was discussed, Ben-Gurion insisted on the need to obtain international guarantees for Israel's security.[12] It should be pointed out, since this is a key to understanding most of Ben-Gurion's moves during the next 18 months, that one of his major reasons for seeking such an alliance was his fear of air raids on Israeli civilian population centres. Having spent a few months in London during the Blitz, he believed that the Israeli population would not be able to withstand a similar onslaught. The need for an "umbrella", meaning reliable air cover for Israeli territory, was uppermost in his mind – and he never placed much trust in the ability of the Israel Air Force to provide it.

In retrospect, then, the spring of 1955 saw the launching of a new Israeli defence policy. Its foundations would be built upon during the following months, according to circumstances and accumulated experience. Eventually, this new policy would come to fruition, a year and a half after its inception, in the form of the Sinai War.

On the Brink of War

We cannot fully explain the motives behind Egypt's actions along the Gaza Strip border during much of 1955 – which consisted mainly of sporadic fire, mine-laying and ambushes of Israeli patrols – although this activity brought the two countries ever closer to the brink of war. Was this Egypt's real intention? It seems doubtful, but no satisfactory explanation seems to offer itself. Egyptian President Gamal Abdel Nasser claimed that his troops felt threatened following the Gaza raid, and therefore were more prone to open fire. He could not, as he told the UN Chief of Observers, General E.L.M. Burns, instruct his army to desist.[13] Correspondingly, IDF reactions in this sector became more violent during the spring of 1955. Still, we must assume that there was more to this situation than a mere desire to respond in kind locally.

From early April to mid-May, the Gaza Strip frontier was relatively quiet, and Dayan found no pretext to launch any sizable operation. The few border incidents that did take place, some of them Israeli initiatives, did not involve casualties – and in the past casualties had often determined the scope of Israeli retaliations. The Chief of Staff kept Ben-Gurion constantly briefed on the situation along the borders, trying to spur him to act. At the time, though, the Minister of Defence was less worried than either the Prime Minister or the Chief of Staff by current security problems. Sharett and Dayan showed far greater concern over possible escalation due to border incidents,[14] the former viewing it as a danger, the latter as a prospect. Ben-Gurion's mind dwelt on larger matters.

With all that, the frontier did not remain quiet for any length of time. After three IDF officers were killed when their vehicle hit a land mine on the patrol road, on May 17, Israel launched another major retaliatory raid, the first since Operation Black Arrow.

Then suddenly there was calm. During the following months, until mid-August, no significant incident was recorded on the Israeli-Egyptian border.[15] Again, it is difficult to pinpoint the reasons for Egypt's policy shift. As noted above, we have no direct knowledge of Nasser's motives – just a short time earlier he had flatly refused to commit himself to pacifying the border – although Egypt's behaviour may have been connected with moves then afoot to bring its arms deal with Czechoslovakia to a successful conclusion. Be that as it may, in late June Nasser authorised Colonel Saleh Gohar, head of the Palestine Desk in Egypt's Ministry of War, to conduct, on his behalf, negotiations with Israel for a localised agreement to terminate border incidents. The "Gaza talks", which went on till mid-August 1955, contributed to tranquillity by their very existence. The dynamics of the so-called "local commanders' agreement" were far more important than the results, which were negligible. Nevertheless, one thing remains clear: while this give-and-take went on, there was no attempt, either by Egypt or Israel, to heat up the frontier.[16]

Ben-Gurion's restraint during this period was due in the main to the election campaign then under way. Retaliation and electioneering were a poor mix, and while the campaign continued the possibility of border incidents escalating into full-scale war was much diminished. Finally, though, the elections were held, on 26 July 1955, Ben-Gurion's party won a plurality, and he was charged with forming and heading a new coalition government (Sharett remained head of the caretaker government for the unusually lengthy coalition negotiations, which dragged on until November).

In mid-August 1955, barely three weeks after the elections – the timing could not have been accidental – tension again began to mount along the Israel-Egypt border. Now a new element was added to the volatile mix. Besides renewed clashes between Egyptian troops and Israeli patrols, organised infiltration into Israel began by terror squads, called *fedayeen* (meaning "those who sacrifice themselves"), masterminded by the Egyptian authorities in the Gaza Strip. The infiltrators were mainly Palestinians from the National Guard, or else belonged to the squads which the Egyptians had previously tried to prevent from entering Israeli territory.

From August 1955, then, the Israeli defence doctrine was put to the test on an unprecedented scale. Current-security incidents brought Israel and Egypt to the brink of war. Towards the end of that month, Dayan's ideas about the linkage between basic defence and current security seemed to acquire heightened credibility. Early in the morning of August 22, an Egyptian position opened fire on an IDF patrol near Kibbutz Mefalsim, opposite Gaza City. In response, acting on standing orders, the patrol commander led his force across the border, attacking and taking the Egyptian position. The Egyptians reacted with an artillery barrage of several hours, directed against both the area of the skirmish and Kibbutz Nahal-Oz. Egyptian responsibility for the deterioration on the front line seemed quite clear. Sharett, after much hesitation, accepted this view and ordered a retaliatory raid. What he did not know is that the night before (August 20–21), an IDF force had attacked an Egyptian Army camp near Rafah, with orders to kill Egyptian soldiers. The raid failed. We have no confirmation from Egyptian sources, but it stands to reason that Egypt's decision to open fire, after such a lengthy period of quiet, was motivated by this raid.[17]

Egypt reacted furiously to the August 22 incident. Between the 25th and the 30th of that month 16 Israelis were killed, along the front line and inland, by marauding *fedayeen*. In addition, the Egyptians used artillery and light-weapons fire, set ambushes and laid land mines near the Gaza Strip. Egyptian troops seized two hills inside Israeli territory, in the Sabha area south of the Nitsana demilitarised zone – far from the Gaza Strip. Egyptian jet fighters penetrated Israeli airspace, and one of them was shot down.[18]

The IDF was not surprised either by the Egyptian reaction or by the flurry of terrorist activity – this was apparently just what had been expected.[19] Then, on August 31, the Ben-Gurion-Dayan defence policy achieved its almost inevitable result, and on a large scale. IDF troops attacked the Khan Yunis fortress in the southern Gaza Strip, blowing up part of the building as well as a nearby fuel depot; they also hit a hospital, buildings in a nearby village and an Egyptian Army post. All told, 72 Egyptians were killed and 58 wounded. The raiding force sustained 1 dead and 17 wounded.[20]

Early in September 1955, current-security incidents brought the situation ever closer to war. For four days running, from September 1st to the 4th, the Gaza Strip frontier was subjected to incessant artillery exchanges. Israel and Egypt were caught up in a dynamic which looked certain to bring war.[21] On September 1, two Egyptian jet fighters were shot down. The next day, Dayan instructed his second-in-command, Major General Haim Laskov, to prepare a fast counter-move in the Eilat area at Israel's southern tip, in the light of intelligence indications that Egypt was planning to move against the town. Speed was of the essence, Dayan emphasised, because of a possible intervention by external powers, which would enforce an immediate ceasefire and freeze the situation on the ground. On September 3, the IDF's Intelligence Branch apprised the leadership that Egypt was about to undertake a surprise move, on land or in the air, "tonight or tomorrow".[22]

Ben-Gurion instructed Dayan to convey an ultimatum to Egypt, through General Burns: If the Egyptians persisted in carrying out operations within Israeli territory, the IDF would move into the Gaza Strip. Ben-Gurion was referring only to the northern part of the Strip, under the assumption that the entry of Israeli forces would suffice to empty the area of civilians – they would flee from the combat zone southwards, into Sinai. The IDF began to prepare for this contingency, calling up reserves, working out countermoves against possible Syrian or

Jordanian intervention and setting up a military government framework to administer the Gaza Strip after its capture. But on September 4, the Gaza sector became calm again after both sides decided to accept Burns's repeated calls for a ceasefire. In Israel, Ben-Gurion seemed on the verge of completing his coalition negotiations, while Egypt's Nasser was busy concluding his major arms deal with Czechoslovakia.[23]

In conclusion, the events of August–September 1955, and the subsequent relative tranquillity on Israel's borders (more with Egypt and Syria, less so with Jordan) left little room for Dayan's initiatives to turn routine security incidents into a *casus belli*. Sharett's suspicions notwithstanding, Dayan took no significant step without authorisation. But from this time the domestic balance of power was clear-cut: it tilted strongly towards the Ben-Gurion–Dayan defence doctrine. Sharett, the "lame duck" Prime Minister, could not be as forceful as before. The writing was on the wall, for both his policy and his political career.[24]

2

The Egyptian–Czech Deal

Soviet Penetration

Some time during the second half of September 1955, Egypt signed with Czechoslovakia an arms deal of unprecedented proportions, in Middle Eastern terms. It was obvious that this deal represented, in a major way, Soviet penetration into the Middle East, and hence an end to Western control of arms sales to the region; in effect, it also spelled the end of Western hegemony in this sensitive part of the world. All the efforts invested by Britain and the United States (including the Baghdad Pact and Plan Alpha) to consolidate a uniform anti-Soviet front in the Middle East and thus block Soviet encroachment in the Mediterranean region and Africa suddenly proved useless. In one fell swoop the USSR outflanked the Western powers, reaching out directly to the leader of the Arab world.

Already in August information was received, in Israel and in the US, to the effect that the USSR had made certain proposals to Egypt. As a matter of fact, the Soviets had apparently offered to sell arms to Egypt as early as 1953, and the Czech deal had been in the making since at least late 1954. Nevertheless, Nasser's public announcement of the deal, on 27 September 1955, stunned both the Western powers and Israel. Nasser's determined objection to Western policy *vis-à-vis* the Middle East, and the successful conclusion, from his point of view, of his negotiations with Britain for the latter's withdrawal from the Suez Canal Zone, made him the obvious candidate for Soviet courting. In May 1955, information received in the West indicated that the Soviets had offered Egypt everything available in their conventional arsenal, in any quantities desired. It was also known that an Egyptian high-level delegation was about to visit the Soviet Union. It was clear that Nasser was not merely trying to put pressure on the West; his intentions were quite real.

Evidently it was American efforts to make Egypt abandon the secret negotiations that induced Nasser to disclose the deal in September. By this *fait accompli* the Egyptian President robbed the United States of the possibility of exerting additional pressure on him. In Israel the Cabinet convened for an emergency meeting (October 3), but several more weeks were to pass before the government and the defence establishment grasped the real significance of the Czech–Egyptian deal.[1]

In the air, the deal included some 100–150 MiG jet fighters, most of them of the 15 series, but also some of the more advanced 17 series; about 50 Il-28 medium bombers; some 70 Il-14 transport aircraft; relatively advanced anti-aircraft guns; and a number of training and liaison aircraft. The MiG-15, which had proved its worth in the Korean War, was armed with one 37mm and two 23mm guns, and had bomb- and rocket-racks under its wings. Its maximum speed was a subsonic 1,000 kph, and its operational ceiling was some 50,000 feet. The MiG-17, though similar in most features, was better suited for ground attack. The Il-28 bomber, which was feared most by Israel, had a payload of about 2 tonnes and an operational range of about 1,100 km – that is, it could reach almost any point in Israeli territory from bases in the Sinai. Its maximum speed was 930 kph, and its operational ceiling was about 33,000 feet. Israel, at the time, had only 19 jet fighters, all of them near-obsolete British Meteors.

On land, the deal included 230 T-34 tanks, some 200 armoured personnel carriers (APCs) and 600 artillery pieces of various types. The T-34, a World War II veteran, was armed with an 85mm gun and one machine-gun. As for the Egyptian Navy, it would receive several destroyers, submarines and torpedo boats. Israel had no submarines at the time, nor did it have any tanks capable of dealing with the T-34.[2]

The impact of the Egyptian–Czech deal on the Israeli public and the country's decision-makers quickly relegated routine security to a lower priority on the national agenda. From now on, the Israeli leadership would have to focus their sights on national survival.

"A Sombre Visage"

By early October 1955, Israel was thinking more readily in terms of initiating a war. Everything that transpired during 1955, and in particular the anxieties of September–October, encouraged the Israelis to push forward their plans for war under conditions of their own choosing. Some support came from abroad: In a cable that was received on 1 October 1955, the CIA's Kermit Roosevelt described US confusion following the announcement of the arms deal, adding that "if, when Soviet arms are received by Egypt, you will choose to hit them, no one will challenge you."

Prime Minister Sharett, albeit unintentionally, further exacerbated Israeli anxieties; in a political statement to the Knesset on October 18,

Sharett referred to "major happenings in the Middle East, bringing forth a sombre visage of major, nay, decisive superiority in military force obtained by the strongest amongst our enemies, confronting us with dangers the likes of which we have not known since our War of Independence". Such a reaction by the usually reticent Sharett clearly reflected – and heightened – Israel's feeling of being seriously threatened by the news from Egypt.[3]

At the same time, Egypt's blockade of Israel reached a new peak in September 1955, when Cairo announced that the airspace above the Gulf of Eilat (in addition to the waterway) was henceforth closed to flights to and from Israel. September and October also saw an intensification of Egyptian-inspired terrorist activities, this time across the Jordanian border. The Syrians, too, were flexing their muscles east of the Sea of Galilee, and there was terrorist activity even on the Lebanese border.

During this time the IDF executed three major reprisal raids. On the night of October 27–28, following an Egyptian raid on an Israeli police outpost at the Nitsana demilitarised zone, Israeli troops attacked Egyptian positions near Kuntileh, killing 11 Egyptian soldiers and taking 29 prisoners. On the night of November 2–3, the IDF attacked Egyptian troops who deployed on the Israeli side of the Nitsana DMZ and beyond. This time, 70 Egyptians were killed and 49 captured. The attacking force lost six dead and some 30 wounded. During the raid, Israeli troops penetrated Egyptian territory. Dayan wanted them to dig in, but Ben-Gurion would not authorise that. When the Egyptian Army launched its counter-attack, at dawn, the Israelis were no longer there, so Dayan's intention to escalate the situation was foiled. Later on there was an Israeli raid on Syrian positions on the eastern shore of the Sea of Galilee (11–12 December 1955), in which 54 Syrian soldiers were killed and 30 taken prisoner, the IDF suffering six fatalities. Egypt, the presumptive leader of the Arab world, did not react to what had been a major Israeli operation against a sister-nation.[4]

As for the IDF, its operational planning for an Israeli-initiated war had begun during the spring of 1955, and by the autumn of that year the plans had reached a fairly advanced stage. Procedures for emergency reserves mobilisation and for other contingencies were worked out, and battle plans for the Gaza Strip and the Straits of Tiran were readied. The reworked plans were code-named Shahar for the Gaza Strip and Omer (or Zohar) for the Straits.[5]

A war-like atmosphere prevailed in Israel. The mass media were full of reports about the Egyptian arms deal. Sharett, having warned the Knesset that Israel must obtain "arms now!", hurried to Geneva, where a summit conference of the Great Powers was taking place, to plead

Israel's case in talks with some of the foreign ministers in attendance. At the same time, an emergency fundraising campaign was launched, the Defence Fund, to which even schoolchildren donated their pocket money, in order to buy arms for the IDF. Thus the groundwork was laid in Israel, intentionally and otherwise, for an initiated war.

Even Sharett considered briefly, in view of the Czech arms deal and the border turbulence, whether Israel should capture the Gaza Strip "if the Egyptians do not desist from their murderous shenanigans". Still, he was hesitant, unlike Ben-Gurion and Dayan, who during October 1955 took a huge step towards an Israeli-initiated war.[6]

"Israel Will Choose the Time and the Place"

During the autumn of 1955, as the political-strategic doctrine advocating an Israeli-initiated war was reaching maturity, Ben-Gurion and Dayan found an almost perfect opportunity to carry it out, in the wake of Egypt's announcement of a full blockade of the Straits of Tiran. Between October 1955 and January 1956, discussions of the subject focused on a concrete plan which the IDF was ready to implement: Operation Omer to lift the Egyptian blockade. On October 23, Ben-Gurion instructed Dayan to stand ready to execute Omer – virtually the logical consequence of the prevailing atmosphere. The operation was set for December 25. On November 13, Ben-Gurion told Dayan to postpone execution until the end of the following January. On December 22, Dayan informed the IDF and Ben-Gurion that there would be another delay, of indefinite duration. Finally, at a Cabinet meeting, on January 8, the operation was cancelled altogether.[7]

What happened between October 1955 – when Dayan was told by Ben-Gurion that speedy execution was essential – and January 1956, when Omer was scrapped? During the autumn of 1955, Dayan regarded his war policy as a given, and even tried to expand Omer to involve the capture of other parts of the Sinai Peninsula. In one of their meetings early in November, Dayan heard from Ben-Gurion that "when one attacks, no questions are asked", which he took as encouragement to go on expanding his war plans.[8]

However, a careful examination reveals that Ben-Gurion cautiously remained within the parameters of the operational discussion, never committing himself to Dayan for anything further than taking over the Straits of Tiran. On the other side, Nasser did not let himself be provoked by Israel, shown most strikingly in his not reacting forcefully to the Gaza or Khan Yunis raids, as described in the previous chapter. And even when he almost slipped, following Khan Yunis, Ben-Gurion helped him out by instructing Dayan to reduce tension along the border.

"In a Month or Two"

During November, cracks began to appear in Ben-Gurion's hard-line posture. The issue of initiating a war was no longer clear-cut, as far as he was concerned. On November 8, the Minister of Defence (and Prime Minister, since the previous week) could still tell Dayan and Peres: "We are sick and tired of [international] condemnations, we want to have our men take positions securely adjacent to Egypt [proper, i.e., along the Suez Canal] and the Red Sea". Dayan promised him then and there, "We shall be ready in six weeks" (that is, the end of December). In reply, Ben-Gurion ordered him "to make all preparations as soon as possible". But a few days later (November 13) Ben-Gurion ordered the operation to be postponed by one month.

Ben-Gurion's diary entry on November 30 was painfully hesitant: "It may be that in a month or two . . . we shall reach this question, war or no war." Throughout the month, Ben-Gurion endeavoured to make it clear to Dayan that an Israeli-initiated war was out of the question for the moment. Finally, on December 1 he instructed the Chief of Staff to prepare for a defensive war, based on the assumption that Egypt would be the attacking side.

Dayan, resigning himself to the fact that the Minister of Defence was no longer supportive of "war now", including Operation Omer, took the necessary steps. On December 22, he informed Ben-Gurion that the force earmarked for Omer (the 39th Infantry Brigade) could not be kept on permanent but indefinite alert. Moreover, he explained that, for operational reasons, if the decision to go ahead were to be made again, the operation could not be launched before late February 1956, since he would have to reorganise the forces now being disbanded. Furthermore, in late December the General Staff was preparing its regular half-year work plan, which included the assumption that neither Omer nor Shahar (the latter, it will be recalled, relating to the Gaza Strip) would be carried out.[9]

These developments resulted from the weekly Cabinet meeting of Sunday, 4 December 1955. Ben-Gurion, having reassumed the premiership on November 2, had spent the intervening month re-examining Israeli policy on a wide range of issues. On this particular day, he raised for discussion the country's policy objectives in defence, immigration absorption and settlement. The main discussion involved a question of principle: an Israeli-initiated war – yes or no? It transpired that the majority of Cabinet ministers were disinclined to support the Ben-Gurion–Dayan approach favouring that option. The resolution adopted declared that "Israel will choose the time and the place it deems appropriate"; in other words, Dayan's policy was not officially set aside by the Cabinet, but nevertheless it was indefinitely postponed. At the same time, however, a conclusion was reached which portended the eventual cancellation of Operation Omer: at this stage, it was not in Israel's interest to initiate a war. Ben-Gurion remarked, with evident satisfaction, that in the matter of postponing such a war, "there is a uniform Cabinet policy."[10]

Since December 4, when an Israeli-initiated war was ruled out as an immediate option, Ben-Gurion had endeavoured to scuttle Operation Omer without hurting the IDF too much. The Prime Minister was concerned about morale in the armed forces, particularly in the higher echelons, due to the uncertainty surrounding Omer and the order to return to a defensive posture. And not without reason, to judge by the following sentiment, uttered by the head of Southern Command, Colonel Meir 'Amit (on a later occasion): "We, who prided ourselves on offence, found ourselves all of a sudden digging in, despite the fact that all our preparations were for a war of motion. The IDF was not too good at defence." The change was palpable: since early December 1995, the Government of Israel, at the behest of the Prime Minister and Defence Minister, had instituted a saliently defensive policy.[10]

There was, however, a real problem with the blockade of the Straits of Tiran, which earlier had dovetailed conveniently with the policy of an Israeli-initiated war, but remained unresolved after that policy was aborted in December 1955. Ben-Gurion now decided to make a clean separation between the two issues. Henceforth, as in the period which antedated the original shift of policy, Egypt's blockade of the Straits of Tiran was no longer considered a *casus belli* in and of itself.

By the end of 1955, the question of greatest concern to Ben-Gurion was not whether, and how, Operation Omer to break the blockade would be implemented. His major cause for worry was now the war-like atmosphere prevailing in the country. Fundamental to this worry was Egypt's huge arms deal with Czechoslovakia. It seems that Dayan and the General Staff were not yet aware of Ben-Gurion's change of mind. This would come later, during the winter of 1956.

Still, it was not a rapid turnabout. Ben-Gurion had gradually prepared Dayan for a forthcoming change in his policy during their discussions in November. The disagreement between the two leaders about the possible timing for an Israeli-initiated war reveals their differing attitudes towards the major process then under way: the tilt in the balance of power (real or only imaginary in the Israeli mind, it does not matter) between Israel and Egypt. Since early November 1955, Ben-Gurion, having reassumed supreme responsibility for Israeli policy, including defence policy and its underlying strategy, had to redefine the direction of that policy, as he had undertaken to do in the election campaign and again during the coalition negotiations. Indeed he did so, but the new thrust was no longer what he had championed when he held only the defence portfolio. His current attitude required the IDF to be strengthened, because of the Egyptian–Czech deal, as a *sine qua non* for an Israeli-initiated war. During November, a frustrated Dayan began to perceive that the distance between himself and his superior was widening. Without Ben-Gurion's support, his hard-line policy was all but doomed. Efforts which had been cultivated for many months were about to be uprooted.

Yet, despite this setback, the policy of a war initiated by Israel did not disappear altogether; it remained the preferred basis for ongoing strategic and operative planning, even for Ben-Gurion. After all, it was his Cabinet which was to authorise, less than a year later, just such a war. Still, during the winter of 1956 the IDF was preparing for a defensive war. At the same time, despite its new orders, the military continued to give preference, in its preparations, to a possible Israeli initiative, if and when approved by Cabinet.[11]

"There Will Be War in the Summer"

Since the announcement of the Egyptian–Czech arms deal, it had been an Israeli assumption that Egypt intended to go to war. On 26 October 1955, Dayan told the General Staff that "Egypt would not have made such a deal for trivial reasons". A few weeks later, at a regular Cabinet meeting, Ben-Gurion said: "I assume the [Egyptians] will attack in the early summer, we must not assume that they will not, common sense says they may attack once they feel they have a chance of winning". And in April 1956, Ben-Gurion wrote to the Director-General of the Prime Minister's Office, Teddy Kollek (who was then in America, helping the Foreign Office's ultimately unsuccessful effort to secure an arms deal with the US): "There is concrete reason to believe that Nasser will attack in June or July, together with Syria, Jordan and Saudi Arabia."[12]

This prevalent feeling did not correspond with developments in Egypt. True, Israel's expectation of war did have some basis in intelligence reports, but stemmed more from genuine concern over the Egyptian military build-up. This was combined with a desire to foment an atmosphere of public alarm to serve the policy of a deliberately provoked war, not least because of the setback that policy had sustained in the wake of the Egyptian arms deal. The efforts by Dayan and Peres in this direction proved, in retrospect, to be a self-fulfilling prophecy.[13]

While Ben-Gurion himself did not want war in the winter of 1956, he did not challenge the IDF's assessment that war would erupt during the next summer, at Egypt's initiative. The Chief of Intelligence, Colonel

Yehoshafat Harkabi, would say later that he used to "preach" (as he put it) constantly to the Chief of Staff and the Prime Minister that Nasser intended war. Harkabi's evaluation was that once the Egyptians felt they had absorbed sufficient arms and enjoyed material superiority – they would attack. It was this perception that led Ben-Gurion to reject the possibility of initiating a war and to adopt a defensive strategy (absorb and repulse the first blow, move swiftly to a counter-offensive) based on the assumption that Egypt would strike first. The IDF was talking about war during the period from January to June 1956. Israel, during the winter and spring of 1956, was preparing itself for an inevitable war – started by Egypt.[14]

In 1958, two years after the events here described, the Chief of Staff's aide, Lt.-Colonel Mordechai Bar-On, described the atmosphere then prevailing in Israel:

> From [October 1955] onwards, the whole nation, and in particular the IDF, was living under the threat and strain of this motto: "There will be war in the summer of 1956." Everyone was talking about this forthcoming war with complete certainty, as though it was just one stage in a thoroughly worked-out plan, which was moving inexorably according to its own fixed timetable. Indeed, many believed that Nasser had planned the whole thing in advance, so that his decision to assume the financial and political burden of the Czech deal could only be explained as being part and parcel of his explicit plan to attack Israel in the summer of 1956.
>
> Even those who should have known better, who should have realised that there are no fixed plans in politics, that extended timetables are unrealistic, were nevertheless convinced that Israel and the IDF should be making their preparations according to this timetable of "war in the summer of 1956". Everybody was talking about "the threat of war looming over Israel" and political parties were proposing emergency programmes to forestall this danger. Committees and conventions were sounding the alarm. Editorials and columnists dealt with it incessantly, and even in private conversations and letters one could feel this awareness of danger looming large.[15]

Sharett, still the Foreign Minister at the time, argued that this very atmosphere, the sense of emergency and the repeated assertions of the dire need to obtain arms, were bound to lead to war – even without any objective necessity. It was his view that successful efforts to purchase arms and build up the IDF were enhanced by the public's mental acceptance of war's inevitability. It did not matter what kind of war it would be, Israeli-initiated or otherwise; what mattered was the Israeli public's willingness – against a background of fundraising for arms, calls for volunteers to help in the fortification of border settlements, and increasing hostility towards Nasser – to accept the fact that war was at hand.[16]

There is no definitive answer to the question of whether Nasser was really preparing his armed forces for war in the summer of 1956. However, the fact that the Suez Crisis broke out, in late July 1956, at Egypt's initiative, would seem to indicate that the Egyptians did not intend to mobilise their forces for an attack on Israel at the same time: the two events were incompatible. Furthermore, Egyptian deployment in the Sinai was by and large a reflection of Israel's posture. When the IDF switched to defensive deployment, the Egyptians responded in kind: having reinforced their forces in the Sinai in case of war against Israel during October to December 1955, they began redeploying them back to mainland Egypt as of early 1956, the better to defend the Canal following British withdrawal.[17]

During the winter of 1956, Dayan and Peres concluded that only a major tilt in the balance of power could restore Ben-Gurion's confidence and induce him to again support an Israeli-initiated war. The policy of escalation had failed. Neither the struggle for freedom of navigation nor the Egyptian–Czech arms deal were able to generate war – on the contrary, the latter actually accounted for Ben-Gurion's *volte-face*. The obvious solution was to find a source for arms purchases of unprecedented scope, preferably a source that could also ensure diplomatic support. In other words, a significant ally was required – a second-level power or better. Ben-Gurion, the author of this appraisal of the situation, was willing to support Dayan in this – and only in this – respect, even if it became necessary to proceed outside normal channels.

"The Most Hostile Government in the World"

When the Cabinet decided against Dayan's war initiative, its chief concerns involved not only the need to redress the balance of armament, following the Egyptian–Czech deal, but also the fear of a third party joining in on the side of Israel's enemies. In particular, Ben-Gurion's worries focused not only on the military aspects of the deal, but also on its implications for the Great Powers' policy towards the Middle East. Even though he thought it unlikely that the USSR would actually attack Israel, Soviet policy gave rise to considerable misgivings in Israel. It was hard to accept the complete (though by no means sudden) turnabout in Moscow's attitude, since the USSR had been one of Israel's major supporters in its early days of statehood. Indeed, the irony was that Israel had obtained most of its arms from Czechoslovakia, with Soviet acquiescence, during its War of Independence only a few years earlier. Both Ben-Gurion and Sharett found it difficult to regard the Soviet

Union as an enemy. At the same time, no one in the mainstream of Israeli politics proposed that the government go back to a policy of reliance on the USSR. The idea of asking the Soviets for arms had been raised, only to be rejected out of hand.[18]

As mentioned above, during the winter of 1955, Ben-Gurion, while continuing to support the idea that Israel should foment a war, set a condition for the realisation of this policy, one which did much to determine the events that followed: Israel, he insisted, would not initiate a major military operation without significant support by one Great Power at least. This was required, again, not only to prepare adequately for war, but equally to counterbalance possible external intervention – and not necessarily by the Soviet Union. When a left-wing hard-line party, Ahdut Ha'Avoda, urged Ben-Gurion to preempt Nasser by going to war immediately, he replied: "Such a view is not unacceptable, in principle or in practice. It is, however, problematic in one respect: possible British involvement in such a war." Indeed, Ben-Gurion continued to be haunted by misgivings about Britain until the Sinai War and even during the hostilities, as related further on.[19]

Britain at this time was engaged in a process of rapid withdrawal from the Suez Canal Zone, and its possible reaction to a war between Israel and Egypt was central to Ben-Gurion's considerations. Memories of the recent past, namely the part Britain had played during its last years as the Mandatory Power in Palestine, inclined him to consider Britain an enemy. The British, he believed, in their present state of decline, would do anything to maintain what was left of their hold on the Suez Canal. There was no doubt in his mind that an Israeli attack on Egypt would prompt Britain to come to the latter's aid – at least to the extent of taking out the Israeli Air Force. In his evaluation, "After the Arab nations, this is for us the most hostile government in the world. ... I feel that [Prime Minister Anthony] Eden wants to be rid of us; he will not do it himself, but he will be happy if somebody else will do it."

Thus, neutralising the British danger would remove a major obstacle on the road to a future war initiated by Israel: "How could we go to Eilat to do this thing we have decided on [breaking the blockade], will this not bring about British intervention? Will we be able to obtain weapons afterwards?"[20]

The alliance Ben-Gurion sought could not be only declarative; its chief expression must be in arms supplies. The effort to secure an arms source provides the explanation for Ben-Gurion's apparently inexplicable moves during the first few months after reassuming the premiership. It is not that he submitted to a Cabinet majority in early December; it was he who brought about the Cabinet discussion of the fundamentals of Israel's defence policy, and he, too, who proposed postponing a war to a more appropriate time, when the IDF would be adequately equipped.[21]

As a matter of fact, already in early November, immediately after he formally became Prime Minister, Ben-Gurion withdrew his support for Dayan's policy of provoking a war and turned his complete attention to the arms supply problem. This was the most urgent issue, he felt. It was always Ben-Gurion's way to focus on one issue at the time, whatever he deemed most critical at any given juncture. Deliberately ignoring other subjects, he turned every discussion towards the need for arms. The paramount question, as he saw it, was "what do we need and how much will it cost us, so that we can match Egypt's growing power?"[22] But as of late 1955, Ben-Gurion could not see any meaningful ally ready to support Israel, come what may – not even France, which was already negotiating with Israel over the supply of tanks, aircraft and other equipment.

Since arms supplies were the main priority, and since most potential sources were in the West, Israel was quite disturbed by the Anglo-American Plan Alpha. The plan involved Israeli territorial concessions but not, as far as Israel could see, any meaningful *quid pro quo* for itself. Ben-Gurion even thought it possible that the US (and perhaps France as well) would offer to sell arms to Egypt, in order to counterbalance Soviet influence there. Plan Alpha did not even mention peace; rather, it spoke of Arab "acceptance of Israel's existence". It said nothing about arms supplies or about a binding defence pact between Israel and either of the two powers behind the plan. Even Sharett maintained that "Israel [is] in no way prepared unilaterally to give up any piece of its land." Plan Alpha had not yet been made public, but the US Secretary of State John Foster Dulles referred to it in a speech on 26 August 1955, as did British Prime Minister Anthony Eden in his Guildhall Address on November 9.[23]

"Dissident Tendencies"

Still, the latter part of 1955 saw some improvement in Israel's arms procurement situation. Several deals had already been concluded with France, and the United States, following a period of calm along the borders, was now willing to allow Israel to purchase American-licensed aircraft produced in other countries, such as Canada. These developments only strengthened Ben-Gurion in his belief that the time was not yet ripe for war: Israel, he insisted, must use this opportunity to restore the arms balance which had been undone by the Egyptian–Czech deal. Until the spring of 1956, it was a cornerstone of his policy that neither current-security problems nor the freedom of navigation issue could constitute a *casus belli* so long as Israel lacked an ally – meaning a provider of sufficient arms to create at least a feeling of strategic balance *vis-à-vis* the surrounding confrontation states, Egypt first and foremost. In view of the types and quantities of arms sought by Israel, the old method – buying whatever was available on the second-hand market – was no longer good enough; Israel now sought an ally who could and would meet its special needs.

It had been decided earlier that the Foreign Ministry would be in charge of these efforts *vis-à-vis* the United States, while the Ministry of Defence would try to obtain arms from France. Now it seemed that the Foreign Ministry had failed, and the Prime Minister decided to give full backing to intensive involvement by the Ministry of Defence in Israel's foreign relations. Peres and Dayan had been prime movers in developing a network of relationships with the French defence establishment; Ben-Gurion gave them the go-ahead, since their efforts seemed to promise the only way to regain a strategic balance with Egypt. Indeed, their endeavours soon began to bear fruit, becoming a highly significant component in Israel's defence policy.[24]

On 10 April 1956, Israel was due to receive its first Mystère jet fighters from France; for the first time, the Israel Air Force would receive planes which had come straight off the production line, rather than leftovers and war surplus as before. Around the same time, in the midst of a massive terrorist campaign instigated by Egypt, Ben-Gurion convened a meeting with Sharett, Dayan, Peres and Israeli Ambassador to Paris Ya'akov Tzur. They discussed Israel's arms needs and the prospects of fulfilling them, in view of the international situation. Ben-Gurion's position at the time was crystal-clear: "I have no other topic [for discussion], I see this subject [arms] as the main problem." As the meeting concluded, the Prime Minister "officially relieved the Foreign Ministry of any involvement in arms purchases, placing this completely under the responsibility of the Ministry of Defence."[25]

This was not entirely to the liking of either the Israeli or the French Foreign Ministry. Not surprisingly, Quai d'Orsay looked askance at the direct links which were developing between Israeli officials and French political and military leaders. Ambassador Tzur wrote, "Quite a few times I was warned by [Prime Minister] Guy Mollet and [Foreign Minister Christian] Pineau, not to make direct contacts with the Ministry of Defence without their knowledge. Therefore, I let our Defence people [Peres and Yosef Nahmias, head of the Israeli Ministry of Defence liaison office in Paris] pursue these contacts." However, there were limits to Tzur's patience, especially when he found out that a dramatic change had taken place in Israel's relations with France, as described below, unbeknownst to him. Afterwards, when Golda Meir took over the Foreign Ministry from Sharett, Tzur would warn her about "the dissident tendencies of some of our Defence people".[26]

Ben-Gurion was aware of this problematic situation. He wrote to Peres, when the latter was in Paris, that he was against a proposed visit by Dayan to France, since "this may make Pineau even angrier". Still, Ben-Gurion was not particular about details in a scheme of activities which he had generally approved. Foreign Minister Sharett, on the other hand, strongly objected to the entire operation, a position which cut him off from the emerging main thrust of Israeli foreign policy.[27]

To repeat, Ben-Gurion believed in no other way except immediate arms purchases: "There is nothing to do but [purchase] arms, all efforts [must be] concentrated on this." Sharett, the Foreign Minister (and ex-Prime Minister), could not deliver the goods, quite literally, whereas Peres could and did. Sharett's reservations about the developments in relations with France, serving what was for Ben-Gurion the supreme national interest, deepened the chasm between the two leaders. Their differences over defence policy were long-standing by the spring of 1956, but Sharett's objections to the way arms deals were concluded with France, coupled with his own failure to procure arms from the United States, were the last straw.

Shortly afterwards, in June 1956, Sharett was removed from office and left the Cabinet.[28] In an effort to placate angry party members, Ben-Gurion explained Sharett's sacking in terms which shed some light on his own attitude at the time, shortly before the outbreak of the Suez Crisis: "A negative attitude of 'waiting it out' is not enough. In the long run, doing nothing may be far more dangerous than any bold, fateful deed – such as fomenting a war."[29]

3

The Israeli Deal

Arms Purchases and Diplomacy

Since coming out of retirement, it was the firm opinion of Prime Minister Ben-Gurion that if Israel were to initiate a war in the autumn of 1955, its already slim prospects of receiving modern arms from Western powers would be still further diminished. On the other hand, if the balance of arms were redressed, an Israeli-initiated war should become possible again. Thus, as we saw, by the winter of 1956 arms supplies was the central theme of Israeli defence policy. It received high priority in terms of budgeting, and this opened potential new sources to the Ministry of Defence and the IDF – now only one major problem remained: finding a willing supplier. Dayan and Peres were aware that this was probably a unique opportunity to strengthen the IDF. They took it upon themselves to find a seller, and it turned out to be France.[1]

Arms purchases also took precedence over diplomatic considerations, relegating to the sidelines such issues as concluding a defence pact with a major power, or international mediation with Israel's Arab neighbours. Mediation efforts were in fact undertaken in the early part of 1956, including a mission by Robert Anderson, personal representative of the President of the United States, in January, and by UN Secretary-General Dag Hammarskjöld, in April. Both missions failed dismally.

The two diplomats addressed current security issues, when they should have been dealing with the fundamentals of the Arab-Israeli conflict. Anderson found out that what Israel actually wanted from the United States was arms, not mediation with Nasser. Not only Ben-Gurion, but even Foreign Minister Sharett could hardly be bothered with diplomacy. The arms procurement efforts directed at France were already producing good results, diminishing the chances of success for any mediators, however high-ranking.[2]

Arms purchases from France entered a new phase in April 1956, when Israel took delivery of the first Mystère IVA jet fighters. The scale of the supply was unprecedented in Israel. As for France's motive, it can be found in Paris' suspicions of Nasser's involvement in the Algerian revolt, as well as in the ongoing political crisis in France itself. This crisis generated constant friction among government ministries and departments, and between them and various external agencies. Ministers came and went in an endless roundabout, so it was impossible to develop a consistent policy.

In this situation, Shimon Peres, the Israeli official in charge of relations with France (at least as far as arms purchases were concerned), sought to strike up personal relationships with senior officials in the French Ministry of Defence; as civil servants, they remained close even during the ministerial revolving door period. But Peres soon discovered that even the shaky Fourth Republic still was a democracy, and there was no substitute for ties with elected officials. Turning his efforts there, he was eventually well-connected with both permanent and elected officials in the French Ministry of Defence.[3]

Peres' road was far from smooth; there were many ups and downs before the peak was attained in the summer of 1956. While the French defence establishment had made a promising response to Israeli arms requests already in 1954, showing a willingness to give them a sympathetic hearing, in early 1956 Israeli expectations were still quite low. Even in April, when the first Mystères arrived, Israel did not dare regard the event as a breakthrough. The Israeli evaluation was that the French Foreign Ministry would not let the newly formed special relationship between the two defence establishments come to fruition, in terms of meaningful arms supplies.

As Peres was to write later about the winter and spring of 1956: French "defence institutions will be delighted to fill any further orders from us, and will promise delivery . . . The only obstacle is the Foreign Ministry, which does everything it can to ensure that our requests are turned down, using underhanded methods."[4]

The breakthrough finally came in June 1956. The two countries signed an agreement which Israel viewed as signifying a full-fledged alliance. As France's troubles in Algeria were becoming more aggravated by the day, Israel managed to persuade the French that it could be quite useful to them – both in intelligence and in actual military operations – in their struggle against Nasser, whom the French regarded (mistakenly, it would later emerge) as practically the fomenter of the Algerian revolt. When a measure of stability was achieved in French politics, with the inauguration of Guy Mollet's socialist government, protracted and wearisome French-Israeli negotiations were finally concluded.The French Defence and Foreign Affairs Ministries now decided that US views on arms sales should no longer be heeded. Henceforth there was nothing to hinder sales to Israel, subject to French interests – and payment in cash, of course.[5] The idea to turn the French entanglement in Algeria to Israel's advantage was conceived by Peres. Having discovered that France had an unexpected glut of jet fighters, following the cancellation of an Indian order for 200 Mystères, he developed a dramatic plan, jointly with Dayan, to increase arms purchases from France: they now discussed quantities which could balance the Egyptian deal with Czechoslovakia. Moreover, the transaction would be only part of a comprehensive Franco-Israeli pact. In exchange for French arms sales, Israel would render France every possible assistance in its struggle against the Algerian rebels and their ostensible sponsor, Nasser.

By late May 1956, they had acquainted Ben-Gurion with the plan and been authorised by him (not without hesitation) to discuss it with the French. Basically, the idea addressed Israel's two foremost concerns: creating an alliance with a major power, and obtaining arms of significant quality and quantity. Nothing, as shown earlier, loomed more crucially in Ben-Gurion's mind at the time. Still the Prime Minister remained hesitant, even as late as October 1956, when the prospects for a war of Israel's choosing were better than in May–June. The final decision was his, and he was worried. It was more convenient for him to let Dayan and Peres move forward while he himself restrained and cautioned them, setting the limits of risk at each new step forward.

Dayan and Peres flew to Paris on 22 June 1956, taking with them the Chief of Military Intelligence, Colonel Yehoshafat Harkabi. For three days, secret discussions took place in the town of Vermars, south of Paris. The French side included representatives of the Ministry of Defence, the armed forces and the intelligence agencies. It was chaired, not coincidentally, by Pierre Boursicot, head of the French counter-espionage agency SDECE.

By the end of the Vermars talks, the scope of French arms sales to Israel, a timetable for delivery and methods of shipment had been concluded. Israel, for its part, agreed to co-operate with France, in both intelligence and covert military operations, in its struggle in Algeria and against Nasser. In order to avoid the need to have the agreement approved by the respective Cabinets, it was deemed an intelligence accord and signed by the two chiefs of intelligence: Boursicot and Harkabi.[6] Ben-Gurion proved willing to approve the agreement, despite his reservations: "There are a lot of fantastic and unnecessary things there, completely baseless. But in this I rely on the common sense of our people on the spot. Fine, we shall go into this business. It's a slightly dangerous adventure, but there's nothing we can do, the same can be said about our very existence here."[7]

"The French Invasion"

Following the Vermars agreement, Israel's relations with France took on two distinct aspects. The credit side of the deal, as far as Israel was concerned, was called by the Israelis "Operation Ge'ut" (High Tide), or informally "the French invasion". Everything to do with arms purchases was now handled by the Ministry of Defence, with Peres and Nahmias, Peres' representative in Paris, in charge. In exchange for its help in suppressing the Algerian revolt, Israel demanded and received, among other items, 200 AMX-13 light tanks, 72 Mystère 4A jet fighters, and great quantities of ammunition. It was agreed that deliveries would commence in July and be completed by early 1957. This massive deal was a tremendous boost to Israel's confidence.

However, in view of future developments (particularly the Suez Crisis), Israel's political and military collaboration with France in dealing with Nasser and the Algerian rebels, was no less significant. This was dubbed "Operation Zayit" (olive), and was under the direct control of the Chief of Staff. Zayit included information exchanges, including the deployment of an Israeli intelligence network in North Africa to be made available to the French; joint operations with the French against enemy objectives in North Africa in general, and in Egypt in particular; and "liquidation" operations against Algerian leaders in Europe.[8]

Of all these objectives, the most urgent (for France) and the most sensitive (for both parties) was joint military action against Egypt. Already in Vermars the French delegation produced a list of possible targets. The Israelis promised that a senior IDF officer would give them operative suggestions within eight days. On June 27, Dayan apprised the Joint Operations staff, GHQ, of his principal ideas for IDF collaboration with the French against Nasser and the Algerian rebels:

> There is an inherent difference between targets on the Tripoli coast [site of a camp of the Algerian rebels] or in Egypt proper. The former require operations in the nature of a combat raid, whereas the latter can be undertaken only with underground methods. The former are relatively easy to carry out, and while they are more complicated politically, they enable Israel and France the better to collaborate in terms of division of political and operational responsibilities. ...
>
> Israel should put forward, against the list of objectives in which France is interested, an "orders" list of its own, for joint execution. This is needed both in order to emphasise our equal partnership in obligations and benefits, and in order to avoid our becoming a "hit contractor" who gets his filthy lucre in armaments.[9]

No less important, Dayan added, such a presentation at an early stage would enable Israel to refuse any operation it prefers not to carry out. The French, for their part, could avoid any operation suggested by Israel which they dislike – in order not to create a rupture in the relationship. "Israel insists on full equality in demands, acceptances, refusals and failures."

As for France's target list, the only criterion for Israel's acceptance or refusal of a proposed operation should be the prospects of carrying it out successfully, without overly compromising the operatives' safety and anonymity. Israel would not reject any operation just because it appeared unreasonable, unjustified or not worth the effort, militarily or politically. It was up to the French to propose their targets as they saw fit. Israel reserved the right to make its own demands, asking the French in turn to accept its evaluation of their necessity or value.

Dayan went on to explain that Israel faced an array of military problems which were unrelated to the collaboration with France, especially along the frontiers. It was not in Israel's interest to involve France in the search for a solution to these problems. Should Israel desire to break the blockade in the Straits of Eilat, or seize the Gaza Strip, or execute a retaliatory raid, or hit enemy armoured forces in the Sinai – it would do so alone, without soliciting French help, permission or advice. "It is necessary to make this absolutely clear, in order to maintain Israel's operational sovereignty, to reserve to ourselves freedom of action in the military sphere and keep politically 'clean' our direct operations in the arena where we confront our enemies, as well as our international relations in general."

Dayan knew perfectly well that collaboration with France could bring about the war he so much desired, and since this seemed to him the preferred option, he wanted to ensure that war would not break out prematurely, due to Egyptian initiative or runaway escalation. From now on, it was more convenient for him to abide by Ben-Gurion's rules for an Israeli-initiated war:

> The preferred operations will [be ones which will] not force Nasser's hand, make him launch retaliatory operations or go to war. Sinking an Egyptian ship will bring about naval operations against Israeli civilian maritime transport, whereas blowing up an installation in Cairo may remain an isolated incident. We shall therefore prefer, within Egypt proper, underground-like activities. The boiling point in Egypt-Israel relations should be reached later on, when Israel, having absorbed its new French weaponry, will be able to move in a carefully calculated way, both in terms of its military deployment and its system of political and propaganda groundwork.[10]

"Provide Us with Arms, and We Will Make War"

While Israel found the list of targets presented by France for joint military operations (discussed in detail below) somewhat bizarre, it did not diminish the willingness to collaborate. To reap the expected benefits – arms and diplomatic support – Ben-Gurion and Dayan were ready to go a long way indeed.

On June 29, Dayan met with Ben-Gurion in order to get his approval of the instructions he would issue regarding military co-operation. The Prime Minister gave his assent, but demanded great caution and avoidance of any premature commitments. He advised Dayan to present, at this early stage, only targets of overriding interest to the IDF: "It is better that we let [France] take the lead, rather than be ourselves the shakers and movers." As for Israel's provoking a war, the Prime Minister now showed an eagerness which had been conspicuously absent during the previous months – since the 4 December 1955 Cabinet decision to reject that policy. Israel, he said now, was willing to risk an all-out war, on one condition: "The French should be aware that if we become entangled in war with Nasser as a result of our involvement in their operations, they must provide us with arms, freely and without any restrictions, and we will make war." With this in mind, Dayan issued his written instructions to press ahead with this military co-operation.

On July 1, the Deputy Chief of Operations, GHQ, Colonel Meir Zore'a, flew to Paris; his brief allowed him to prepare operational plans, but not to agree to any form of implementation. His opposite number was Colonel Morelan. In Paris, he discovered that the list of targets presented by the French in Vermars had been hastily prepared: the French began to treat collaboration with Israel seriously only after assuring themselves that the Israelis were indeed ready to go along. Eventually, from a modified target list, Zore'a and his hosts chose for execution raids on the broadcasting stations of Radio Damascus and Radio Cairo, and on an FLN training camp on the Libyan coast, between Tripoli and the Tunisian border.

The idea of hitting Radio Damascus was part of an intended Western (mainly Anglo-American) move against Syria, coincidental with but independent of the Anglo-French strike against Egypt. The aim was to prevent Syria from drifting into the arms of the Soviet Union. France, which traditionally wielded influence in Syria, was partially involved in the preparations for Operation Straggle, which was due to begin, by chance or by design, on the same day the Sinai War started – 29 October 1956.[11]

Targeting the radio stations was a propaganda move. It was not the French intention to blow up broadcasting facilities (which were situated in the countryside) and thus get both stations off the air for a time. Rather, they wanted to hit the main studios and head offices, in downtown Damascus and Cairo, delivering a warning which could not be ignored. "France was looking for a show of force against Egypt's propaganda," said Zore'a. The French drew up operational plans, gathered intelligence, and even prepared the charges for use in blowing up the stations. However, they wanted Israel to do the actual work – for the sake of "deniability". Given the situation between Israel and the Arab states involved, they believed, Israel could carry out such an operation without generating the kind of serious political repercussions which would harm France, should its role be discovered. The French were even willing to assist in smuggling the hit squads into the target countries, as long as they were Israelis.

As for the Libyan operation, this would be executed by a French force; the IDF was only asked to send an agent to gather necessary information, and then lead the French force to its target. Regarding other targets on his list, Morelan told Zore'a that at this stage, it was a question of intelligence gathering only.[12]

On the whole, Israel was glad to see the French list of demands so drastically reduced. Nor was there much concern about the operation in Libya. However, Ben-Gurion and Dayan could not accept the French position on the operations in downtown Damascus and Cairo. From the outset they had been worried that Israel would become a "hit contractor" for the French and would bear the entire political burden to boot, and now it seemed that their fears were justified. Furthermore, the French wanted implementation within a month or two, meaning that Israel would risk an all-out war even before the arrival of the promised arms shipments. In hurried consultations it was finally decided not to shut the door on France's requests – Israel wanted above all to avoid doing anything liable to jeopardise the arms shipments – but to try to delay the final decision on implementation for a while, and at the same time emphasise the principle of full equality and joint responsibility.[13]

A few days later the French withdrew the Tripoli plan, for reasons of their own, but still insisted on annihilating the broadcast stations. On July 7, Ben-Gurion chaired a meeting in his office which dealt with this question, prior to the dispatch to Paris of a senior Israeli liaison officer, Colonel Yuval Ne'eman, the Deputy Chief of Intelligence. It was decided that Israel would participate only if one of the attacks was carried out by the French. As for Israel's own target list, the decision was made to confine this solely to operations Israel could not execute without French assistance, thus ruling out strikes against Egyptian tanks, destroyers or submarines.

Accordingly, Ne'eman was instructed to present to the French a list of requests for assistance in case of all-out war against Egypt, or in the event of "drastic operations". They would be readied as "operations on hold for the time being", to be launched at Israel's request. Among the possibilities mentioned was the use of the French naval base at Djibouti and of French submarines, to lift the blockade in the Straits of Tiran or attack Egyptian naval bases at Alexandria and Suez.[14]

On July 8, Zore'a met again with his counterpart Morelan. He was surprised to learn that the French officer viewed Israel's demands as completely reasonable, "showing once again that a just and firm attitude cannot lose, and usually also adds dignity and importance". The two officers concluded that:

> The procedure for approval of operations will comprise four stages:
> Stage I – Both parties will approve a target presented by either of them as a concrete objective, namely an objective intended for execution, for which all relevant information should be gathered, and then planning will begin.
> Stage II – Planning stage. An operational examination of possibilities, odds [of success] and methods will take place. At the end of this stage, the [intelligence] services of both parties will declare the operation ready for execution.
> Stage III – Approval in principle by the "managements" in both countries, namely the supreme political authorities. This approval will allow the services to make final preparations, set the day and ready the operation to start once final approval is given.
> Stage IV – Final, concrete political approval by the "managements", followed by implementation.[15]

With this arrangement both sides could exercise full control over each consecutive stage, or even halt the entire operation because of changed political or military circumstances, without reneging on the agreement as a whole. It was further agreed at the July 8 meeting that the attacks on the Damascus and Cairo radio stations had already passed through Stage I. For this Israeli concession, the French accepted the principle of mutuality: Israel would carry out the operation in Cairo, the French in Damascus. Ben-Gurion then agreed that Israel would assist the French in their operation, in exchange for similar assistance from France to Israel at Cairo. All other targets were consigned to the first procedural stage. Israel was satisfied – the pace was moderated, as it had intended. The French, for their part, agreed to examine the list of targets presented by Israel.[16]

Planning at a "European Pace"

On July 11, Zore'a returned from Paris, having accomplished his mission there. Ne'eman arrived in the French capital on the same day, to assume his duties as Israel's permanent liaison officer for Zayit (military co-operation). Zore'a had laid the groundwork of a methodology for liaison, planning and implementation, and had built up French confidence in Israel's serious attitude and willingness to act. It was now up to Ne'eman further to put flesh on the skeleton of the Morelan-Zore'a guidelines.[17] With Ne'eman's arrival in Paris, the emphasis shifted to the development of intelligence co-operation, particularly with regard to Egypt. In this sphere, there had already been intensive links between the two nations, but of a different nature. For instance, the French internal security service, DST, was in touch with the Israeli Mossad, which had been involved in organising illegal immigration of Jews from North Africa and self-defence before they left. Occasionally, the Mossad would provide DST with intelligence information not directly related to these areas of co-operation. Now links were forged between the IDF's Intelligence Branch and the French counter-intelligence service, SDECE, a duality which could have produced much confusion and wasted effort. To prevent this, the IDF received exclusivity in relations with the SDECE.[18]

Acting on his brief to get co-operation under way, Ne'eman went into action with great gusto. This puzzled his French counterparts: France, despite its urgent needs, went about its business at a "European pace", Ne'eman noted. Arriving in Israel on July 20 to report, Ne'eman told his superiors that the division of labour between the raids on Cairo and Damascus had been finalised, including arrangements for mutual assistance. The two countries began to prepare their respective operations, set for simultaneous execution in late September or early October. Israel, in addition, presented the information in its possession regarding certain other objectives, for planning purposes only. The French had reaffirmed their willingness to operate on Israel's behalf against the Egyptian navy, as well as instructing the Israeli Navy in techniques of eliminating destroyers and submarines. Ne'eman was authorised to reply that Israel did not need this kind of assistance at the moment, but would take a rain cheque.[19]

As for intelligence co-operation, it was agreed that both nations would exchange intelligence reviews on a weekly basis. A procedure was also introduced for the transfer of urgent material. Finally, Ne'eman reported, towards the end of July France would make some major decisions about how to prosecute the Algerian war outside Algeria proper. This would have an acute effect on collaboration with

Israel, since France's very need for Israel was intimately bound up with the Algerian problem in the first place. However, Paris's review of its Algeria policy was pre-empted by the outbreak of the Suez Crisis a few days later.[20]

Ne'eman also reported that the two sides had agreed to exchange situation assessments and issues requiring further examination. The intelligence co-operation would encompass most of the issues which were of concern to either party, in both the concrete and theoretical spheres. Reporting that the idea of "personal" terror was now dormant, Ne'eman was instructed to let it lie. As Dayan put it, "don't stir things up, don't awaken it until [the French] please." But Ne'eman, not wishing to appear artless, looked into the matter and discovered that in any event the "contracts" were not practicable at this stage.[21]

"A Tangled Web of Mistakes, Suspicions and Malice"

Immediately after Vermars, Dayan and Peres apprised Isser Har'el, the chief of the Mossad, of the secret intelligence collaboration. It was agreed to let the French arrange their own division of labour, but to work out the corresponding arrangements in Israel without interfering in French affairs. Eventually it was decided that the Intelligence Branch would be responsible for all intelligence co-operation with France, in coordination with the Mossad, which was well-placed to develop an effective ring in North Africa, both for intelligence gathering and for "liquidating" FLN leaders in Algeria.[22]

It was therefore decided that assassination attempts in Europe would be entrusted to the Mossad – subject to prior approval by the Chief of Staff. Har'el was asked to provide Dayan, by July 8, with full details about the existing Jewish immigration network in Algeria. Har'el's suggestion to expand the scope of the information being delivered to the French to include regions outside the Arab world, was deferred for later consideration. For the time being, the scope of intelligence collaboration agreed on with the French would remain intact.[23]

Already on July 10, Israel provided France with information about an arms-carrying plane about to lift off from Rome for Algeria. The French reached the plane, but were unable to stop it. Nevertheless, this episode earned Israel much respect.[24]

Once Ben-Gurion decided to give the IDF (i.e., the Chief of Staff) exclusive responsibility for all Zayit affairs, with Peres already in charge of Ge'ut matters, the two acquired total control over Israel's relations with France, central to which was the secret military alliance between the two nations. Secrecy was of paramount importance – not only because of the nature of the co-operation, but also because Israel was reluctant to appear in world public opinion as a collaborator in the suppression of an anti-colonial rebellion. It was therefore decided to restrict the number of "need-to-know" personnel to an absolute minimum, compartmentalise the various spheres of activity, formulate well-defined channels of communication and designate all cables and letters as "for your eyes only". On July 3 the Chief of Staff ordered that no contacts with the "partners" be undertaken without his authorisation: "It is necessary that the people of Israel speak to their friends in one tongue, otherwise the situation will get out of control, and eventually we shall find ourselves enmeshed in a tangled web of mistakes, suspicions and malice."[25]

It was also decided that all correspondence relating to arms procurement (Ge'ut) would be handled by Peres and Nahmias of the Ministry of Defence, even if the subject concerned IDF officers. Zayit and "Yona" (unloading French arms in Israel) was to be handled by the Chief of Intelligence and Ne'eman in Paris, with notifications to Peres. All Zayit cables were to be forwarded immediately to the Chief of Staff. All these compartmentalisation procedures were finalised by July 5, and on the 12th were approved by the Prime Minister.[26]

"Remember, our Object is War against Nasser"

The linkage between Zayit (intelligence collaboration) and Ge'ut (arms procurement) was self-evident. Progress in Zayit supported Ge'ut, almost as a precondition.

The entire situation was unprecedented, as far as Israel was concerned. Colonel Harkabi made this clear in his summation of the Vermars talks: "We must remember that our object is war against Nasser. It is our interest to hit him on all fronts, since it does not matter, as far as he is concerned, whether he was beaten on the Libya front or on the Israel front. And we cannot achieve co-operation with France in the war against Nasser if we restrict this war only to matters which interest us. If we want to have the French involved in our war, we must involve ourselves in theirs."[27]

When the Israeli delegation returned from Vermars, Shaul Avigur, advisor to the Minister of Defence for special affairs,* criticised the agreement, saying that the same arms could have been obtained without all the extraneous commitments. To which Dayan replied, "In the past the People of Israel has paid more for things which have not been done

---

* Actually, Avigur was much more than that. Regarded by Ben-Gurion as a paragon of integrity, he was consulted on questions of conscience, ethics and propriety. Which does not mean that his advice was invariably accepted.

than for things which have been done, only to be proven later to have been errors."[28]

Thus, in June 1956 the foundations were laid for wide-ranging political and military co-operation between Israel and France. Dayan saw this alliance as "a relief. We shall get weapons, plenty of weapons, good weapons, and soon. Within a year we shall have a brand-new air force and armoured corps, defensive and offensive weapons. We shall be relieved of the hardships created by Egypt's alliance with the USSR." For Dayan, there was also relief from another difficult situation: it seemed that the reason which had made the Cabinet reject his policy of an Israeli-initiated war – namely, the Czech deal – was about to be made irrelevant.[29] Still, Ben-Gurion would not readopt this posture now, at least not explicitly. He was still of two minds regarding an Israeli-initiated war. While never rejecting it on principle, he could not regard the IDF's rearmament as sufficient reason to go to war. At the same time, it is reasonable to suppose that in giving his approval to a deal with France that involved – was contingent upon – military collaboration against Egypt, the Prime Minister took into account the possibility of Israel's being dragged into a war by France. Already on June 29, just after the Vermars agreement was signed, he told the Chief of Staff that he would not reject pre-emptive action, should this be required under the terms of the alliance with France. Nevertheless, in order to cross the threshold from this posture to a war of Israel's choosing, Ben-Gurion needed another push.[30]

Events soon transpired that put the Israeli-French deal in a completely new light. It should be remembered, however, when we move on to examine the Suez Crisis, that this international development was unrelated to the tightening links between Israel and France. The really far-reaching agreements, which bore such a weighty military significance in practical terms, were concluded prior to the Suez Crisis. Those agreements created the infrastructure for operational co-operation between France and Israel. Joint working procedures had been hammered out, a liaison system put in place, and in Israel the defence establishment had been given exclusivity with regard to relations with France, bypassing the Foreign Ministry. Above and beyond this, the Israeli negotiators' success in Paris had reinforced the substantive posture authored by Dayan and Peres – a posture which called for Israel to provoke a war.

During June and July 1956, there was much reason for optimism in Israel's Ministry of Defence and in the IDF. True, the government had not yet decided explicitly to support an Israeli-initiated war. But the new armament, and the collaboration with France, were factors which could not be ignored.

4

The Suez Crisis

From Crisis to War

In the early summer of 1956, while Egypt was busily enhancing its relations with the Soviet Bloc and Israel was entering a mainly anti-Egypt alliance with France, the Suez Crisis broke out, bringing about a fundamental change in Egypt's international situation. It was this turn of events which made it possible for Israel and France to start the war they each desired, under the most favourable conditions for them. The Suez Crisis alienated Egypt from the Western Powers, which even considered going to war against it – and Israel could now seize the opportunity. We shall review briefly the events which led to war, and afterwards elaborate on each phase of the developments in turn.

A Perfectly Legitimate Move

On 26 July 1956, an international furore erupted over the question of ownership of the Suez Canal Company: this came to be known as the Suez Crisis. On that day Nasser, in a major public address marking Egypt's Revolution Day, announced the nationalisation of the Suez Canal Company by the Government of Egypt. Essentially, this was Nasser's reaction to a US decision to withdraw its promised financial support for a prestigious Egyptian development project, the high dam at Aswan. At the same time, it was a logical extension of the series of moves which had brought about the withdrawal of British troops from the Suez Canal Zone during the previous year, as well as a major step towards establishing Egypt in a leadership position among the Arab nations in particular, and the non-aligned nations in general. More critically, it also meant depriving France and Britain of their vested interests in the Suez Canal. As British jurists were forced to concede, however, it was a perfectly legitimate move.[1]

The Suez Canal Company (properly, *La Compagnie Universelle du Canal Maritime de Suez*) operated the Canal as an Egyptian-registered public company, yet most of its shares were held by foreigners: the British Government held a 44 per cent share, while most of the rest was in private French hands. Technically, there could be little doubt as to the legality of the nationalisation. The British Government wanted to present a case resting on legal as well as political grounds, but could find not a firm juridical foothold. Asked to provide a brief, the legal counsellor of the British Foreign Office found himself in an awkward position; he could only inform his superiors that their intention to attack Egypt had no legal justification.

Still, the British and French governments, and others in the international community, were outraged at the liquidation of the "special regime" which had prevailed in the Suez Canal Zone since the turn of the century. This regime had afforded France and Britain a unique position in the Canal Zone and, as a result, throughout the Middle East. Most importantly, the Canal was then the main artery for the flow of oil from the Persian Gulf to Europe. Britain, in particular, tended to regard its special position in the Canal as the guarantee of the free flow of oil. And besides, the Canal was a major source of revenue. Some two-thirds of the passage fees went to the Canal Company's bank accounts in Paris and London.

The Suez Crisis was the most serious international flare-up since the end of the Korean war, earlier in the decade. It lasted some eight months, from its beginning, in late July 1956, until Israel's completion of its withdrawal from the Sinai by early March 1957. The crisis had several peaks, the Sinai War being just one of them – though, historically speaking, undoubtedly the most acute. Furthermore, the war brought about the most dangerous rift in NATO's history, between the US and its closest European allies, Britain and France, and also marked the decline of both those two countries from their former position as powers of the first rank. Nonetheless, some other peak events in the crisis should be noted, as they seemed quite important at the time: the establishment of the Union of Suez Canal Users in a conference convened in London; the mediation efforts by the Menzies Commission, which visited Cairo in September on behalf of the Users; and the reactions of the two superpowers, the US and the USSR, to the Sinai War.[2]

Generally speaking, the reactions of each concerned party to the crisis formed an on-going process, though with many ups and downs. The duration and nature of each side's involvement in the crisis differed. Thus, Israel did not consider itself involved at all in the Suez Crisis when it began, but came to play a major role later on. On the other hand, several countries which played a substantial role at the beginning, such as Italy or Australia, were subsequently shunted to the sidelines. Most important, the Suez Crisis began as a political dispute, but subsequently deteriorated into a military conflict. As a result, a central place was occupied by those countries that were willing to use military force: this was not a universal reaction among the states that saw themselves as injured parties, and some of them condemned those who were ready to resort to violence. In time, it transpired that only three countries – France, Britain and Israel – seriously considered the military option. And they finally acted on it, within the framework of a secret military alliance fraught with lies, intrigues and half-truths.

Each of the combatant states had its own distinctive motives for taking military action against Egypt. Israel's were discussed in earlier chapters, and it should again been noted that though Israel had been denied passage in the Suez Canal since its establishment, this was by no means its major reason for going to war against Egypt; its agenda was far more existential than that. And nearly the same can be said of France.

"Failure in the Suez is Tantamount to Failure in Algeria"

For the French, as we have seen, the Sinai War was the extension of another, far more important conflict from their perspective: the uprising in Algeria. The revolt which broke out in this "Overseas Department" on 1 November 1954, had escalated into all-out war during the period under discussion. Eventually, that conflict would end in France's evacuation of Algeria in August 1962. For the purposes of this study, the key fact is that the French believed Nasser to be a major moving force behind the Algerian rebels, a fact of which Israel was keenly aware. Just a few days after the outbreak of the Suez Crisis, Peres told Ben-Gurion that "the French tend to take Nasser's decision [to nationalise the Canal Company] far more seriously than the newspapers indicate; for them, failure in the Suez is tantamount to failure in Algeria".[3]

Thus the Algerian war was approaching its third year when the Suez Crisis broke out. All told, six French Prime Ministers were replaced because of the Algerian crisis, the Fourth Republic fell, and the Fifth Republic, headed by de Gaulle, who was propelled to the Presidency in its wake, survived by the skin of its teeth. Internal disagreements about Algeria's future brought France to the brink of civil war. Officially, Algeria had been regarded as an integral part of Metropolitan France, an "Overseas Department", rather than a colony. In the mid-1950s its population included more than a million French citizens (some of them of Spanish, Italian and Jewish extraction), the so-called *Pieds Noirs*. Most of them had left by the time the war ended. The number of casualties incurred was probably about a million, the majority Muslims.[4]

France had been in control of Algeria since 1830. At first it was an ordinary French colony, but as the number of French and other European settlers increased, and their desire to be considered full-fledged French citizens intensified, Algeria was annexed to France in the 1870s. Its status became that of a Department, which was subject – like all the other, mainland Departments – to the authority of the Ministry for Internal Affairs. Algeria differed from its neighbours to the east and west, Tunisia and Morocco, which in this period retained their status as French protectorates, eventually controlled by the Foreign Ministry in Paris, until they gained independence in 1956. Algeria, comprising three sub-Departments, was entitled to send representatives to the French National Assembly. In time, this right was extended to Muslim residents as well, though the number of their representatives was the same as those of the *Pieds Noirs*: eight million or more Muslims were thus represented by the same number of delegates as one million European settlers.[5]

For many in the French nation, and not only the *Pieds Noirs*, Algeria was an inseparable part of France. According to Jacques Soustelle, the French Governor-General of Algeria from February 1955 to February 1956, "Algeria and its inhabitants are an integral part of France . . . as much as Provence or Bretagne."[6] Thus, as many in France saw it, the Algerian war was being fought over part of their homeland, and the conflict represented a substantial threat to Metropolitan France. By 1956, Algeria was France's paramount political and military problem. Guy Mollet's Socialist government, which had assumed office in January 1956, made the granting of any further privileges to Algeria's Muslim majority conditional upon the cessation of their violent revolt. Mollet appointed Robert Lacoste, a well-known hard-liner, Governor-General of Algeria, and Lacoste immediately began to organise a sweeping military campaign to terminate the insurrection. He announced his intention to deploy an army of 500,000 in Algeria (in fact, the number of French troops there by the end of 1956 was 200,000).[7]

What connection was there, if any, between Nasser, the Suez Crisis and the Algerian war? Frustrated by their inability to turn the tide of uprising, the French began to seek external causes for its increasing scope. Egypt was the obvious bogeyman: on 3 November 1954, when the revolt was barely three days old, the government of France already made an official protest (for the first, but not the last time) to the Egyptian government: even at this early stage Radio Cairo (*Saut al-Arab*, the "Voice of the Arabs") was urging the rebels on with inflammatory broadcasts.[8]

By April 1955, Nasser had become a prominent leader of the nonaligned nations. After he persuaded their conference at Bandung to adopt a resolution siding with the rebels, it became an article of faith for the French that Nasser was providing comprehensive support (i.e., material as well as moral) to the Algerian rebels. Although having little evidence, Paris was convinced that more than mere rhetoric was involved. By 1956, then, Nasser was France's chief excuse for not being able to quell the revolt.

Nor was this entirely an idle propaganda claim. France believed that Nasser, besides permitting exiled rebel leaders such as Ferhat 'Abbas and Ahmad Ben-Bella to conduct propaganda from Cairo, was providing military aid to the rebel organisation, the FLN (Front de Libération Nationale). In late November 1955, during a parliamentary crisis which brought down the government of Edgar Faure, the Minister of the Interior (who was in charge of Algerian affairs, as explained above) Maurice Bourgès-Maunoury delivered a tough speech to the National Assembly, in which he revealed hitherto secret "information" (quite false, as it turned out) about the extent of Nasser's support of the rebels, including alleged arms deliveries.[9]

Already embroiled in a bitter war in Algeria, France was all the more inclined to use military force at Suez. By early 1956, the prevailing opinion in France – which was to gather momentum in the months to come – was that Nasser and his house guest Ben-Bella were "the moving forces behind the Algerian revolt".[10]

"Defeating Nasser was more Important than Winning Ten Battles in Algeria"

Nevertheless, the French Cabinet was not in full agreement as to how Nasser should be handled. Christian Pineau, the Foreign Minister in Mollet's new government, did not wish to begin his term in office by engineering a major débacle in France's relations with the Arab world – precisely because of the Algerian revolt. Pineau accepted the prevailing view in the Quai d'Orsay: that France should effect a rapprochement with Nasser to ensure that he would refrain from further intervention in Algeria. According to this approach, France should even fulfil its obligation, under an old agreement, to sell certain arms to Egypt. Pineau also declared that his government would coop-erate closely with the US and Britain in Middle Eastern affairs, in the spirit of the May 1950 Tripartite Declaration, according to which Britain, France and the US would act to prevent changes being made to bound-aries in the Middle East.

However, Bourgès-Maunoury, now Minister of Defence, took the opposite approach. He wanted to bring as much pressure as possible to bear on Nasser, to force him to stop meddling in Algerian affairs. His attitude was to gain much support during the next few months, while the Mollet government's frustration with Algeria grew apace. It was this attitude, and this frustration, which accounted for France's tighter links with Israel.

Meanwhile in Israel, during the winter of 1956, another difference of opinion was almost at its height. The Foreign Ministry argued that Israel should invest its main arms procurement efforts in the United States, whereas the Ministry of Defence and the IDF thought prospects in France were better. Early in March 1956, Israel's Ambassador to Paris, Ya'akov Tzur, and the head of the Defence Ministry delegation there, Yosef Nahmias, paid a visit to the French Minister of Defence. Tzur was impressed that Bourgès-Maunoury was taking quite a different tack from Pineau, as he tended to place at least some of the responsibility for Israel's security on the Americans and showed little concern for France's relations with the Arab states. According to Tzur, Bourgès-Maunoury told them: "As for the Arabs – we shall not win them over anyway. What could they do to France that they haven't done already?"[11]

In April 1956, Tzur heard from Guy Mollet that "Middle Eastern affairs are no longer marginal to French policy. Nasser's active intervention in North Africa goes directly for Algeria's bleeding jugular, and there is no need any longer to convince France that the enhancement of his prestige and strength with Soviet arms is a danger to Mediterranean security, even beyond the boundaries of Israel and its neighbours." It was shortly after this that French-Israeli relations entered a new phase, as related above.[12]

Tzur also said that later in April 1956, Lacoste himself sent a personal representative to Israel, to learn how Israel could contribute to the French effort in Algeria. On June 8, after the emissary had returned to France, Tzur met with Lacoste at the latter's invitation. The connection was clear: "[Lacoste] was quite concerned about Nasser's growing influence and military capabilities. [He] asked for details about our army and its deterrence capabilities." Tzur discussed with him the differences of opinion in France's top leadership, between those who supported arms sales to Israel and those who were hesitant. Lacoste remained noncommittal, for an obvious reason: for the French, Israel's arming was a function of its ability to contribute to their struggle against Nasser. Tzur was not involved in the secret negotiations which Peres was conducting at the time with the heads of the French defence establishment. On the other hand, he was better informed about the prevailing mood in France, and therefore had a better perspective from which to view the changing attitude towards Israel.[13]

In the eyes of many in France, the Suez Crisis was immediately linked with Algeria. For the French, the timing was excellent: now they had a good excuse to settle accounts with Nasser. From the start of the crisis, it was clear that France was willing to allocate some of its troops in Algeria for a military move in the Suez Canal Zone.[14]

The evaluation that made success in Algeria contingent upon Nasser's removal was born within the French armed forces. However, full co-operation between the military and political establishments was achieved primarily because both the French government and public opinion tended to accept this connection. Thus, General André Beaufre, who would be second-in-command to Britain's General Hugh Stockwell, commanding officer of the land forces in Operation Musketeer – the Anglo-French part of the Sinai/Suez War – was a leading proponent of this view. Beaufre had been a senior officer with the French Army in Algeria prior to Suez, and returned there afterwards; he firmly believed that the supreme command of the Algerian revolt was based in Cairo, enjoying active support from Egyptian intelligence.

As early as June 28, French Ambassador to London Jacques Cheauvelle explained to British and American officials that if Nasser were to get away with nationalising the Canal, France would no longer be able to contain the Algerian revolt. The same notion appeared in a memo written by Foreign Minister Pineau for a tripartite meeting (with his British and American counterparts) on 30 July 1956. Pineau even went further when he told his interlocutors that, as far as France was concerned, "defeating Nasser is more important than winning ten battles in Algeria." In short, the French regarded Nasser as the linchpin of the revolt; the nationalisation crisis only strengthened them in their views.[15]

Nasser and the Algerian Revolt

Statements made after the event by French military leaders show clearly their mounting frustration over developments in Algeria. They were especially upset that their government did not give the Army sufficient support to enable it to bring its full weight to bear on the uprising. Both Army and government needed an excuse for their on-going failure in Algeria, and Nasser provided them with one. Thus the Suez Crisis became, for French military leadership, an opportunity to settle accounts with Nasser for his supposedly active support of the revolt.

The ultimately dismal conclusion of *l'affaire Suez* only heightened French frustration, particularly within the Army, which would lurch out of control in the "generals' rebellion" of 1961. Yet, in the course of the Suez Crisis, French soldiers and politicians still shared certain views about how France should conduct its war in Algeria. For one thing, both groups believed that Nasser's removal would deal a severe blow to the revolt, materially and morally.[16] One should bear in mind that French military frustrations were older than the Algerian revolt; they had been festering since April 1940 and, 14 years later, the humiliating defeat at Dien Bien Phu. The Army simply could not afford another débacle in Algeria. Viewed in this light, any excuse – sound or otherwise – would do. When joint planning towards an Anglo-French war against Egypt began, it became clear to the British that besides all the French protestations about freedom of navigation in the Suez Canal and Nasser's insufferable arrogance, their real concern was Algeria (as noted above, the Israelis too were quick to realise this). In this sense, the French were better situated than the British: for them, Suez was just another crisis in an on-going war, a second front, in a manner of speaking. Unlike the British, they did not have to put domestic public opinion on a war footing.[17]

It was only after the war had ended that Algerian rebel leaders revealed how little support they had actually received from Nasser. For practical reasons, they could not have expressed their disappointment earlier, for they dearly needed whatever aid they got. In retrospect, however, it turned out that besides his rhetoric, amplified by Egyptian radio broadcasts, Nasser's aid to the rebels had been meagre indeed. Abdelkader Chanderli, one of the uprising's political leaders who in 1956 had been in charge of arms purchases in Yugoslavia, later said that Nasser's assistance had been "negligible, [but] because of the need for solidarity, we could not say so". According to British historian Alistair Horne, Morocco and Tunisia, which gained their independence from France in March 1956, were far more significant purveyors of aid to the FLN than Egypt.[18]

Still, it was convenient for the Algerian rebels – and for Nasser himself – to maintain the pretence, and radio broadcasts from Cairo may possibly have had some impact in Algeria. But more important, the same perception was useful for the French as well: the revolt was so difficult to crush because it was feeding on external support – otherwise it would have long since crumbled. For the present discussion, it does not really matter how much actual support Nasser gave the Algerian rebels. What does matter is that it was an article of faith with the French, which brought them to conclude a military agreement with Israel in June 1956, and that this later developed into joint moves towards war, culminating in the Sinai War itself.[19]

For the French, Nasser's removal from power had become such a vital objective as to make a military alliance with Israel (which, as the French were well aware, was willing to go to war against Egypt), with all its consequences for Franco-Arab relations, worthwhile. French Chief of Staff from 1954 until March 1956, General Pierre Guillaumat stated that

France's decision to arm Israel had predated the Suez Crisis, and was related to the Algerian situation. In May 1955, he told Peres and Colonel Emanuel Nishri, Israel's military attaché in Paris, that significant assistance was bound to generate Arab protests and demands, but "he indicated that the Arabs were enemies to France as well as to Israel . . . their policies have always been hostile." His Israeli interlocutors judged this, at the time, to be a very unusual turn of phrase.[20]

In a state of confrontation between France and the Arab world, Israel could provide much-needed, and firm, support. France's already close relations with Israel (which actually predated the state's establishment in 1948) grew even closer as the crisis progressed. Earlier arms deals, signed in 1954 and 1955, were replaced by larger ones, and there was diplomatic support as well. One should also mention that on a personal level, quite a few French leaders at the time (such as Mollet, Bourgès-Maunoury and Abel Thomas, the Director-General of the Ministry of Defence) had not long before been Resistance leaders, and therefore were sympathetic now to the Jewish state.[21]

For its part, Israel naturally found it convenient to nurture French animosity towards Nasser. Although Israel was first requested (as far as we know) to provide intelligence about the revolt only during the spring of 1956, when French anti-Nasser sentiments were already running high, it did make its own contribution: information passed on to Paris served to strengthen the feeling prevailing there that Nasser should be removed.[22]

At the time, Israel tended to accept French assumptions regarding Nasser's role as the chief external supporter of the Algerian revolt. The Israelis also conjectured that there were differences of opinion in France, notably between Quai d'Orsay and the military, as to how to deal with external supporters of the rebels in general, and with Nasser in particular; these internal debates, Israeli leaders thought, should be exploited. It is interesting to compare this French internal debate with a similar dispute which took place in Israel at the same time, again between the Foreign Ministry and the military, and again regarding ways and means for handling Nasser, as described in previous chapters. It was no coincidence that the special relationship between the two countries began with the personal ties which had developed between Bourgès-Maunoury and Thomas on the one hand, and Peres and Dayan on the other. One thing they all had in common was a great dislike for the attitudes struck by their respective foreign ministries.[23]

"Mediterranean Tides"

Central to Israeli-French negotiations prior to the Sinai War was Israel's request for arms: a lot of arms, as soon as possible. Yet all these discussions, with their ups and downs, were overshadowed by Algeria. Whatever Israel could contribute to France was bound up with the revolt, including intelligence information about Egypt and possible operational assistance in a strike against that country. Israel's ability to provide the French with relevant intelligence was thus a major component in the development of its alliance with France. Diplomatic relations between France and Egypt were quite correct throughout this period, so that France found it quite difficult to take an overt stand against Egypt. A third party was needed to supply information and even carry out sabotage operations if need be. Years later, Israeli Chief of Intelligence Harkabi could not remember clearly his first meeting with SDECE chief Boursicot; yet he recalled very well how impressed his French interlocutor had been when Harkabi mentioned some anecdotal titbit about Nasser and French agents in North Africa. It just sprang into Harkabi's mind during the conversation, but it served well to convince the Frenchman that relations with people who possess this kind of information should be cultivated.[24]

Israel having proved, in this way and others, by early May 1956, how helpful it could be as an intelligence source, the final barriers were removed from the road to the Zayit–Ge'ut defence pact. And when the Suez Crisis broke out less than three months later, the French were already actively preparing a move of their own against Nasser.[25]

Yet another factor in the increasingly tight co-operation between the two nations, again with Algeria in the background, was France's desire to sell arms, which was almost as strong as Israel's desire to purchase them. In this respect, France was virtually unique among the nations Israel turned to for arms, not to mention political support. On 3 June 1956, just before the Zayit–Ge'ut agreement was signed, the French government announced – following a heated debate in the National Assembly about continued arms deliveries to Egypt (the general subject was, of course, Algeria) – that it would no longer consider making arms deals with any Arab country. This, needless to say, was a heavy blow to France's military industries, and having Israel as a major, cash-paying customer went a long way towards softening the blow.[26]

The hard-pressed French Army, so heavily involved in Algeria, required funding for a special research-and-development project: it had to tailor its weaponry and other equipment to the special needs of anti-guerrilla warfare. The Army's modern equipment was better suited for World War II-style battlefields, and was not really appropriate for combat against small hit-and-run groups operating in familiar territory. It was clear from the start that tanks and jet fighters would not do, and the French wanted to equip themselves with American helicopters –

they had none of their own. In order to finance a transaction of that scope, France had had to sell other aircraft to all comers. Israel's strong desire to purchase precisely those weapons which the French now had little use for meshed beautifully with French intentions.[27]

Here, then, was another motive underlying the Vermars conference and the French-Israeli co-operation pact of June 1956. In Vermars, the cards were laid on the table: both parties shared an interest in the downfall of Nasser's regime, or at least in curbing his ambitions. Strengthening Israel with modern weaponry, should by itself weaken Egypt.[28]

In the final analysis, France's willingness to respond to Israel's arms requests from 1955 onwards, including the agreement and the actual arms deliveries of June 1956, as well as the joint operation against Egypt in October, was related to Paris' belief that linking up with Israel would facilitate the war in Algeria. Generally speaking, even today the entire *affaire Suez* is for the French but a chapter in their Algerian story. By the same token, the dismal political and military failure in Suez is overshadowed by France's more significant defeat – its humiliating withdrawal from Algeria in 1962.[29]

Relations between the two nations grew closer as war drew nearer. While Israeli representatives were handling the mass of details involved in military collaboration, there were also emotional expressions reflecting the community of interests on which the June 1956 agreement had been based. Thus Ben-Gurion spoke in early October 1956 about the "spiritual links which connect us with the home of that great revolution which gave mankind the Declaration of Human Rights." Yet, all concerned, including Ben-Gurion, seemed to understand that it was France's involvement in Algeria, rather than any spiritual bond, which had engendered the special relationship on the eve of the Sinai War, as well as (afterwards) France's support of Israel during the war itself.

The "Algerian connection" between France and Israel prior to the Suez Crisis was probably best summed up in a remark by Maurice Bourgès-Maunoury to Peres during the autumn of 1955, when the former was still Minister of the Interior in the Faure government: "Mediterranean tides rise and ebb on France's shores and Israel's at the same rhythm; and murky waters ought to be contained, lest they exceed their boundaries."[30]

It was the Algerian problem that made the difference between France's posture on the Suez Crisis and that of the other nations involved. Nonetheless, Britain also expressed a desire to resolve the Suez situation by force, as explained below. This suited the French very well, as it was their view – throughout the crisis – that they could not "go it alone", or even with just Israel's help. They sorely needed Britain.

There were several reasons for this: first and foremost, most of the French Army was tied up in Algeria, beside the forces involved in other colonial duties in Africa and elsewhere. Consequently, the French Army could not allocate to a possible invasion of the Suez Canal the entire force deemed necessary by planners to cope with the Egyptian Army. The British Army, on the other hand, was by and large "available for war".

The French also lacked launching bases near the theatre of operations. Their nearest military facilities were in North Africa – well out of range for their jet fighters, even their bombers. Britain, on the other hand, maintained bases in Cyprus and Malta, even in Libya. A possible deployment of French forces to Israel would have entailed not only serious political problems, but also military ones. The strategic assets Israel could offer at the time amounted to one deepwater harbour (at Haifa), three air bases and one international airport – a total of only four jet-certifiable runways, barely enough for the IDF's needs, let alone for use by the French at the same time.

Finally, it was clear to France that an attack on Egypt would place it in an awkward international position, generating a severe American rebuke, to say nothing of the USSR. France could not risk possible confrontation with the Soviet Union without support from a major NATO ally – if not the US, at least the UK. For all these reasons, France was intent from the very beginning on not going to war without British participation. Indeed, France was willing to acknowledge British domi-nation, political as well as military, and play second fiddle to Britain's leadership, in view of the aforementioned advantages: Britain's ability to allocate troops and bases, and its special relationship with the United States. Against this background, all Israeli efforts to persuade the French to proceed with them alone were doomed to failure.

An Unsettled Account with Nasser: The British Perspective

From the very beginning of the Suez Crisis, the British had vacillated in attempting to find the appropriate response to Nasser's unilateral move. While the French interest in Egypt was indirect, Britain had a large number of direct interests there. Just a few weeks earlier, in June 1956, the lengthy British presence in Egypt (dating from 1882) had come to a close, when the last British troops withdrew from the Suez Canal Zone following an agreement signed in October 1954.

The history of Britain's role in the Suez Crisis is characterised by deep differences within the country's political leadership, which made it impossible for Her Majesty's Government to pursue a uniform, consistent policy on Suez. In fact, British policy towards Egypt had been uncertain since the early 1950s, particularly with regard to the Suez Canal. Britain's position in Egypt has changed markedly during this time, and prior to the Suez Crisis the major feature in Anglo-Egyptian relations was the talks about the future arrangements for the Canal, which culminated in the British withdrawal, but had begun a few years earlier, at Egypt's insistence.

Basically, the Egyptians wanted to modify the 1936 agreement on the Canal, which they deemed incompatible with their sovereignty, since it entailed no mutuality of obligation and privilege. That is to say, the 1936 agreement addressed primarily Britain's prerogatives in the Suez Canal, with little reference to Egypt's rights. Most important, the agreement allowed Britain to maintain in the Canal Zone military bases which enjoyed extra-territorial status.

British animosity to Nasser and his regime is traceable to these negotiations, which soon developed into talks about an agreement for British withdrawal from the Canal Zone. The agreement played a subtly negative role in the Suez Crisis. After all, Eden (during his term as Foreign Secretary, 1951–5) sought, like his predecessor Bevin (1945–51), to extricate Britain from Egypt, as part of the more general process of post-World War II empire dissolution. Nevertheless, the Anglo-Egyptian agreement left a bad taste in many an English mouth, and became utterly unpalatable when the Canal Company was nationalised in July 1956. In part, timing was the issue: the Canal was nationalised barely six weeks after the withdrawal of the last British troops from the Canal Zone (June 13), that is to say, immediately after Britain had faithfully executed its part of the 1954 agreement.[31]

The reduction of the British presence in the Middle East after World War II stood in sharp contrast to, as London perceived it, the Suez Canal's exceptional importance for Britain's security and economy. Britain's major source of oil was the Persian Gulf, and all of that oil came through the Suez Canal (this was before the era of supertankers). Britain was thus the single largest Canal user, at least in terms of oil bound for Europe, accounting for more than 20 per cent of the oil passing through the Canal in 1955.

Britain's vested interests in Egypt overall and in the Suez Canal in particular, had given rise to a large British community in the country. As Britain's presence in Egypt began to decline and talks about the withdrawal of British troops from the Canal Zone intensified, concern arose about how to protect this community, should the need arise. By the end of 1952, following the Officers' Revolt in Egypt in which the king was deposed, Plan Rodeo had already been worked out. It called for a brief occupation of Cairo and Alexandria and the seizure of the roads to the two cities from the Suez Canal Zone, in order to evacuate British subjects to the Canal Zone, which was then still under British military control. The plan acknowledged that Britain could not, and would not, occupy the whole of Egypt, but its implementation would suffice, not only to protect British life, but also to prevent any government from taking over in Egypt against Britain's wishes.

The officer in charge of planning Rodeo was General Sir Brian Robertson, Commander in Chief of British Army Forces in the Middle East. In April 1953, Prime Minister Churchill appointed him Britain's chief negotiator in the talks with Egypt about the future of the Canal Zone. Earlier, Sir Brian was the commander of the British Occupation Zone in Germany, where he had played a major part in working out the *status quo* arrangement with the USSR. He wished to introduce a similar arrangement with Egypt, which would not involve coercion, at least not overtly, while at the same time preparing for the possible use of force in order to ensure that the prospective Suez Canal arrangement would be satisfactory to Britain. Thus, in the early 1950s, British policy *vis-à-vis* Egypt always tended to prefer accommodation to the use of force.

Foothold

The British Army, under Robertson, wished to maintain a foothold in Egypt. Churchill warned that without any military bases in Egypt, Britain would find it exceedingly difficult to return, should it have to defend the Suez Canal in its interests. Robertson tried to persuade decision makers in London to take a firm stance, up to a point, in order to secure for Britain something of a military presence. Churchill was even more adamant, willing to stick by his guns even in the face of American displeasure – Washington refused to support this British position – and the risk of the negotiations' collapse. However, Churchill's own Cabinet refused to accept his approach.[32]

In the end, Britain was humiliated. British negotiators were powerless, achieving nothing whatsoever, while the Egyptians, secure in the knowledge that Britain could not call on American support, agreed to nothing short of complete British withdrawal. The British were furious; their desire "to teach Egypt a lesson" harks back directly to this point. Churchill even broached the idea of conquering Egypt and then withdrawing immediately, just to cut the Egyptians down to size. But reason prevailed, and the British made major concessions (also to the United States, which felt that an unwanted Western presence would do more harm than good in Egypt). In the end, they were able to obtain Egyptian consent to a vague clause allowing for a British return to the Canal Zone under certain conditions. The troops involved were then redeployed in locales – Cyprus, Jordan and Libya – which could have been interpreted as threatening to Egypt.[33]

In any event, when the Suez Crisis broke out the idea of occupying Egypt, in whole or in part, was no novelty to the British government or military. As a matter of fact, Plan Rodeo provided a convenient starting-point for the making of Operation Musketeer, beginning in August 1956. During the entire lengthy but on-going process of negotiations over the future of the Suez Canal Zone – first with King Faruq, then with the Free Officers under General Neguib – Britain never relinquished its military option of moving in by force in order to "pacify" Egypt. Despite the winds of change following World War II, British "imperial instincts" were apparently still functioning during the negotiations with Egypt. Those instincts dictated much of the Foreign Office's attitude even before the Egyptian revolution, and more so afterwards, since the new Egyptian regime obviously had an anti-British potential.

The question of intervention came up immediately after the revolution, but was rejected: Egypt's new government agreed to resume negotiations, and Britain elected to make arrangements with various countries in the region without recourse to coercion. Thus, its agreement to make Libya an independent kingdom, in 1951, left some military bases there in British hands.

Britain's view that an agreed settlement was preferable to one achieved by force was in part due to its conclusion that, from the British point of view, the feasible alternative governments in Egypt would have been even worse: whether headed by the fundamentalist Muslim Brotherhood, or another Wafd-style secular regime, which would be inherently weak. Nevertheless, the situation rankled the British, and their policy towards Egypt throughout the Canal negotiations and later on was encumbered by severe misgivings about Egypt's leaders, none of whom was regarded in London as trustworthy.[34]

Against this general mistrust, Gamal Abdel Nasser looked to the British like a leader who could both sign an agreement and uphold it. It was not Nasser who led the Free Officers' revolt in 1952; the junta leader, at least nominally, was the popular General Muhammad Neguib. But to the British officials who had met him the younger, more ambitious Nasser seemed to be a modern statesman who understood that he could not seriously tackle his nation's severe domestic problems as long as foreign troops were based there. Therefore, he would be grateful to the British if they left and would abide by his agreement with them.

Nasser had never made a secret of his resentment of British infringement of Egyptian sovereignty; but Robert Hankey, who now headed the British negotiating team, chose to discern in him a deep admiration for

Britain. It was this trust in Nasser personally, coupled with the realisation that this might be the last chance to conclude a lasting agreement with Egypt, that led Britain finally to sign an agreement which left it empty-handed.[35]

Having lionised Nasser as "our last gamble", British leaders made him personally the focus of hopes that were shattered even before the Suez Crisis: great expectations tend to produce great disappointments. Particularly so with Sir Anthony Eden, who returned in October 1953 (having recovered from a serious illness) to the Foreign Office, where he masterminded the conclusion of the negotiations with Egypt. Eden – with the support of the Ministry of Defence and the military, and against the views of the Prime Minister, other Cabinet members and the "Suez lobby" in Parliament – based the entire agreement on Nasser's credibility. In April 1954, Nasser replaced Neguib as head of state, and in June the British Cabinet ratified the draft agreement. A final version was agreed on in July and officially signed in October.

Eden's moves were particularly significant because the Prime Minister did not trust Nasser at all. Churchill even thought about provoking Nasser into attacking British troops in the Canal Zone, to give him a pretext for war, but Nasser did nothing that might justify an attack. In the meantime, Egyptian negotiators hinted that Britain could retain the right to return to its former bases under certain circumstances, such as an attack by a third party on one of Britain's allies in the Middle East, including Turkey (a member of NATO). This compromise enabled Britain to pull out its troops (80,000 in 1954) from the Canal Zone without losing too much face, but it was dependent entirely upon Nasser's good will. As the British evaluated his situation, he would do anything in order to make them leave, and it would be worth his while to abide by the agreement even after their complete withdrawal.[36]

Britain's lack of insistence in the negotiations could also be explained by the feeling that in a nuclear world, the presence or otherwise of several thousand troops, in this remote place or that, was no longer meaningful: this seems to have been Churchill's view. Also, the Prime Minister's physical condition was deteriorating rapidly, and he could no longer dominate his Cabinet colleagues as before. In the end, Churchill succumbed to the combined pressure of the Foreign and Defence ministries.[37]

"Special Relationship"

British policy in the Middle East in general, and at Suez in particular, was dominated at the time by a strong need for alignment with American policy. The United States, however, while looking for stable, pro-West regimes in the region, took a very different approach from the traditional British orientation. The result was that Britain's "special relationship" with the US caused its policy vis-à-vis Egypt to be indecisive. On the one hand, Britain was co-author of Plan Alpha, which sought a peaceful settlement to the Arab-Israeli conflict, in a way that would cater to Western interests in the region; for both America and Britain, Nasser was the Arab linchpin in such a plan. At the same time, in order to preserve their standing and economic interests (particularly oil) in the Middle East, the British made efforts (which enjoyed American consent, though not actual support) to construct the "Northern Tier" (later to be called the Baghdad Pact) – a defence pact with Iraq and Turkey. Seeking to protect Western interests in the Middle East from the Soviet Union, this alliance relied heavily on Iraq, Egypt's rival for leadership of the Arab world. Needless to say, Egypt preferred to stay out of the Baghdad Pact. Moreover, Nasser's reservations about Plan Alpha were mainly due to his misgivings concerning the Baghdad Pact.[38]

Thus a duality loomed between the need to secure British interests by resolving the Arab-Israeli conflict, on the one hand, and by creating an anti-Soviet alliance, on the other – a situation reflected in the 1954 Anglo-Egyptian agreement. At the time of the agreement, the British assumed that Egypt would become a major component of their proposed regional defence pact, and that solving the Canal problem and allowing Egypt to concentrate on its domestic problems would pave they way to Western-sponsored mediation of the Arab-Israeli conflict. Egypt's objection to the Baghdad Pact, and its arms deal with Czechoslovakia, shattered these British assumptions.

It was not only the Suez Canal agreement that collapsed in 1956: the chances of creating an effective pro-Western alliance in the Middle East were sharply reduced, while the Arab-Israeli conflict took on a new dimension, quite alarming to the British, when Israel's relations with France began to bloom. Britain was quite frustrated, and there was much distress in London over the collapse of a carefully and patiently worked-out scheme.[39]

"Threaten, Bribe, Get Rid Of"

Until the outbreak of the Suez Crisis, it was the Foreign Office that determined British policy towards Nasser. Foreign Minister Eden had been, as mentioned above, the architect of the 1954 withdrawal agreement. Even later on, after becoming Prime Minister, Eden usually saw eye to eye with Whitehall. Traditionally, the Foreign Office's chief concern was the flow of oil from the Persian Gulf. Naturally, its pundits were anxious to please Nasser. In this regard, the chief policy-maker was Sir Evelyn Shuckburgh, assistant under-secretary in charge of Middle Eastern affairs.

Immediately after the Egyptian–Czech deal became known, in September 1955, Sir Evelyn expressed his willingness to pay a high price – even to abandon whatever commitment there was to Israel in Plan Alpha – for the sake of maintaining relations with Nasser intact. But a few days later, when the unprecedented scope of the deal was learned, and Nasser adamantly rejected British entreaties to cancel it, a different attitude began to take shape, which would come to full fruition ten months later, when Britain invaded Egypt. Shuckburgh himself, after some hesitation, developed a proposal for a new policy towards Egypt: "We should first threaten Nasser, then bribe him, and if both fail, get rid of him."[40]

As the Suez Crisis unfolded, Britain's posture reflected most of all its indignation, anger and severe disappointment. There is no other explanation for the harsh reactions towards Nasser and his regime by policy-makers in Britain. Eden and others saw the nationalisation of the Canal as an epoch-making event, the way they saw, in retrospect, some of the crises which preceded (and ushered in) World War II. Harold Macmillan, then Chancellor of the Exchequer (and subsequently Eden's successor as Prime Minister), spoke of war over Britain's economic future, using terms such as "existential danger".[41] And in the background, there was always the clause in the 1954 agreement which allowed Britain to send its troops back to the Canal Zone, should an allied nation in the region be attacked – including Egypt itself.

Sir Anthony Eden

The role played by Anthony Eden, the British Prime Minister during the Suez Crisis, was extraordinary, both in terms of the impact of his personality on the development of the crisis, and in terms of the impact of the crisis on his personal fortunes, as well as his government's. Critics and supporters alike agree that he exercised a unique influence over the Suez affair. British historian Lord Balogh regards Eden as the "linchpin" of the Suez Crisis.[42] By July 1956, Eden had been Prime Minister for some 15 months, and somewhat of a disappointment. He had been waiting for the job for a very long time, in Churchill's gigantic shadow, and when he got his chance expectations ran high – he could not but fail to meet them all. Furthermore, in the 1950s Eden was unwell, sometimes working under the influence of various medications. At the same time, he was motivated by a strong desire to vindicate the reputation he had gained during the 1930s.[43]

Many historians concur that Eden was a captive of his own legend, as the Foreign Minister who had resigned from Chamberlain's Cabinet because of its policy of appeasement towards Nazi Germany. Eden was not alone in regarding Nasser as a small-scale replica of the German Führer, a "mini-Hitler" who must be pushed out of the way before he could wreak serious damage. Yet it was not Eden who dubbed Nasser "Hitler". At the time, it was quite usual in Britain to attach this appellation to any ruler who seemed to jeopardise world peace, which was still thought of as *Pax Britannica*. Eden's commitment to his own past, as well as the personal insult he had endured from Nasser – since it was he, Eden, who had masterminded the agreement which Nasser had signed just a couple of years earlier and now broke – made for what might easily be considered an overreaction, wholly disproportionate to anything Nasser did or stood for.[44]

Moreover, Eden basically believed, as did many in Britain at the time, that "the Arabs only understand force". Still, political expediency, plus the fact that he did not regard Israel's existence as an essential British interest, led him to orient his Middle East policy towards the Arab states in general and Egypt in particular, until the winter of 1956. During the 1940s, Eden had consistently objected to the creation of a Jewish state, even in part of then-Palestine. His attitude towards Israel was reflected in his habit of using the words "the Jews" in reference to it; only during the Suez Crisis did the British Prime Minister make himself use the word "Israel" more often.[45]

As noted earlier, the two guidelines which had directed Eden's "Egypt policy" prior to the conclusion of the agreement for British withdrawal from the Suez Canal Zone, in October 1954, were highly significant in shaping his approach during the Suez Crisis: his decision to put his trust in Nasser personally, and his insistence on a "back door", namely, the clause allowing British troops to return to the Canal Zone under certain circumstances. As a matter of fact, in order to include this clause in the final agreement Eden was forced to make large concessions, such as forcing a hasty withdrawal on his Army – within 20 months, quite a short order as the Army saw it, operationally and logistically (which in turn was to influence, later on, the preparations for Operation Musketeer) – just to please Nasser. And now, when the Suez Crisis broke out, Nasser showed that he would not live up to Eden's expectations.[46]

It cannot be said that none of this could have been foreseen in advance. As we saw, since early 1955, Nasser had made no secret of his opposition to British policy in the Middle East, particularly the Northern Tier effort. But then came two moves which set Eden utterly against Nasser:

1. Nasser's thankless attitude, as Eden saw it, towards a joint proposal made in December 1955 by the US, Britain and the World Bank, to construct a high dam on the Nile at Aswan, in southern Egypt. This proposal was indeed intended to put Nasser to the test: in exchange for financing this huge development project, which was expected at the time to solve major economic and social problems in Egypt, the West sought appropriate policy *quid pro quos*, in the form of Egypt's attitude towards the Western system of alliances in the region. Nasser, though, would not modify his foreign policy.
2. The removal of Sir John Glubb as Commander in Chief of Jordan's armed forces (then called the "Arab Legion") on 1 March 1956. This, for Eden, was the last straw. "Glubb Pasha", a British officer, was the founder of the Legion and its highest ranking officer for 25 years. His removal had to do with a major policy shift in Jordan, Britain's closest ally in the Middle East, towards Nasser. As a matter of fact, the British attributed Glubb's removal to direct Egyptian pressure (although this was an assumption they never bothered to investigate seriously).

Be that as it may, March 1956 marks a turning point; from then on, British policy towards Egypt mirrored Eden's fierce personal hostility towards Nasser. Already at this stage, Eden wanted Nasser's regime in Egypt destroyed. More than three months before the Americans reached their decision to cancel their grant to build the Aswan High Dam – the official reason was the nationalisation of the Suez Canal Company – Eden had known for a certainty that the Aswan project was dead and buried. Thus, Anglo-Egyptian relations were in a critical state months before the Suez Crisis.

Eden was punished following the Sinai War: his political career came to an end in early 1957. Undoubtedly, by taking upon himself such a central role in the crisis from the start, he also had to assume paramount responsibility for its eventual failure. In fact, his policy was fraught with contradictions from the outset: hostility towards Nasser but continuing overtures towards the Arab nations; resentment of "the Jews" but willingness to collaborate (albeit indirectly) with Israel; lack of respect for the French but dependence on France as an indispensable ally in the war against Egypt; dependence on domestic public opinion while spreading lies all over. British historians attribute Eden's behaviour to his personality and to his psychological, perhaps also his physical, condition. Such a diagnosis is obviously difficult to substantiate; but surely Eden's central role in the Suez Crisis makes his personal attitude, as well as his diplomatic, political and military moves during the crisis, crucial to any understanding of its unfolding.

Someone Else's Problem: The Israeli Perspective

"We Should Not Interfere in the Suez Affair"

At the outbreak of the Suez Crisis, the Israeli leadership was totally absorbed with two closely related developments – tightening its political ties with France, and strengthening the IDF as a result. There were several ramifications to the close links forged with France in the political sphere; for our purposes, the most significant were the major arms deal, code-named Ge'ut in Israel, and what seemed at the time imminent Israeli assistance to the French in their war against the Algerian rebels and their allies – code-named Zayit.

Thanks to Ge'ut, the IDF underwent a rapid build-up, particularly in the Armoured Corps and Air Force. By late July 1956, when the Suez Crisis broke out, the IDF was busy integrating its new equipment and expanding its formations. An absorption process of this scope could not co-exist with heightened operational activity: war at this time was, therefore, if only for technical reasons, the lowest of the IDF's priorities.

On the face of it, Israel had, in the summer of 1956, all it could ask for: rapid rearmament, a reduced Egyptian military presence on its frontier (most of Egypt's forces had been pulled back from the Sinai to the Canal Zone in advance of nationalisation), and relative quiet in the routine security sphere. As for the Suez Crisis, Ben-Gurion expressed the general view when he stated, immediately after the nationalisation, that it was not in Israel's interest to involve itself in this affair. Indeed, there was probably quiet satisfaction in Israel at the sight of Nasser embroiling himself so deeply with the Western powers and the other Canal users. Perhaps his downfall would be accomplished without Israel's lifting a finger.

As an added bonus, international attention was drawn away from the Arab-Israeli conflict, at least for a while. When Ben-Gurion remarked to Dayan, on 9 August 1956, that "We have more time now. Nasser is busy with England," Dayan concurred: "We should not interfere in the Suez affair."[1]

Yet Israel soon realised that, like it or not, it was deeply involved in the Suez Crisis. Because of its on-going conflict with Egypt – its willingness since the winter of 1955, at least in principle, to make war against Egypt – and its special relations with France, Israel could hardly be just a spectator on the sidelines.

"This Is Our Bondage to Our Suppliers"

On the eve of the crisis, Israeli leaders felt that quite soon, perhaps within six months, it would be possible to foment a war, even before the arms balance was fully restored. At the end of 1955, as we saw, Ben-Gurion did not discard the policy of an Israeli-initiated war; circumstances induced him only to suspend temporarily the IDF's preparations for such a conflict. By July 1956 (see chapter 3) Israel had resumed its militant posture, thanks mainly to the alliance with France and the unprecedented arms bonanza. The importance Ben-Gurion attached to the emerging relationship with France can be gleaned from a seemingly trivial event. Always dismissive of the pomp and circumstance of office, the Prime Minister habitually declined all invitations to attend ceremonial occasions; he went only where state business called him. Yet in 1956 he accepted French Ambassador Pierre Gilbert's invitation to attend the traditional July 14 reception at the French Embassy – after turning down, just ten days earlier, a similar invitation from the American Ambassador.[2]

At the same time, Israel modified its official assessment of how the Great Powers would react to a war of its initiating. Ben-Gurion was more optimistic than he had been several months before: he now estimated that neither the US nor the USSR would commit troops to the region. As a worst-case scenario, he thought that the UN, at Britain's instigation, would try to force Israel to make territorial concessions or take in a large number of Palestinian refugees. And then, said Ben-Gurion, Nasser might go to war, under the pretext of Israel's non-compliance with such a UN resolution. In that case, Israel should pre-empt. Moreover, prior to the Suez Crisis Ben-Gurion had thought that Nasser would attack only if he were militarily ready and only if the international atmosphere was conducive – again, due to British pressures. No one thought at the time in terms of a possible deterioration in Anglo-Egyptian relations.[3]

Now that his fears about future arms supplies to an "aggressor" Israel had been assuaged, the only remaining problem was almost a technicality: the sooner the French delivered their promised goods, the sooner

Israel would be poised to initiate war. Besides military preparedness, there was also the question of detailed operational planning, but this was already in place, by and large, and required only some updating. Problems of technical absorption of armament notwithstanding, Israel would be ready for war as soon as the new equipment arrived.

At the same time it was clear, at least to Ben-Gurion, that the French deal might curtail Israel's freedom of action. Just as the Soviet Union had acquired influence in Egypt through the Czech arms deal, so did France in Israel. During a discussion on spare parts to be supplied by the French, Ben-Gurion said: "This is our bondage to our suppliers. And the same goes for Egypt – the Egyptians are now subservient to Russia." The implication was that an Israeli decision to go to war would no longer be autonomous, for better or for worse.[4]

Dayan, for his part, was quick to take advantage of the new circumstances. When the Prime Minister convened a meeting of the General Staff to instruct the IDF to resume its preparations for a possible Israeli-provoked war, the Chief of Staff reminded him of the *casus belli* of the previous year: freedom of navigation in the Straits of Eilat and freedom to use the Jordan River waters as Israel saw fit. Now Dayan added yet another cause: "In the event of the disintegration of [the Kingdom of] Jordan – not a war initiated by them against us – with [the armies of] Iraq and Syria and other nations moving into Jordan, so that Jordan ceases to be Jordan, what role will Israel play? What will our policy be in such an eventuality?" Ben-Gurion replied that above and beyond the obvious aim of securing East Jerusalem and Mount Scopus, "certainly our initial inclination will be to reach at least the Jordan [River]. But we cannot ignore the fact that there are many Arab inhabitants in this area [i.e., the West Bank]. . . .Yet all this is conditional, I do not know if any serious person could make a firm commitment now."[5]

So Israel had three possible *casus belli*, two of them related to its eastern frontier. On the whole, said Ben-Gurion (just a few days before the nationalisation of the Canal), "what concerns us, in immediate political terms, is not so much Egypt as the [possible] disintegration of Jordan and Syria." The Suez Crisis, then, furnished Israel with yet another potential cause for war.[6]

Dayan still held fast to his view that Israel had the capability to initiate a war at its own discretion, irrespective of the question of absorbing the new armament. Ben-Gurion, though, took great pains to explain to him that he saw things differently, and gave Dayan strict orders not to provoke Egypt. It was clear, even to the Chief of Staff, that Ben-Gurion did not think Israel would be ready for war within the next six months – not before the first part of 1957, at the earliest. Nevertheless, what had been in June a cautious re-exploration of a possible Israeli-initiated war began to gain momentum by July. The question, just before the outbreak of the Suez Crisis, was not whether Israel would launch a war of its choosing, but when, and in what circumstances.[7]

"He Still Thinks It's Dutch"

All discussions about the fundamentals of national defence policy were conducted within a very narrow circle which included the Prime Minister and Minister of Defence, the Director-General of the Ministry of Defence, the Chief of Staff and a few General Staff officers. No politicians were involved, not even Cabinet ministers, to say nothing of the media and the general public. Thus there was no discussion of a pre-emptive war, prior to the Suez Crisis, in the Cabinet plenum, the Knesset, the various councils of the ruling party, Mapai, or any other civilian body. The secret of Israel's new ties with France was divulged only to the new Foreign Minister, Golda Meir (but to no other officials of her ministry, other than Ambassador Tzur in Paris), and Minister of Finance Levi Eshkol.[8]

Still, after the inception of the Suez Crisis, some secrets were gradually uncovered. It was felt, within this small group, that a cautious unveiling of the new French connection could be useful in the new atmosphere of confrontation between Egypt and the Western powers; the result was that certain information about a new supplier of arms to Israel was leaked. On July 30, Ben-Gurion called in Israel's daily newspaper editors for an off-the-record briefing.* He told them that Israel had signed a deal for tanks, jet fighters and artillery, but refused to disclose the supplier. The "Old Man" seems to have actually thought he could get away with it, but the number of reasonable possibilities was just too small. Whatever direct information was missing, indirect sources and common sense could provide, and the general grapevine became hyperactive. In late August, Dayan told Ben-Gurion how the rumour was spreading:

> I have a cousin in Kibbutz Geva, his name is Amnon, and he told me a story the other day. He has this friend, a lorry driver in Kibbutz Hanita. When he met this fellow, this is what he heard from him: "Listen, I must tell you something." And now, everybody in Geva knows that a French ship came into Haifa harbour last night with 1,200 tons of crates . . . [9]

---

* There was no television in Israel then, and radio was state-controlled. All the newspapers were subject to military censorship, although in the atmosphere of a nation under siege no editor would have dreamt of exposing a military secret just because it was "fit to print".

However, Mapai, the party's Knesset caucus and indeed the Knesset itself were too preoccupied with the brutal dismissal of Foreign Minister Sharett to turn their attention to the goings-on between Israel and France.

The Cabinet was first informed of the arms deal on 19 August 1956, in the midst of the Suez Crisis. The Knesset heard about it only on October 15, a fortnight before the start of the Sinai War. Looking back at the records of discussions in the Knesset and in other political bodies, one is struck by their irrelevance. The reason is that the senior level of the defence establishment was generally able to keep secret (or at least, out of printed records) whatever it wanted kept secret. There were indeed rumours about a major arms deal, which served the leadership's purposes; but even the few who had to be brought in knew nothing about Israel's promises in return. Or at any rate, those who were in the know kept mum.

Once again, as he had done earlier when contemplating the moribund Operation Omer, and as Eden was doing in Britain at the same time, Ben-Gurion was pushing military plans with serious political ramifications to the limits of democratic practice. In late 1955 the issue had been an Israeli-initiated war, but now it was a political alliance involving far-reaching military commitments.[10]

On the night of 24 July 1956, two days before Nasser declared the nationalisation of the Suez Canal Company, the first French arms shipment reached Israel. In order to maintain secrecy, the site chosen for unloading was a small, out-of-the-way port at the mouth of the Kishon River, near Haifa, rather than the naval base within the larger commercial harbour at Haifa proper. The French sent a landing craft to the site, capable of unloading cargo without proper port facilities. This first delivery included 30 AMX-13 tanks and 60 tons of equipment.

On hand were Ben-Gurion, Dayan and Peres, as well as French Ambassador Gilbert. The relief felt by these Israeli leaders must have been enormous. The public mood in Israel since the announcement of the Czech–Egyptian arms deal some eight months earlier, was desperate. Egypt's massive rearmament, combined with a terrorist campaign masterminded by Cairo, created the feeling in Israel that war was imminent – and that the IDF was inadequately prepared, in terms of modern weaponry.

While Dayan was more confident – quite sure, in fact – that the IDF could handle any Egyptian threat even in its present state, if only he was given a free hand, Ben-Gurion was worried. In particular, he was concerned about air raids; as mentioned, he had been in London during the Blitz, an experience which had left a lasting impression on him. He was convinced that Israel's civilian population would buckle under a similar campaign. Hence his decision to give Peres a free hand to conduct a foreign policy of his own, with one purpose in mind – to obtain arms for the IDF, and in particular aircraft.

Now this policy was coming to fruition. Yet, frustratingly, the fruits had to be kept secret from the public he had sought to reassure. The solution Ben-Gurion found was ingenious: on that night of June 24 he invited as a witness to the unloading Israel's unofficial poet laureate, Nathan Alterman. Alterman occupied a unique place in Israeli politics. Beside his serious work, Alterman was also a political commentator. His weekly Friday newspaper "column", usually written in verse, was avidly read and discussed. The relationship between Ben-Gurion and Alterman can only be described as one of mutual admiration, although, mindful of the biblical significance of both their first names, Nathan would occasionally chastise David for perceived wrongdoing.

Not this time, however. Alterman was invited in order to commemorate the occasion, although he was asked not to publish his verse just yet. Later on, when Ben-Gurion decided to reveal to his Cabinet, and still later to the Knesset and the general public, that Israel was getting arms from somewhere, rather than make a direct statement he took the unusual step of reading out Alterman's poem about "iron, plenty of iron, new iron. Long barrelled, thundering on chains of steel. Coming from afar . . . and upon landfall, becoming Jewish strength".[11]

The next vessel docked on July 30 bearing 30 more tanks and spares; it was met by Golda Meir. Four days later, on August 3, a shipment of more than one thousand tons of artillery shells arrived. It seemed that the French were abiding by the Ge'ut timetable, and a deliberate war was rapidly becoming a real possibility. Indeed, in retrospect, it was becoming real faster than anyone in Israel could imagine, as the Suez Crisis unfolded and the alliance between France and Israel became ever more concrete.

Subsequently, more politicians were allowed to witness the miracle, although there never was a thorough discussion of Israel's arms supplies in Cabinet – even the source of the arms was not revealed. On August 31, Dayan asked Ben-Gurion how Minister of Justice Rosen liked what he saw at the Kishon port. Ben-Gurion: "He's full of admiration. He still thinks it's Dutch."[12]

"We Should Treat Them as Brothers"

On August 3, Peres came back from France, where he discussed the possibility of purchasing Vautour fighter-bombers for the air force. Peres told Ben-Gurion that on August 1, his opposite number Abel Thomas gave him the following information:

1.   The British and the French have decided in principle on a joint military action to take over the Canal Zone.
2.   This operation was expected to start about three weeks hence.
3.   The British have made it a condition that Israel will not be involved, or even informed, so as not to cause all Arab nations unite around Nasser.[13]

Despite this, Thomas asked Peres if Israel would participate in a possible action against Nasser – in planning and advice, or more, should the need arise. The French Director-General requested that a high-ranking Israeli officer visit Paris for immediate consultations.

Already on July 27 (just one day after the nationalisation), Peres had apparently heard from Bourgès-Maunoury some clear hints about French willingness to consider Israel a partner in a proposed military move against Egypt. Peres even took it upon himself, there and then, to promise Israeli co-operation in such a scheme. Yet, because he was not authorised to make such a commitment, and because the French minister's questions were not broached officially, this information was not conveyed to Ben-Gurion until Thomas, undoubtedly on behalf of his superior, made his semi-official overtures. This time Peres gave no firm answer, other than promising to put the question to Ben-Gurion.[14]

These were not the only hints of possible collaboration from the French side. On July 27, members of the Israeli Ministry of Defence mission in Paris were informed by their French counterparts – as representatives of an allied nation – that a French delegation was to visit London the following day to hold consultations about a possible joint military move against Egypt. The delegation would include a number of military experts, meaning that real action might follow. Having revealed this much, the French officials came to the point: they asked the Israelis urgently for information about the Egyptian Army's deployment.

In this way, Israel's military alliance with France became operative. A special annex to the Zayit agreement covered the exchange of intelligence information between the two nations. Israel was determined to prove it could live up to its promises. Although Israel did not then have the necessary reconnaissance aircraft to cover the distance involved, a Meteor jet fighter was especially fitted for the mission and sent out "with an escort of old, slow, cumbersome Mosquitos, at great risk – just to vindicate French trust". Later on, Israeli Mosquitos overflew the Canal Zone and Meteors flew to the heart of Egypt on photo-reconnaissance missions.

A few days later, the French enquired about the possibility of using Haifa harbour for their purposes. Ben-Gurion immediately consented to this request as well. At that stage, as noted above, the Prime Minister showed little interest in the Suez Crisis. To judge by his willingness to respond favourably to French operational requests, the crisis did nothing to change his mind about a possible future Israeli-initiated war against Egypt, with French participation.[15]

At the same time, Israel's acquiescence to French requests, in the spirit of the agreement between the two nations, was not yet tantamount to an Israeli commitment to move against Nasser immediately. The question of timing, which was directly related to the IDF's absorption of its newly acquired armament, was critical to the Prime Minister. Israel was careful, until then, to keep its distance from this incipient Anglo-French military planning. Evidently the British demanded Israel's exclusion, and the assumption that the French wanted to come to London with their Israeli "dowry" solely to impress their British interlocutors had a calming effect on Ben-Gurion.

Nevertheless, already in June 1956 it was clear that Israel's agreement with France held out the possibility that Israel would have to go into action because of considerations which were not exclusively its own. Ben-Gurion was careful to restrict collaboration with the French at this stage to the supply of intelligence information only, as agreed earlier that month. He was quite generous in this respect, even instructing Dayan to provide the French with any useful information, whether they had asked for it specifically or not. As he said to the Chief of Staff,

> Overall, we should treat [the French] all along as brothers; the assistance and aid which they give us, and our partnership with them [within the secret framework of Zayit-Ge'ut] are absolutely essential to us.[16]

Despite this, in internal discussions Ben-Gurion showed no sign, as yet, of willingness to involve Israel in any political or military Anglo-French (and possibly American as well) move. Since, however, the objectives of such a move would be favourable to Israel, he did not oppose it in public, either.[17]

Ben-Gurion was hesitant (and remained so during the next few months). In any event, he had never seen Israel's way clear to a totally independent military move, even before the Suez Crisis. His thinking now was that any military action by the Western powers, if they decided to move at all, would be intended only to exert political pressure. Western abstention from concrete military action would obviously exempt Israel from participation at an inconvenient time. He noted in his diary that "somehow I find it difficult to believe that Eden will carry out his intention [to attack Egypt]." Then he added, "The Anglo-French force is just a scarecrow." Even French Ambassador Gilbert, a strong supporter of Franco-Israeli collaboration, thought that a joint move would be dependent upon American consent, which made the entire affair unrealistic.[18]

Thus, despite the strong hints which began to emanate from Paris immediately after the nationalisation, Ben-Gurion preferred, as of early August, to keep Israel out of the wider picture. He would rather provide secret aid to the French and let them and the British do the job – bring about Nasser's downfall.[19] Dayan and Peres saw things in a different light. They viewed the Suez Crisis as their long-awaited opportunity to initiate a war. As noted above, Peres hastily agreed to what looked like a French proposal to involve Israel in a war against Egypt. For him, this was a natural extension of the Vermars agreement, signed just a few weeks earlier. It was Peres who let the French understand, already in June and again in July, that Israel was willing to go a long way with them.

Dayan, too, saw the nationalisation of the Canal as an opportunity to push his policies ahead with renewed vigour. On July 28, Dayan's mother passed away. The next day, immediately after the funeral, Dayan met with Ben-Gurion and put to him three proposals in a single vein – war. Dayan proposed that Israel (a) conquer the entire Sinai Peninsula, up to the Canal, which would then be placed under international administration; (b) break the blockade and seize the Straits of Tiran; and (c) take the Gaza Strip. It was the first time on the record that the idea was broached to use the crisis as an opportunity to take over the whole of Sinai. Ben-Gurion, in his response, reiterated what he had told the General Staff on July 19: an Israeli-initiated war – yes, but not now. "For now we have to restrain ourselves, complete the French arms deal, grow stronger – and then look for the appropriate opportunity to lash out [at Nasser]."[20]

"Technical Problems"

During the second week of August it became apparent that the French were not going to meet the Ge'ut timetable. Not the least implication of this unforeseen delay, in view of Ben-Gurion's basic attitude, was that Israel could not go to war until much later than originally anticipated. On August 7, the French informed the Israelis that the deliveries promised for the following week would be delayed by technical problems. The next shipments would arrive only towards the end of the month. Peres hastened to report this to Ben-Gurion and his immediate aides, who became quite alarmed. They were gravely disappointed – but just as gravely suspicious.

Ben-Gurion: "The excuses for one [ship] could be genuine. But if it's two – that is a completely different matter . . . I have no quarrel with France, but this is something we discussed, we paid money for it, and if they want to delay deliveries – they should at least have suggested [an alternative]."

Peres: "We must talk about it, both here and [in France], because this may be very serious . . . there is much concern about what is to follow."

Dayan: "Perhaps there is something behind all this."

It was feared that the reason for the delay was that the Americans had caught a whiff of the deal; perhaps the US Sixth Fleet in the Mediterranean was somehow involved. We know today that while the Sixth Fleet did not discover the French arms deliveries to Israel, they were recorded by U-2 spy planes, which the Americans began to use in August against their NATO allies. So the Americans knew about France's arms supplies to Israel, but did not interfere.[21]

Somehow, it never occurred to the Israelis that the technical problems were, in fact, genuine. One problem was that as soon as the French began marshalling their own forces for a possible move against Egypt, they needed all their cargo vessels for themselves. Moving troops and equipment from Algeria to Cyprus, the proposed staging area, required a large number of ships, which naturally came in part at Israel's expense. Dayan was relieved when all this was clarified in due course, while Ben-Gurion noted dryly, "Delay due to technical, not political reasons."

Some shipments did arrive during August, but the pace was slower than originally planned. The fourth Ge'ut ship arrived on August 13, the next on the 20th, and shortly the Israelis were informed that there would be no more shipments before mid-September. Then the French said that they would be able to resume shipments only five days after they went to war against Egypt. Israel was in a quandary: there was no certainty that the French would attack Egypt at all, or, if they did, when. And no Israeli participation was conceivable without arms in far greater quantities. Israel therefore decided to use its own craft, regular cargo ships, although this meant unloading inside Haifa harbour, since the navy had no landing craft; secrecy was thus compromised.[22] Still, there was good news in the air: the Ge'ut timetable was met and the transfer of 36 Mystère 4A fighters was completed on schedule, these could fly in directly. All told, by late August the Israel Air Force had 60 such planes, though only 12 of them were combat-ready by that time.[23]

When two allied nations are involved in conflict with a common enemy, their collaboration tends to develop a dynamic of its own. On August 15, Ben-Gurion authorised a joint French-Israeli operation. It was agreed that the French would make available to Israel two Vautour fighter-bombers, with long-range flight capability (Israel was then negotiating to acquire Vautours), and that Israeli pilots would use them to fly photo-reconnaissance missions over the Suez Canal. Ultimately the mission was aborted, as the French concluded that they had no Vautours to spare, but the Israeli consent was quite significant in itself, for two reasons: (1) the scope of military collaboration (Zayit) was expanded to include aerial missions (till then, only land and covert operations were discussed); and (2) this was Israel's first concrete agreement to collaborate with the French directly in the context of the Suez Crisis.[24]

"A la guerre comme à la guerre"

During late August and early September 1956, there were increasing indications that France and Britain were indeed determined to move militarily against Nasser, as soon as diplomatic efforts had spent themselves. Israel pinned little hope on the results of the Suez Canal Users' Conference in London – in which representatives of 18 countries met under American pressure to find a solution to the crisis – or in the resulting mission by Australian Prime Minister Robert Menzies to Cairo in an effort to get Nasser to revoke the nationalisation (the mission indeed failed). It was becoming clearer by the day that diplomacy was going to prove futile. By late August, Israel was weighing three possible scenarios: (1) the UN Secretary-General's evaluation that the world would eventually habituate itself to the Canal's nationalisation, and that things would therefore return to normal; (2) the Western powers' pressures would bear fruit, which Israel would enjoy, without war, i.e., Nasser would remain in power but the Canal, and perhaps even the Straits of Tiran, would be opened to Israeli shipping; or (3) the London conference would fail, France and Britain would go to war against Egypt – and Israel would, most probably, be invited to join in. Not a few Israelis preferred this last option. On August 21, Israel's Ambassador in London was informed by the Director-General of the Foreign Ministry: "The Minister . . . considers it possible . . . that representatives of the Big Three will declare, upon the adoption of the [Users' Conference] resolution, that any demand for freedom of navigation include the cessation of all interference with Israeli shipping and commerce."[25]

Yet Ben-Gurion was hesitant. On the one hand, he did not curb the ever-intensifying activities of Dayan and Peres (see below); on the other hand, his doubts about French and British determination were not dispelled. Even though his semi-official biographer, and other authors, have chosen to ignore Ben-Gurion's state of mind at the time, it seems that Israel's Prime Minister and Minister of Defence was highly confused during August and early September of 1956. As Peres wrote:

> Ever since the time we began negotiating with the French about a joint move, Ben-Gurion has taken a strange, even contradictory position. He was rather critical of any proposal and cable[d report], but never ruled out, even encouraged, any move to get us closer [to joint military action] . . . Neither Moshe [Dayan] nor I were clear about Ben-Gurion's overall attitude, which put the pressure on Moshe, in particular, to demand and eventually get from the French better and better conditions.[26]

In short, by late August 1956, Israel, namely Ben-Gurion, preferred a wait-and-see posture, committing itself to nothing, as long as it was not directly involved in the crisis. But the pace of events soon made that position untenable.

"Utmost Willingness to Support"

The fact that Israel preferred to await further developments in the Suez Crisis did not impede the progress of French/Israeli preparations for attacks on broadcasting stations in Cairo and Damascus, within the framework of the Zayit agreement. Throughout August, the IDF mission in Paris worked hand in hand with Mourelin and the SDECE on raids intended to knock out Radio Cairo (Israeli responsibility) and Radio Damascus (French responsibility); both attacks were set for early September. Operational plans had already been approved, and matériel and agents were positioned in Egypt, at least (it is not clear whether the French had done the same in Syria). All that remained was to co-ordinate the raids and get the authorisation of the two governments for both missions.

When the Suez Crisis broke out Israel decided, as noted above, to stand by its commitments to France. Despite the risk now inherent in this joint operation – of Israel's becoming directly involved in the crisis – Ben-Gurion instructed Colonel Yuval Ne'eman, the head of the IDF mission in Paris, "to proceed with preparations at full speed". The desire to prove Israel's worth to the French overrode all other considerations.[27]

It was France, rather than Israel, that suddenly decided to back out. Paris, involved in the Algeria rebellion and on the brink of war with Egypt, wanted to avoid further friction with the Arab world. The Chief of Staff's aide noted ruefully in his diary, "The French decided to call off their operation in Syria, but not in Egypt, since there is going to be war there anyway." Thus, on August 20, Ne'eman was informed that the Damascus mission was being postponed, "but they [did] ask that Israel do its part [in Cairo]."[28] Ben-Gurion, who was reluctant to involve Israel in the crisis anyway, immediately called off the Israeli raid. The reasons he gave Dayan for this decision shed light on his entire attitude towards

Israeli-French collaboration, and they would serve Dayan as broad guidelines in future developments:

> So long as [the division of] political responsibilities between France and Israel [was] carefully observed, Israel was willing to take risks for missions which served the French interest, for the sake of friendship. But as soon as France backed out of its willingness to do its share, Israel was left to bear the brunt of political risk and diplomatic responsibility, at a time when Egypt is the focus of international attention." [Ben-Gurion added that] an Israeli operation at this time, when the world is clamouring against British and French preparations for war, will be regarded by the entire world as a base provocation, an attempt to grind our own axe.[29]

The Israeli mission in Paris could not understand why the operation had been called off. Colonel Nishri, the Military Attaché, sent the following cable to Ne'eman, who was in Israel to inform Dayan personally about France's decision:

> I now have grave doubts about the entire future of collaboration [with France] . . . Our decision to back out will be regarded as a sign of incompetence and deceit, especially in view of the fact that the French made good on all their promises. There is no reasonable argument for [a linkage] between the [French] postponement and an Israeli one. The only condition we put forward at the time was full partnership in both operations . . . The matériel is already in place in Egypt, and there was mutual agreement during all previous stages of implementation. I suggest you bring it up for reconsideration before returning [to Paris].[30]

In addition to a message apprising the French of Israel's decision, Ne'eman also brought with him the Chief of Staff's response to Nishri's complaint:

> I hope you will be proven wrong in your assumptions. The Government of Israel, just like the Government of France, is fully entitled to reconsider its moves in the face of current events. There is no justification now for the [Cairo raid]. Its benefits would be negligible, whereas the chances of failure in moving in, execution and moving out will be much greater than in ordinary times – the whole world, including Israel, is now in conflict with Egypt. Israel was not yet recognised as a partner in this campaign. If we are going to become partners, we shall come in through the front door, in an operation whose prospective benefits exceed its chances of possible disgraceful failure. Such considerations do not normally exist in our hostile relationship with Egypt. Therefore, if things return to normal, we shall be able to carry out [the raid].[31]

Dayan's comments, as well as Ben-Gurion's reactions, reveal much about the way the Chief of Staff saw, by late August 1956, the development of the Suez Crisis and Israel's role in it.

When Ne'eman met with his French counterparts, even before he had a chance to say his piece, they suggested that Israel postpone its raid on Radio Cairo. The interpretation later placed on this move by the Chief of Staff's bureau was that "[our] allies went to great lengths to present their case as a legitimate one in terms of international law, and the French were worried about British disapproval and possible loss of control over events." Probably the fact that France was just then making up its mind about accepting Israel as a full-fledged partner in the Anglo-French military move against Egypt, as related below, also had something to do with this particular suggestion.

On August 29, Ne'eman cabled Dayan:

> The French called off the [Cairo raid] . . . Asked permission to use instruments prepared in Cairo for Canal affairs [Operation Musketeer]. I gave permission, and they thanked me greatly. The Lord preserveth the simple.[32]

Dayan was still worried; in view of the growing likelihood of Israeli collaboration with France as it coped with the deteriorating crisis, he was anxious to create a sense of full equality, whereas Ne'eman and his co-workers seemed to him over-anxious to indulge the French. He replied to Ne'eman:

> For future reference, I want to straighten you out on this. In this particular instance, our partners suddenly decided to reconsider and reasoned that the time was not ripe for this raid, while this very notion had been rejected by Emanuel [Nishri]. As things stand now, it seems that objectively speaking, our considerations were equally valid. Yet Emanuel must have thought that the right to reconsider in such instances is reserved exclusively to our partners, while we must carry out their wishes unhesitatingly, and any refusal on our part necessarily means dishonesty and shirking our responsibilities.
>
> I am worried by this baseless notion. We are not hired agents who have already been paid, and now must deliver the goods. We paid for everything we got [in the weapons sphere], and these operations are a separate matter, where both parties must equally show good will, readiness to take risks, and utmost willingness to support each other's interests. But in any case, each party is free to consider matters and decide, based on such considerations, whether the operation is worthwhile. No refusal or postponement can be regarded as welching on a given promise.[33]

Although this joint planning did not mature into actual implementation, it did lay the foundation for military liaison between France and Israel. Equally important, it helped the Israeli leadership define for itself the parameters of such co-operation.

6

Vive la France et Israel

"We Won't Go Unless Invited"

French requests from Israel, from the outbreak of the Suez Crisis until September 1956, were in the main for assistance that could be regarded as Israeli commitments contained in the June 1956 agreement. As explained above, besides the Ge'ut machinery, which handled arms purchases, the two countries had set up another apparatus, called Zayit, which channelled information and handled joint military planning, albeit limited in scope. Colonel Yuval Ne'eman, the head of the IDF mission in Paris, was the linchpin in this regular channel of communication between the two armed forces, which required no mediation by the diplomatic sphere.[1]

In the realm of intelligence information, until September the French requested details to enhance their joint planning with Britain on Operation Musketeer: data on the Egyptian Army and assistance in photo-reconnaissance missions. Dependent on the British for long-range flights and for the use of air bases in the Canal area, they looked for other possibilities as well, mainly the use of Israeli facilities. Ben-Gurion ordered that all their requests be viewed favourably, "as though they are our brothers".[2]

A turning point was reached on August 31, when the French first discussed a possible military move in which Israel would be directly involved. On Saturday, September 1, an urgent cable was brought to Ben-Gurion. It had been sent by Yosef Nahmias, head of the Ministry of Defence mission in Paris, to Peres, who forwarded it immediately to his chief:

> Met yesterday and today with [Abel] Thomas and [Louis] Mangin [Director-General of the Ministry of Defence and personal adviser to the Minister of Defence, respectively]. The following directly from them, with official approval [of the French government]: Re military preparations for Suez, no letup and no regrets, neither British nor French. . . . Admiral

Barjot [second-in-command, joint expeditionary force] intends to invite us to join in the campaign on D+7. Will explain to the British in terms of weakness in some appropriate part of battlefront. Requests meeting with Deputy Chief of Staff, arranged through military channels. All this approved by Bourgès[-Maunoury]. I never reacted to this announcement, but you should be aware that they fully expect us to accept it enthusiastically. Expressed some surprise at our restrained and reserved attitude re Suez. I expressed surprise at their surprise, since we had never been invited to join in on any stage [of planning] . . . There are no doubts here re sincerity of British attitude nor worry about the outcome, since France's main aim is to have Nasser removed, which coincides with British interest.[3]

Having seen this cable, Dayan noted that "for the first time since Nasser announced, on 26 July 1956, the nationalisation of the Suez Canal, the French raise a possibility of our incorporation in the Anglo-French campaign." To the present writer's knowledge, this is also the first time Israel was quasi-officially informed of the Anglo-French Musketeer plan. In all likelihood, the idea of letting Israel in was conceived by Bourgès-Maunoury as a way to encourage Admiral Barjot, who at the time was acutely depressed by British obstacles placed in the way of Musketeer planning. The possibility of Israeli involvement at the appropriate time was much to the admiral's liking.[4]

Ben-Gurion immediately summoned his inner staff (namely, Dayan and Peres) and told them to inform the French that "in principle, we are willing to co-operate".[5] Thus Peres replied to Nahmias, on Ben-Gurion's behalf:

The Old Man approves co-operation of course. As for the person to co-ordinate co-operation with Barjot, this depends on nature of meeting. If this is of unusual importance but does not require on-the-spot decisions, it will be [General] Meir 'Amit [Chief of General Staff Division] who, since there is no Deputy Chief of Staff, is perforce second-in-command. If things are decisive, involving military negotiations rather than information exchanges, Moshe Dayan is ready to come over. Please let me know.[6]

Eventually, General 'Amit went to France, with instructions drawn up by Ben-Gurion himself: "Willingness in principle to help the French with their military operation to the best of our ability. Air bases, use of sea ports, involvement of our troops – if need be – will be decided by Cabinet in Jerusalem". Dayan, who wished to keep the Israeli side of the co-operation under his control, added something of his own, though in the spirit of Ben-Gurion's instructions: "General 'Amit is not authorised to undertake any operational commitment. His job will be to listen to French requests and get full explanations thereof, then, having checked with Israel, will be able to reply and make commitments. Israel's general intention is favourably to respond to French overtures, and this spirit should guide 'Amit. If things get to the point of decision, the question will be considered whether the presence of Chief of Staff is required in Paris."[7]

On September 7, 'Amit, Ne'eman and Nishri met in Paris with Admiral Barjot, General Gazin (Barjot's Chief of Staff) and other French officers involved in the Anglo-French operation. It soon became clear that this was a preliminary discussion only. The French wanted to hear whether Israel was actually willing to join in this operation with them, and also asked for a professional evaluation of IDF capabilities for handling Egyptian forces on their border.[8]

"Most to Our Liking"

The 'Amit–Barjot meeting gave the Franco-Israeli connection a new impetus. Now the Israeli side of the negotiations was taken over by the principals of the June Vermars agreement, Peres and Dayan. On September 18, Peres arrived in Paris and met with French Minister of Defence Bourgès-Maunoury, the moving force, on the French side, for a war with Egypt and for Israeli participation. As it happened, French and British attitudes were then further apart than at any other time during the Suez Crisis, since the British Cabinet found itself in a hopeless political tangle (military preparations still went ahead, albeit ploddingly). The French Minister wanted to keep up military momentum, at the least, and for that he needed Israel. As Peres wrote to Ben-Gurion following the meeting:

> Bourgès-Maunoury invited Yosef [Nahmias] and myself for a private discussion. He said there were signs of British reluctance about the joint military operation, and he was now having new doubts whether it will take place at all. . . . Personally, he thought other ways and other partners have to be found for war against Nasser. He found Anglo-Saxon reservations about having Israel involved in an operation against Nasser altogether excessive. Much more so bearing in mind that all Arab nations would support Egypt anyway, in case of war. His thoughts about alternatives for an Anglo-French operation he has not yet revealed to anyone, but he intends to present them to his Cabinet colleagues once the future of a joint operation with the British has been clarified.[9]

The meeting with Bourgès-Maunoury was a milestone on the French-

Israeli road to war. For the first time, a senior French leader openly discussed possible coordination of the two countries timetables for war. Peres, for his part, expressed Israel's general willingness to participate in a deliberately provoked war against Egypt. All this was certainly far removed from questions of Israeli arms purchases from France, which the two were ostensibly discussing then, as so often before. Oddly, this key meeting is barely mentioned in most histories of the period. Be that as it may, the French Minister of Defence, having made his intentions clear, now moved on to practicalities, particularly the timing of the war as this related to possible French-Israeli collaboration.

Bourgès-Maunoury explained to Peres (who afterward summarised his remarks) that there was "the French timetable, which required immediate action against Nasser, bearing in mind not only the Suez situation but also developments in North Africa . . . There was the English timetable, which preferred continued diplomatic activity for yet another couple of months; and there was the American timetable, which rested on a firm belief that the Iranian oil fields nationalisation experience ought to be repeated, at least in terms of its extended timetable. Bourgès understood that the Israeli timetable was nearer to the English than the French one."

Immediately after this discussion, it seems, the French Minister of Defence sat down to compose a happy birthday telegram to Ben-Gurion, who would turn seventy about three weeks later. This was hardly conventional diplomatic procedure. Was it Peres who whispered in Bourgès-Maunoury's ear that such a gesture would be welcome? This stands to reason but is difficult to prove. In any event, the "birthday cable" went down in history as the first invitation (though not yet official) by a French leader to Israel to co-operate in a military move: "The Egyptian problem stands out as an increasingly serious issue for both our nations. I am delighted that there is something we can do together to protect our common interests. For my part, I shall cherish [the June agreement] in the future as in the past, using every opportunity to promote active co-operation which will be beneficial to both our nations." Forwarding this to Ben-Gurion, immediately after taking his leave from Bourgès-Maunoury, Peres emphasised the French Minister's "question of timetables".[10]

On September 21, Ben-Gurion cabled to Peres his response to Bourgès-Maunoury's proposals and congratulations alike. The key phrase indicated to Dayan and Peres that their plan was working. "As for the three timetables – it is the French timetable that is most to our liking," Ben-Gurion wrote. "If they move out at a time which is convenient to them, we shall stand by them to the best of our ability."[11]

Thus the degree of collaboration rose another notch. In retrospect, it seems that the timing was indeed propitious. Peres met with the French Minister of Defence just before the second, and final, London Conference of Suez Canal Users, in September. On September 22 – immediately after Bourgès-Maunoury received Ben-Gurion's reply, as fate would have it – the French Cabinet convened to hear Foreign Minister Pineau's report of the abortive London Conference. Bitterly disappointed – particularly with American and British attitudes towards the resolution of the Suez Crisis – Pineau now tended to support the way out of the deadlock proposed by the Minister of Defence: to examine the possibility of military co-operation with Israel. It was resolved to approach the government of Israel, "secretly but officially", and ask for a high-level consultation, with a view towards a joint military move against Egypt.[12]

Peres, who returned to France from a brief visit to the United States, was thus asked on September 23 to forward this request, with a proposed date already in mind: October 15. It was agreed, however, that a "high level" should not mean the highest level. The French Minister suggested that the "supreme authority [the two prime ministers] be kept in reserve, in order that negotiations be more flexible".[13]

Upon his return to Israel, on September 25, Peres immediately reported to Ben-Gurion, who subsequently wrote in his diary: "What [Peres] told me may be fateful". On the same day, following a Cabinet meeting (which authorised another retaliatory raid against Jordan, to take place that night), Ben-Gurion convened the Mapai ministers for a secret meeting; two ministers representing an allied party, Ahdut Ha'Avoda, were also invited. Without going into detail, the Prime Minister discussed the French proposal for a joint military move against Egypt and the invitation for a high-level meeting.[14]

Some participants expressed their fear of external military intervention by the USSR, Albania (*sic!*), or China. Others had misgivings about Perfidious Albion, or worried that other Arab nations might become involved. Sharett, however, was no longer in the Cabinet, and Ben-Gurion's chief opponent now was a weaker personality, Zalman Aranne, the Minister of Education, whose express objections to any military move initiated by Israel and France carried little weight. In his reply, Ben-Gurion explained his chief consideration for undertaking this military action: "In my opinion, this is our first chance to have an ally . . . thanks to whom we are not altogether helpless now."[15] Already on September 28, an Israeli high-level delegation left for Paris. Its instructions were formulated by Ben-Gurion in consultation with Dayan and Peres, and its codename, SIDON, was a Hebrew acronym for "France and Israel lay out their arms".[16]

The instructions of the SIDON delegation were that:

1. Israel cannot go to war without an ally;
2. Israel is severely handicapped in terms of air power, sea power and armour;
3. Israel is very worried about possible reactions by Britain and its Middle Eastern allies;
4. Israel cannot afford even a single defeat on the battlefield;
5. Israel is concerned about Soviet reaction to war against Egypt. How do the French evaluate the situation?

Although Ben-Gurion urged the delegation to conduct negotiations positively and give full expression to his willingness for military co-operation with the French, his instructions can be read as a summation of his apprehensions about an Israeli-initiated war.[17]

In an effort to introduce a note of flexibility, Dayan added three "operational instructions" of his own, indicating a somewhat different attitude, less reliant upon Israel's new European ally:

1. War will be conducted in separate French and Israeli theatres, even if agreement is reached on a joint supreme command. Dayan saw fit to mention that this applied to air power as well – the area where Israel was most dependent upon France.
2. If the French will take care of the Canal Zone, and if Israel will have the required matériel, it will undertake to seize the whole of Sinai on its own.
3. No linkage is to be made between arms deliveries from France and Israeli participation in a war against Egypt.

Dayan fully understood that the June 1956 agreement between France and Israel did not compel Israel to go to war merely at French insistence. However, he anticipated such pressure on Israel from Paris. His chief aim, apparently, was to secure for Israel the greatest possible military (and political) freedom of action in case of war.[18]

"The Only Thing Clarified"

On the evening of September 28, the four members of the SIDON delegation left Israel. The mission was headed by Foreign Minister Golda Meir and included Dayan, Peres and Minister of Transport Moshe Carmel, an ex-general and the only French-speaking minister in the Israeli Cabinet; they were accompanied by Dayan's Chief of Bureau, Lt.-Colonel Mordechai Bar-On. They boarded a French bomber which had landed secretly in Israel, and were flown to Bizerta, a French air base in Tunisia, where they transferred to a more comfortable plane, once used by De Gaulle, which took them to Paris. The first leg of this journey, besides the discomfort caused by an aircraft never intended for passengers, was marked by a bizarre accident. Carmel, on his way to the lavatory, fell into the bomb bay and nearly plunged into the sea. He barely managed to hold on to the rim, until (after a very short time, though to him it must have seemed an eternity) a passing crew member rescued him. Some of Carmel's ribs were broken; he was treated in Bizerta, but there was no question of sending him back to Israel without compromising the entire mission. Thus he went on to the conference, where he bravely endeavoured to carry out his mission as an interpreter, aided by Nahmias, the head of the Ministry of Defence mission in France. The circumstances of his injury would long remain a state secret.

A hotel was found for the delegation in St. Germain, near Paris, and the talks were conducted at the nearby residence of Colonel Mangin, a senior advisor to Bourgès-Maunoury. The French side consisted of the Minister of Defence, Foreign Minister Pineau and General Maurice Challe, the Deputy Chief of Staff, previously head of the Air Force and now in charge of military coordination with both Britain and Israel.[19]

As the talks proceeded, the Israeli side felt ever more strongly that indeed, Israel was about to fight a war alongside France. As it turned out, the French approach was convenient for Israel, even if there were slight differences of emphasis. Still, before a full understanding could be reached, each party had to overcome internal differences among the leaders of their respective defence establishments – who had spearheaded the collaboration from the outset – and their Foreign Ministry colleagues. A kind of coalition evolved at St. Germain between Dayan and Peres, on the Israeli side, and Bourgès-Maunoury and Challe, on the French side, which faced a parallel coalition between Foreign Ministers Meir and Pineau. Even more than the French Foreign Minister himself, civil servants at Quai d'Orsay objected to any collaboration with Israel, or indeed to any military move against Egypt. (Eventually, at British insistence, the French Foreign Ministry was excluded from all further involvement in the war preparations, and Pineau took part in discussions on a personal basis, as "advisor for external affairs" to Prime Minister Mollet.)[20]

Small wonder, then, that the Israeli delegation felt something of a letdown following the opening session of the joint discussions, on Sunday morning, September 30, which was chaired by Pineau. His statement was not as clear-cut as the Israelis must have expected, and was amenable to several different interpretations. Although not ruling out a possible French-Israeli military move against Egypt, Pineau was careful to stress that at this stage discussions were theoretical only, and there was still the possibility of a French-British move, without Israel. At the end of that morning's session Dayan remarked that "the only thing clarified was that the situation is unclear".[21]

Meir, who from the start was deeply suspicious of the whole idea of military collaboration with France – probably a product of her deep mistrust of Shimon Peres, the concept's architect on the Israeli side – found in the session sufficient confirmation for her views, which remained unchanged during the next few days. Furthermore, she regarded the absence of Prime Minister Mollet (contrary to a previous understanding, she thought) as a sign of insincerity on the French side. As far as she was concerned, "the discussions ended with no concrete results," as she subsequently reported to Ben-Gurion. According to her biographer, "[i]n early October, she won a minor victory. Ben-Gurion was ready to call off the entire operation."[22]

In fact, there was no basis for the Israelis' expectations of a higher level of French representation than their own. Peres, though (anxious to placate Meir, restore his credibility and prevent any untoward development prejudicial to the joint move), arranged for Meir to meet with Mollet the next day.[23]

Dayan's aide, Lt.-Colonel Bar-On, who took notes for the Israeli delegation, thought that the ambiguity, not to say disappointment, following that first meeting, was due to Pineau's sincerity; as a friend of Israel, he did not want to mislead its representatives in any way. He therefore put all the problems on the table and made no promises he could not keep. Usually, Bar-On reflects Dayan's views, and in many cases Peres's as well. All three realised that despite this honest, and somewhat disappointing, description of the harsh political realities, Pineau was wholly in favour of Israeli involvement in the war. However, he saw no sense in making a concrete political deal, so long as the US took a position which made it difficult for France to act on its own. Pineau was shortly due to leave for what loomed as a difficult session of the UN Security Council, in which France could expect little support for its hard-line stance on the Suez issue, let alone on Algeria. Here, France and the US were thoroughly at loggerheads. And there was still the question of where the British stood, which was none too clear at the moment.[24]

Nevertheless, Pineau did not rule out possible French-Israeli military co-operation in military affairs. He only asked that his Israeli interlocutors consider these secret talks as exploratory only. Things could be finalised, he said, only after the Security Council meeting – that is, on or about October 12. The French had few hopes that the Security Council would act and believed that its inaction would provide them with a pretext for a direct military move. By then, however, little time would remain to implement the Anglo-French plan. Military action, explained

Pineau, must be launched already on October 15, because of political considerations (such as the imminent American presidential elections) as well as technical ones (the expeditionary force had maintained its alert status far too long); and the weather was also a factor.[25]

Military and Political Considerations

Dayan and Peres accepted the views of neither Pineau nor Meir. They had come to St. Germain in order to reach an operative agreement. In the event, their feelings were shared by the French Minister of Defence and his aides, Challe and Mangin. As soon as Pineau left for New York, after the Sunday morning session, these three took charge. From now on, the St. Germain conference would deal with military issues, and this shift would lead to agreement on a joint military move against Egypt.[26]

The afternoon session on September 30 was thus the first working meeting at St. Germain. During this meeting, four participants joined hands to push for a military move: Dayan and Peres on the Israeli side, Bourgès-Maunoury (who had not attended the morning session, but now became chairman in lieu of Pineau) and General Challe on the French side. Also present were Meir and Abel Thomas, as well as the incapacitated Carmel.

Far more determined than Pineau, Bourgès-Maunoury set the tone of this meeting from the beginning: "We must see to it that military expediency will be the overriding consideration, and adjust diplomatic expediency to its needs." He added, "The political outcome will be an upshot of the military approach, so I suggest that a study of the military aspect precede any political conclusions." This, of course, was perfectly in line with the approach taken by Dayan and Peres all along. Dayan hastened to announce that he could not agree more with the French minister's views about the relationship between military planning and political decision-making.[27]

The French Minister of Defence and his Director-General wanted to move on to discuss joint military planning, so that once the political level gave the go-ahead the two nations could move into action. Comments made by Bourgès-Maunoury and Thomas show that they shared the disappointment felt by the Israeli defence establishment representatives: having heard Meir's reserved tone, they must have realised that despite everything they had heard from Peres the Israeli delegation was not mandated to negotiate military collaboration. They urged the Israelis to obtain such a mandate – the sooner the better.[28]

In the meantime, Bourgès-Maunoury had used the meeting to present the main concerns of the French government regarding an action in the Suez, with or without Israel. Central to these, as they had been since the outbreak of the Suez Crisis, were the problems surrounding collaboration with Britain. Both nations had begun preparations already in late July, yet no political decision had been made by the end of September. Operational planning was slowed down, although both countries had placed troops on the alert in Cyprus, Malta and North Africa: "What should concern France in practical terms, and Israel in moral terms [meaning, apparently, the role intended for Israel in the French plan] is that plans be made clear and concrete. Our experience in joint planning with the British has taught us that it is no easy thing to plan joint operations."[29]

Later on, Bourgès-Maunoury said explicitly what Pineau had only hinted at: whereas the Israelis had anticipated simultaneous French and Israeli operations, the French thought that Israel should make the first move, to provide them with a pretext for "intervention". Bourgès-Maunoury put it very simply, as though the method had already been agreed upon: "As for a pretext, which is a major issue for starting an operation, Israel's position is far more convenient [than that of France or Britain]." It was this notion, which was subsequently put to the reluctant British, that induced them, finally, to join the French military move.

The idea of Israel's serving to create the pretext for Anglo-French intervention seems to have been directly linked to another fact made clear at St. Germain: The French were thinking in terms of a joint move with the British, and were prepared to do anything to achieve this. An independent move, or one in which only Israel joined them, was out of the question for Paris, for reasons explained earlier. Apart from practical considerations, such as the availability of air bases and maritime transport, the French would not embark on a venture to which the US so vehemently objected without having the British on their side.

Realising the effect this presentation of the facts by his Minister would have on the Israelis, Thomas immediately interjected: "Whatever future [role Israel will play], we must not waste time, and if the Israeli government accept the plan [to provoke Anglo-French intervention], we must immediately arrange a meeting between our General Staffs, as well as allow Israel to present its demands for maximum readiness, and attend immediately to those demands."[30] "Demands for maximum readiness", needless to say, meant arms supplies.

The two outstanding conclusions of the talks held during the afternoon of September 30 were: (a) that the French would not move without the British; and (b) that they wanted Israel to provide them with a *casus belli*. What had earlier been left unsaid, or only hinted at, was now discussed frankly – under the assumption that all present were thoroughly in favour of a joint military move. Concretely, the French declared their intention to send to Israel, immediately after the conference, a high-level military delegation headed by General Challe, in order to study Israel's capabilities as a useful ally to France in a war against Egypt. In view of Bourgès-Maunoury's view of the relationship between military moves and political decision making, it is not difficult to understand why the French wanted to send a military delegation to Israel, before anything was settled politically.

"A Large Army, but Landbound"

From that point on, the discussion focused on how (not whether) to implement the joint plan. The various speakers seem to have ignored their limited mandates, as Bourgès-Maunoury suggested. By now, the two senior military officers had taken charge – Dayan and Challe. The former asked his counterpart to get to practicalities: "Do you have any idea what you would like the Israeli Army to do in a joint operation? Surely you realise you cannot really expect us to fill in for the British, with our small force. Can you tell us your general intent? How will the French Army, and how will the Israeli Army, operate in this joint offensive?" Dayan apparently went too far. He not only ignored – as Meir had, when speaking earlier – the "pretext plan" suggested by the French, he even turned a blind eye to France's absolute insistence on a joint venture with the British. It was he who spoke of a "joint offensive", which the French never mentioned: they had a reason for referring only to a "joint move".

The French were evasive, Dayan kept pushing. Finally, Bourgès-Maunoury had to admit that he and his staff had not yet considered how to convert existing plans, which involved the British, into a joint operation with Israel. In fact, it is not clear whether the French really had not found the time to consider a tripartite operation, as they claimed, or were still committed to the Anglo-French plan, Musketeer, which they did not want to discuss at all. It is still a moot question whether they ever seriously considered a simultaneous operation jointly with Israel, or wanted Israel only as a lure for Britain.

Bourgès-Maunoury manoeuvred deftly to avoid this issue. He tried to move the discussion to the military nitty-gritty – a comparative evaluation of Israeli vs. Egyptian pilots, for example. He repeatedly stressed that "the question is whether it is desirable that General Challe visit [Israel] in order to work out plans there . . . You must agree that any discussions now take place in a void. Besides, this is a matter for the experts . . . And let us not forget that General Ely [the Chief of Staff] and General Challe can meet with us tomorrow night. Still, I shall be glad to have a glimpse of General Dayan's thinking now."[31]

But Dayan was persistent. He seems to have hoisted Bourgès-

Maunoury by his own petard: you said you wanted a purely military discussion, so let's get on with it. Dayan could see no other purpose to the discussion apart from further military coordination, as both sides realised that progress in this sphere was bound to influence their respective governments. Furthermore, during these talks he could see for himself, for the first time, how the French perceived the IDF, its strengths and weaknesses. Dayan tried to impress on the French how vital their help would be in case of a joint move:

> I want you to know first of all that we are a very small army . . . the Arabs have very bad armies, so in saying that our army is good, I mean in comparison with them . . . We could win, if it's war against Egypt only . . . If we have to deal with Egyptian pilots alone, we could achieve air supremacy. If there will be Czech and Polish pilots in the sky over the Middle East, I hope there will be French ones as well.

As for the forces the IDF could throw into war immediately, the Israeli Chief of Staff added: "If there is war next month, we could send out 30 Mystères, 20 Ouragans and 20 Meteors, and more planes will do us no good because we cannot train enough pilots . . . We can move 6 to 8 brigades to the Egyptian front . . . Even the meagre forces we do have, especially armoured formations, have some critical faults. For instance, our tanks are M-3s, and although the crews are ready, it will be a disaster to send out this obsolete tank against Russian ones . . . The problem is the specific items we lack, not the Egyptians . . . within a fortnight, we can win and achieve air supremacy."

Fully aware of the import of what he had just said, Dayan asked his hosts, "Were you disappointed by my description of the facts?" "Not at all," replied Bourgès-Maunoury.[32]

On this note of sincerity, the French too opened up, frankly spelling out their own difficulties: "We have a large Army, but it is land-bound . . . Any landing, even on a deserted beach with no opposition, is a matter of 10,000 tonnes of supplies . . . We thought of using [air or naval] bases in Cyprus. Now we shall have to change our plans [if Britain would not join in] . . . We have 400,000 [troops] in Algeria, our military situation is much more complex than it was in Napoleon's time." Precisely because of this situation, as well as the French Army's refusal to leave Algeria without large forces for any length of time, the French insisted on the timetable set forth by Pineau, namely D-day on October 15, barely a fortnight away.

Bourgès-Maunoury then added that both sides should start at once discussing practical matters, beginning in Paris and proceeding in Israel, to be concluded again in France. "Thus, if the British quit the game at the last moment, we shall not be forced to improvise on the spot, and France will remain hobbled while Israel is already involved, unable to offer any help".[33]

Going into details did not, needless to say, change anything in either side's basic posture. The French realised full well that Israel had its own interests, and would pursue them by all means. Nevertheless, in between various minor details, Dayan carefully outlined for the French Israel's war aims, in the event of a war, emphasising that Israeli forces would not cross the Canal under any circumstances:

> We intend to undertake any mission anywhere in the territory between our border and the Suez. We have no thoughts beyond the Suez, nor about occupying it for any length of time. We thought about fighting in the Sinai, and reaching the Canal at the most, no further than that . . . In any event, we thought about seizing the Straits of Tiran so as to have an option to reach Suez from the south, and so as to retain, as spoils of victory, the western shore of the Gulf of Eilat in our hands.[34]

"We Can Beat the Egyptians by Ourselves"

This new idea, of reaching Suez from the south, must have been an on-the-spot inspiration by Dayan, ever a master of improvisation. As far as I can ascertain, no such concept had shown up in Israeli military planning until then. Yet this apparently novel concept became the germ of the idea which would resolve the differences between France, Britain and Israel over the kind of Israeli move which would give the two Powers reason to intervene.[35]

Now both sides began to understand each other's intentions and limitations. As the September 30 meeting progressed in a cordial atmosphere, Peres asked the French to make good on their promise – that is, make a definite commitment to provide Israel with even more arms – then and there. For Peres, this was the culmination of the mission he had been sent to accomplish on September 18, but which then had to be sidetracked because of the conference. His questions, however, alarmed his own representative in Paris, Yosef Nahmias, who refused to translate them. But Peres had sufficient command of the French language to ask for himself: "(1) Is France willing to sell us American-made armament, or only French? (2) Is France willing to put aside for the moment the question of finance? Could we not work out a kind of a lend-lease agreement for the equipment, which we shall return if there will be no operation, or use in a joint war if there is one? (3) In view of this new situation, is what we have concluded here with Pineau and

Bourgès final, or need we go through the financial echelon, as we have done in the past?"[36]

Bourgès-Maunoury replied in the affirmative to all three queries, although he took care to make his agreement contingent upon French Army needs and the IDF's absorptive capacity. This issue too the French Minister linked to a French delegation which should leave for Israel immediately. Subsequently, this discussion led to another French-Israeli arms deal, separate from the previous one, Ge'ut, which was concluded during September. The new deal, code-named in Israel SIDON (and later 'EZUZ), finally brought the IDF to a level of armament that enabled it to fight a war by late October 1956.[37]

The immediate outcome of the discussion was that a French delegation, led by General Challe, left for Israel immediately after the conclusion of the St. Germain conference. That same night, Dayan's aide Bar-On conveyed the following to General 'Amit, Chief of Operations, in Israel: "As for the matter that occasioned our trip here: In order to pursue it, we shall be returning early Tuesday morning with 4–5 partners to examine air, sea and land [coordination] and the potential capacity of our bases. All three services must appoint liaison officers who speak their language, for the duration of their stay in [Israel]. They must be high-ranking officers . . . Complete secrecy will pertain regarding our partners' arrival, stay and return."[38]

Now Dayan took another step forward. He asked the French for permission to share the secret with several Ministry of Defence and IDF representatives stationed in Paris; this would promote military collaboration and avoid a possible situation in which political authorisation was given but the military machinery was not yet ready. It was agreed that the military attaché in Paris, Colonel Nishri, would be let in on the secret planning – provided he refrained from using his regular (diplomatic) channels of communication, meaning that the Foreign Ministry should remain in the dark. Also brought in were Col. Ne'eman, Israeli liaison officer in Paris for Zayit affairs, and Lt.-Colonel Yosef Kedar, air attaché in the Israeli mission in Paris.[39]

On the morning of October 1, while Meir was spending her time with Mollet, Dayan and his aides met with General Ely and some of his staff, who were to become liaison officers between their respective services and the IDF: Colonel Mangin was to co-ordinate between the two ministries, General Challe between the general staffs, General Martin between the air forces, and Colonel Simon between the land forces. Collaboration was no longer a theoretical issue; practical preparations began. Still, the new system was based on the Zayit apparatus, which had been operating in Paris since early July, antedating the Suez Crisis.[40]

The Ely–Dayan meeting was intended more as a formal introduction between the two military leaders and as a preparatory discussion with the French delegation about to leave for Israel, but Dayan wanted to get down to details at once. What the Israeli Chief of Staff was trying to convey to his French counterpart was the feeling that France could go to war even without Britain. In this meeting, as in the previous one, with Bourgès-Maunoury, one can discern the difference in attitudes between the Israelis, anxious to lay out maps on the table and draw arrows, and the more reticent French.

Dayan reiterated the points he had made the day before, adding that "we could beat the Egyptians [in the Sinai] in the air and on the land, even if we fought by ourselves: not only without the British, but also without the French". Yet having stressed the IDF's independence, he hastened to point out that "as for assistance, we need more equipment, though I must say that the most important assistance would be a simultaneous French operation". Dayan, who wanted war as soon as possible, feared that emphasising the IDF's weaknesses might deter France from possible collaboration. He therefore repeatedly stressed the IDF's relative capabilities *vis-à-vis* the Egyptian Army. Some time later, he would remark: "I did not know whether the French staff officers knew about the IDF's strength and equipment, but I could see how surprised they were . . . "[41]

The French wanted to hear from Dayan about the theatre of operations and to get his views about the optimal plan of operations. He suggested that Israel handle the entire area east of the Suez Canal, with the French to seize control of the Canal Zone itself and destroy air bases to its west, in Egypt proper. In reply to a question, Dayan advised the French Chief of Staff not to "get embroiled" with the city of Cairo, as this would "create terrible political complications and [therefore] should be avoided". As for timetables, Dayan informed his hosts that if the decision to proceed could only be made after the conclusion of the Security Council discussions, namely October 12, Israel could not be ready before the 20th. Six to seven days were needed to mobilise, Dayan explained.[42]

At the end of the St. Germain conference, French views about a possible military move against Egypt may be summed up as follows: France was unwilling, at this stage, to go to war without Britain. The French attitude towards collaboration with Israel was quite different from the Israeli approach: They did not regard the Israelis as equal partners and were unwilling to act simultaneously. At the same time, they were ready, under certain circumstances, to have Israel operate independently even west of the Suez Canal. The French were interested in Israel as a land base near the theatre of operations, and more importantly, as the provider of a pretext to provoke an Anglo-French war against Egypt. For their part, the French were willing to go to great lengths in providing Israel with arms and ammunition. It was clear to the French that the military in both nations shared a desire to urge their respective political leaderships to make the necessary decisions; they were also aware of the impact military planning and coordination would have on political decision-making. Last, but far from least, the French still concentrated all their thoughts on Algeria, and everything they did was intended to serve that ultimate cause.[43]

"Events Flow Backwards"

During the few weeks between the meeting at St. Germain and the Sèvres conference (see below) – that is, the first three weeks in October – there was a feeling in Israel that everything had come to a standstill because of differences between France and Britain. As Peres later wrote, "It seemed that events were flowing backwards, contrary to expectations: England and France seemed to have despaired of any possible action." In retrospect, it is obvious that the tripartite operation was still viable in early October, albeit with less vitality than before. The Israeli delegation left for home on the evening of October 1, arriving in Israel only at noon on the next day – for secrecy's sake, they flew through Tunisia again. Each side experienced its own misgivings about the military operation, but in Israel, Dayan and Peres were busy translating the St. Germain understandings into a concrete Franco-Israeli commitment.[44]

Foremost on the Dayan–Peres agenda was securing, on a permanent basis, the freedom of action they had enjoyed until then from Ben-Gurion. From that time on, until a final political decision was made (on October 24), they were at pains to ensure Ben-Gurion's unwavering support for their actions. In retrospect, they seem to have been preaching to the converted, but that is not how Dayan and Peres saw it at the time. They genuinely feared that Ben-Gurion might back out.[45]

Those who had been in St. Germain saw the direction of forthcoming events very clearly: a joint Franco-Israeli military move against Egypt. At the same time, the French were making desperate efforts, throughout October, to forge their understanding with Israel into a plan which Britain, too, would find satisfactory. Yet any account of these events which focuses on the political arena alone will be misleading.

The political efforts were to culminate at the Sèvres conference (October 22–24), which is discussed later on. There, British, French and Israeli officials would finalise the modalities of co-operation and set D-day.[46] However, we must also take into account the military understanding achieved at St. Germain between France and Israel, and

the military preparations in Israel, which received a significant boost
following that conference. The impact this dual military aspect had on
the political process in general, and the Sèvres conference in particular,
was crucial. Nothing else can account for the fact that these three parties,
with such radically divergent points of departure, were able to reach
complete agreement at Sèvres so quickly.

It was tacitly assumed by Dayan and Peres, as well as by Bourgès-
Maunoury, Thomas and Challe, that the political leadership must be
made to follow in the wake of advances in the military sphere. Now that
the Israeli delegation was back home, the time had come to implement
this approach.[47] From the airport the members of the St. Germain
mission proceeded directly to the Prime Minister's Office in Jerusalem.
The chief speaker at this first meeting was Foreign Minister Meir. From
her report Ben-Gurion could only conclude that the French had not yet
made up their minds about going to war, still less whether Israel should
be a partner to any such venture. Meir's remarks thus deepened Ben-
Gurion's suspicions. Dayan was careful not to contradict her directly –
he seems to have been more aware than usual of his formal status in this
forum – but he did outline for Ben-Gurion what the French wanted
(whereas Meir had stressed what the French were unwilling to do, in
her view). Dayan went further, taking the opportunity to explain, then
and there, how Israel should prepare for a joint operation – and ignoring
the Foreign Minister's scepticism about such a move. Dayan asked for
permission to set up a joint liaison bureau with the French General Staff,
allow the French to prepare for the use of Israeli air bases, arrange for
further arms shipments from France, as agreed on at St. Germain, and
send Peres to New York so he could stay in close touch with Pineau, who
was there for the Security Council session.[48]

After the meeting, Ben-Gurion noted in his diary a series of dilemmas
concerning the value of a joint operation with France. Central to all these
issues were misgivings about Britain, on the one hand, and commitments already made to France, on the other. Ben-Gurion's notes did not
add up to an outright rejection of a war, but they did cast doubt on the
wisdom of an immediate military action "according to a French
timetable". In conclusion he wrote, "I shall present an outline of my
considerations . . . to General Challe" – he was due to meet the French
military delegation led by Challe that same day.[49]

But Dayan managed to dissuade Ben-Gurion from airing his misgivings in front of the Frenchmen. A short while before that meeting,
Ben-Gurion summoned Dayan and Peres in order to explain his fears to
them; he even spoke about a personal letter he thought of sending to
Mollet. Dayan's reaction to Ben-Gurion's doubts was typical of his
relationship with the Prime Minister in general, and probably reflected

his personal attitude at the time. By his own account, the Chief of Staff all but berated the Prime Minister and Minister of Defence: "I asked him categorically not to [express his doubts to the French, but] to wait until the end of the French delegation's mission so we could hear their firm conclusions. It is very easy now to quench the French government's burning desire to launch a military campaign against Nasser; but to rekindle it again – this will be impossible. I told Ben-Gurion he was over-anxious about air raids [by Egypt against Israel] . . . I may have come on too strong with Ben-Gurion, but I do not regret this."[50]

As a matter of fact, the Prime Minister was not in the least angry with Dayan. On the contrary, he entered Dayan's comments in his diary with obvious satisfaction, as though this was just what he had expected to hear. Far from calling a halt to the military preparations, he encouraged Dayan to carry on.[51]

Ben-Gurion's meeting with the French delegation on October 3 dealt with operational military matters; Ben-Gurion obliged Dayan and kept his doubts to himself. At their second meeting, the following day, Ben-Gurion himself finalised with Mangin, Bourgès-Maunoury's aide, the modalities of liaison between the two ministries of defence. On the same day, the Prime Minister also approved the understandings reached between Dayan and the French on continued military planning. Franco-Israeli collaboration was now well past the sounding-out stage. French arms shipments agreed on at St. Germain were already on their way to Israel, liaison officers had been appointed by the various services and the IDF was busy with its own preparations.[52]

Undoubtedly, military co-operation reached new heights during the visit of the Challe delegation, code-named in Israel "Milk and Honey". One topic of discussion was the British posture. Ben-Gurion asked the French officers whether their troops would be able to operate from Cyprus even if Britain finally decided to stay out. General Challe said that from the military point of view there would be no problem, but as to "whether this base will be made available to France or not, that was a political question which he was not competent to answer." Mangin added that his chief, Bourgès-Maunoury, thought the British might allow the French free use of the Cyprus base, even if that should turn out to be the whole extent of their involvement. Alluding to Eden's inde-cisiveness, Mangin conjectured that "sooner or later Britain will drift into action against Egypt". Still, none of the participants thought it likely that Cyprus would be placed at their disposal without concrete British involvement in the war itself.

Ben-Gurion was concerned about what might happen in Egypt if Nasser were not removed from power but withdrew to Upper Egypt and kept up the fighting from there. Challe explained that in such a case the only possibility would be to hold on to the Canal Zone, which France could not do alone. Ben-Gurion then stated that he would not have Israel go beyond the Canal: "Our part will be to seize the Sinai Peninsula up to the Canal." In that case, Challe said, the French Army would be able to hold one bank of the Canal, as well as a few more key points; and the Canal itself would obviously remain closed to navigation.

Still lurking in the background, though, was one problem which had been worrying both Israel and France: Britain's role in the forthcoming war. Both countries, each for its own reasons, wanted Britain involved: Ben-Gurion sought to neutralise the danger of Britain's siding with the Arabs against Israel, while France thought it would be unwise to back out of the Anglo-French moves already under way in the Mediterranean towards full deployment. The solution was obvious, on both counts: involve Britain. But how could this be done, when Britain wanted to play the role of saviour rather than aggressor and, furthermore, refused to engage in direct contact with Israel? The French did their utmost to persuade Israel to "play the aggressor" and Britain to relax its "rules of engagement". In the meantime, at the conclusion of the Challe delegation's visit to Israel, it was agreed that Peres and Dayan would remain in charge of joint military planning with France.[53]

Military Liaison

Although no new political decisions were made as October progressed, military preparations became ever more concrete. If politically "events are flowing backwards", as Peres put it, militarily things were moving ahead fast. Some time between the St. Germain and Sèvres conferences, Israel's representative at the joint military staff in Paris wrote to Dayan: "Despite [political] appearances, the partners' resolve is unshaken."[54]

Events were no longer confined to internal planning, which could be called off at any time. They had assumed the form of a comprehensive joint planning process, in which a European power was involved. If there was any possible way for Israel to back out, it became far narrower as time wore on. Furthermore, on October 15 Ben-Gurion gave in to public opinion, which was increasingly jittery about the leadership's apparent inaction as security deteriorated rapidly. In a political statement to the Knesset (which made no mention, of course, of any "alliance" with France or a joint move against Egypt) the Prime Minister disclosed – circumspectly, even poetically, as mentioned earlier – that Israel was getting arms, and this, too, was another bridge now burning behind him.[55]

The French did not confine themselves to joint preparations with Israel towards war with Egypt. They examined the capabilities of their new ally using their own devices. Thus were circulated throughout the French Army intelligence reviews about the IDF – particularly in the Air Force, which seemed, as of September 1956, the chief candidate for military collaboration with Israel. The anticipated level of co-operation was far higher than anything envisaged in the Zayit framework agreement.[56]

All in all, the "Milk and Honey" delegation's visit proved satisfactory to both parties. General Challe agreed to speed up the arms deliveries agreed on at St. Germain (code-named 'EZUZ). The French delegation, for its part, was satisfied that the IDF could defeat the Egyptian Army on its own, and therefore could be regarded as a significant partner in any possible military move. It was agreed that in any event, the French Army needed organised bases in Israel.[57]

"Tzavta"

In terms of military liaison, considerable progress was made, with members of the French delegation visiting the various services and making initial contacts for future coordination. The most thorough work was done by General André Martin, Chief of Staff of the French Air Force, with his Israeli counterparts. Co-operation in the air, in contrast to land and sea, was less politically complicated because of its easy deniability. Already in their first meeting, the two parties got down to detailed planning.

In a series of meetings with Colonel Shlomo Lahat, Chief of the Air Staff, who was appointed chief liaison officer for the Israel Air Force (IAF), General Martin laid down the foundations for co-operation between the two air forces. Its parameters were reflected already in Israel's two consecutive war plans, Kadesh 1 and Kadesh 2, and during the war itself. For a start, the French asked the Israelis to allocate bases for their air squadrons. IAF officers described in some detail the structure and operation of the bases. It was also explained to the French that the IAF was incapable of stepping into the RAF's shoes, that is, carrying out extensive missions against Egyptian air bases west of the Canal. The Israelis could defend their own air space (assuming that the French were operating on the western side of the Canal) as well as the Sinai skies, and support their own ground forces there. This meant that the two air forces should launch their operations simultaneously.[58]

Arrangements were made for the reception of French squadrons due to arrive from Cyprus with some 2,000 personnel, mainly ground crews, and for communications and control procedures in war. It was agreed that Israeli ground control would also serve the French. The main control centre would operate bilingually, with French liaison and control officers present. At the conclusion of his visit, General Martin made specific recommendations regarding the establishment of French operative bases in Israel. During October, Colonel Maurice Perdrizet was appointed chief liaison officer with the IAF, under Martin. The Israelis, for their part, set up a liaison staff code-named "Tzavta" (i.e., "companionship"). For Ben-Gurion, whose foremost concern had always been the defence of Israel's air space, these discussions with General Martin proved highly significant in making up his mind about the entire joint move.[59]

Talks on co-operation also took place between representatives of the respective ground forces and navies, but these did not reach the same level of practicality as the air forces. Still, the navy did set up some initial arrangements for liaison and communications, prior to and during war. Haifa harbour was pronounced serviceable for the French, who promised their Israeli counterparts certain necessary equipment, relating mainly to harbour and coastal defence. As for the ground forces, since there was from the start no prospect of joint operations, there was little room for liaison. Colonel Simon, the delegation member in charge of liaising with Israel's ground forces, saw his mission more as a fact-finding one (and was impressed) than as requiring concrete arrangements.[60]

At the concluding meeting General Challe complimented his hosts, but also pointed out a few of the IDF's problems – particularly as regards military planning:

> From what I saw here and in view of your level of training, of which I have heard a lot, it seems to me that the plans shown [to us] are executable. In the air, it seems to be the best that can be done in your circumstances, although I must point out that the plan pushes the limits of the possible. If you lose the element of surprise, and if this will result in your Day One raids attacking empty airfields, your plan will fail. Because of this, I regard surprise as essential.
>
> As for the ground plans, they look good to me . . . It is my conclusion that if the French could undertake the air aspect, the job will be easier and the chances of success will improve. On the ground, it seems, we can offer much less help.
>
> My personal conclusion, and I stress that it is not binding upon my government, is that in the conditions we saw it is possible that the Israelis will capture the Sinai Peninsula and the French will do the same in the Canal, although I am not sure this could be the entire Canal, unless the Egyptian Army completely disintegrates. But here I begin to play the prophet, and it seems wise to stop now.[61]

The foundations for military collaboration, laid in June and bolstered at St. Germain, now gave rise to more concrete agreements on the appointment of liaison officers, mutual recognition arrangements between forces, and fully equipping the IDF for a joint endeavour. The French delegation left Israel on October 4, and the next day Planning Order Kadesh 1 was distributed to the various branches of the IDF. Even before the French left, preparations were begun in France: first orders were written up in the French Air Force for the orderly transfer of ground facilities to Israeli air bases, in advance of the deployment of French aircraft to Israel.

Opération 750

Code-named Kadesh in Israel, the joint operation was called Opération 750 in France – this code-name was maintained throughout, as distinct from Opération 700, the name given Anglo-French collaboration. With the return of the high-ranking military delegation from Israel and the beefing up of the IDF mission in Paris, the French General Staff began discussing the outlines of their collaboration with the IDF in the event of a political decision being made to go ahead with a joint operation. So far, the French had learned from their Israeli counterparts that Israel had no intention of conquering the Canal Zone, since its main interest lay in the Straits of Tiran. In the northern part of the Sinai, the French understood, Israel would send forces along the Abu 'Agueila-Isma'ilia road, up to some 30 miles east of the Canal, no more. An additional effort would be aimed at El-'Arish, in northern Sinai.

The French thought Israel was deluding itself if it believed that Nasser could be brought down by an operation consisting mainly of occupying the Straits of Tiran. They had been given an outline of the Kadesh 1 plan while in Israel, but seem to have misunderstood its fundamentals. Since their Israeli counterparts kept emphasising that Israel had no intention of physically reaching the Canal, reiterating that its chief concern lay in the Straits, it is small wonder that the French got the impression that Israel thought to defeat the Egyptian Army in southern Sinai. But this misunderstanding served Israel's purposes: "Since our objective is the Canal," commented French planners, "it will be desirable for our operation to take place concurrently with the Israelis'. A simultaneous operation will relieve us of major pressure." This approach fit well with the Israeli attitude, as expressed by Dayan at St. Germain, by air force commanders in their discussions with Martin in Israel, and by Ben-Gurion up to and during the Sèvres conference.[62]

On second thought, however, the French generals realised that while such a conclusion might be sound theoretically, it was utterly impractical. Launching both offensives concurrently would mean losing the element of surprise completely – for Israel as well. For one thing, the

French would have to send out their maritime convoys at least 72 hours before D-day. Thus the French had ruled out the simultaneous option even before the British let it be known that they simply refused to consider it. The only option left, then, was the "Israeli pretext" idea, which was rather advantageous for France, politically speaking. Working on their maps, French military planners reached a conclusion which was already an article of faith with the politicians in France and Britain: collaboration with Israel must be kept secret, and they themselves should appear to be intervening in order to separate the warring forces and to be saving the Canal for humankind, rather than acting with Israel against Nasser.[63]

In order to persuade Dayan to withdraw his demand for simultaneity, the French began passing on to him, through his representative in Paris, Colonel Gazit, a series of offers for assistance which would facilitate the so-called "pretext plan" – entailing an IDF-initiated offensive with covert French air support. For instance, the French asked how long it would take to rebuild the railroad from Israel to Gaza, out of commission since 1948; whether the IDF would need French naval support in landing at El-'Arish; and what type of naval support might be needed for IDF operations along the northern Sinai coast. They even considered deploying in Israel more air squadrons than those already decided on. At the same time, the French General Staff requested more intelligence information about the Alexandria harbour, asked whether the marshes east of Port Said were passable for vehicles, and so on.[64]

Still, Israel remained under the impression that France's political will for war was wavering. In fact, the French attitude was marked by divergent points of view: France's military authorities consistently took a more positive approach, the Prime Minister supported the idea but only tacitly, and Quai d'Orsay objected to the entire concept. The French-Israeli connection was effected through the defence establishments of the two countries. France also had objective problems, notably the need to prepare an invasion of Egypt while at the same time providing aid to Israel. Still, the French did their best to allay Israeli fears. They talked nuts-and-bolts: "As for the French Air Force, there are no problems. They are ready to use naval aircraft as well as eight heavy bombers. ... The French Navy [however] cannot undertake an operation against Alexandria as well as a major landing elsewhere. For this reason, besides the difficulties inherent in concentrating a significant French task force in Israel before D-day, there is no possibility of a French attack concurrent with an Israeli one." The French, then, favoured broader collaboration, but no simultaneity. They suggested that Israel make a parachute drop with "a serious force" in Isma'ilia and Port Sa'id, to provide both pretext and support for a subsequent French landing. As if in compensation, the French suggested that one of their units – not a large one – participate in a landing at El-'Arish, then move westward along the railroad to Qantara.[65]

Dayan conveyed these French suggestions to Ben-Gurion, and both replied on October 14. They ruled out completely any drop of Israeli paratroopers in the Canal Zone, let alone to its west. As far as they were concerned, the Canal was solely a French affair. Ben-Gurion also hinted that following the opening stage, the IDF would have missions of its own to execute in the Sinai. Dayan explained that Israel was willing to approach (but not reach) the Canal from the east, and was prepared to forgo French land support, in return for French agreement to launch their operation simultaneously with Israel. In their instructions to their representatives in Paris, both Israeli leaders emphasised that it was imperative, at this stage, to press Israel's demand for simultaneity. Dayan pointed out that "we shall undertake every effort to make it possible for them to operate out of Israel, including various operations in support."

At the same time, Dayan accepted most of the French Army's logistical and operational requests regarding their air activity in Israel. Nor did the Chief of Staff reject France's generous offers of naval support. Even before the Kadesh 1 plan was finalised (on October 16), Dayan asked his planners to see how El-'Arish could be taken with French artillery support from the sea. But on one point Dayan would not budge: the two operations must be concurrent. Israel would not appear as the sole aggressor. Ben-Gurion, well aware of the political implications of the ever tightening military collaboration, repeatedly instructed his representatives – as he had done throughout the crisis – to remind the French that in the final analysis everything depended on his Cabinet's decision.[66]

There was one major reason for the difficulty Israel found in getting the French to formulate plans more to its liking: the fact that a single French planning staff, headed by Vice-Admiral Pierre Barjot and General Gazin, his Chief of Staff, was in charge of both the activities of General Challe *vis-à-vis* Israel, and of General André Beaufre *vis-à-vis* the British Army. Beaufre's people kept reminding their colleagues that they should bear in mind the needs of their partners across the Channel. Co-operation with Britain was ever uppermost in the minds of the French, and they leaned over backwards in their efforts to please London. Already in early September, French Ambassador in Israel Pierre Gilbert told his Israeli counterpart, Ya'akov Tzur, that "the British General Staff is deliberately excluding Israel from all its military preparations, and the French Staff has no choice but to go along with it." This was becoming abundantly clear as October wore on.[67]

"Israel Will Not Start a War on Its Own"

Unclear about the state of Anglo-French preparations for Operation Musketeer, and unable to involve the British in any Franco-Israeli planning, the French and the Israelis found it difficult to proceed with the elaboration of their joint plans. Eden was unable to muster a clear Cabinet majority for a military action against Egypt. It soon became clear that there was little sense in keeping up talks at a relatively low level, when the Israelis had no authority to plan for anything but a simultaneous operation, which the French ruled out, and the French had no clear instructions from their government, which was itself in a difficult spot because of British indecisiveness.[68]

Given this state of affairs, it was felt necessary to clarify the political situation first of all, and then raise the level of military talks. The French now began an intensive effort on two fronts, the political and the military. In France, as in Israel, it was the military that pushed reluctant politicians forward. With Bourgès-Maunoury's go-ahead, Challe flew to New York immediately after his return from Israel. There, he briefed a much surprised Pineau about his visit; the Foreign Minister expressed his support for continued military coordination with Israel and even agreed to try to get the British involved.

Challe's timing was propitious: in the Security Council there was a guaranteed Soviet veto for any anti-Egypt resolution. This, and the increasingly substantive Israeli option, gave the French better grounds for persuading Eden in favour of immediate war. On October 14, a French delegation visited Britain in secret: the untiring General Challe, who had just returned to Paris from New York, and Minister of Labour Albert Gazier, a confidant of both Mollet and Pineau (who was on his way back from New York). Prime Minister Eden received them at his country residence, Chequers.[69]

The day before, October 13, Challe had informed Nahmias of his intended meeting with Eden, in which he proposed to outline the French version of the "pretext idea". Challe was in a hurry: he felt he had to reach Eden before his Foreign Secretary, Selwyn Lloyd, returned from New York, since Lloyd was dead set against any collaboration with Israel. The idea was to convince Eden that involving Israel would be useful, as its actions would furnish the two Western powers with a *casus belli* and thereby also revitalize the almost moribund Anglo-French planning.[70] Challe wasted no time: already on the day he met with Eden, October 14, the French asked the Israelis to send to Paris a senior military officer with broader authority than Colonel Gazit's. Dayan decided to dispatch his second-in-command, General 'Amit, Chief of Operations at the General Staff. With him he sent Ne'eman, who had just returned from Paris to Israel. However, the instructions 'Amit received from both the Minister of Defence and the Chief of Staff gave him little chance to accomplish any more than Gazit had.[71]

Although Ben-Gurion did not completely rule out the possibility of Israeli involvement in subsequent activity in the Canal Zone, his brief to Dayan and 'Amit was quite clear on this point: Israel was ready to move out simultaneously – but not to launch a war on its own. Dayan laid down the law for 'Amit even more explicitly: "Israel moves no ground forces before French ground forces set foot on Egyptian soil. We reach the east bank of the Suez Canal, no more . . . It's none of our business whether [the French] or somebody else sit to the west of the Canal, for all we care the Egyptians can remain there. D-day for ground forces must be the same, there's no arguing about that. Air operations must precede ground D-day. Our reaching the Canal is for me Stage I of the operation. I have no reservations about going on, if further stages will be called for. Obviously, it's up to the French to seize the Canal itself, in whole or in part."[72]

Meanwhile, at Chequers, Eden rejected a French proposal for a simultaneous operation with Israel. He did, though, accept Challe's other idea: an Israeli attack on Egypt in the Sinai, seemingly aimed at the Suez Canal, would be a pretext for Britain and France to intervene in the Canal Zone. As a matter of fact, this was not the first time Eden had heard this idea. Since early August it had been broached several times by the Chancellor of the Exchequer, Harold Macmillan. Previously Eden had rejected the idea, but now he was ready for collaboration of this kind with Israel. The British Prime Minister had reached an impasse *vis-à-vis* both the Americans and British domestic opposition. By now, he was willing to accept help from any quarter, even Israel, though he was aware of the risks this would pose to the British interest. It was agreed that on the very next day, Lloyd and Pineau having by then returned from New York, Eden and Mollet, with their foreign ministers, would meet at the Matignon Palace in Paris.[73]

On that same eventful October 14, General Meir 'Amit and Colonel Yuval Ne'eman left for Paris to meet with General Gazin and other Musketeer planners. What happened there was typical of the way in which preparations for war were to proceed during the next two weeks, and of how the war itself would unfold afterwards. On October 15, General Challe forwarded to Dayan and Peres, through Nahmias, the idea which Eden had found acceptable. He also explained the plan to Musketeer HQ, Paris, but did not authorise the start of work on it and did not want to explain himself: the fact of the collusion and that the operation depended on a prior Israeli provocation was kept secret from Musketeer HQ. On the same day, 'Amit and Gazin and their staffs met.

Although Gazin had been directed to keep working with 'Amit on the simultaneous operation Israel was insisting on, as though nothing had happened, things were by now so confused (and small wonder) that he referred to an advance Israeli move (according to the Challe plan, of which he was already aware). 'Amit, strictly enjoined to discuss a simultaneous operation only, found it impossible to go on. Neither general knew anything about the political negotiations which were under way concurrently with their military talks. Gazin, having realised his mistake, could not explain to 'Amit why he had brought up this notion, other than to say that it made more military sense, in his view (though it didn't). 'Amit, therefore, could not tell Dayan what had made the French raise this "new" proposal.[74]

'Amit, undoubtedly feeling like a babe in the woods, asked to meet with the leaders of the Milk and Honey delegation, hoping to get a clearer picture – the strict compartmentalisation meant that 'Amit, too, did not know all the details – and on October 16 Dayan permitted him to talk with Generals Challe and Martin. Challe explained the new plan to him, but only at the operational level: the French Army would go into action on D-day +3. He also expounded plans for air and ground co-operation, although carefully pointing out that the latter possibility represented something of a problem, because of the difficulties the French had encountered in getting the British to take even a positively neutral stance towards Israel. 'Amit reminded his hosts that agreement on a simultaneous operation had been reached in Israel. Martin allowed that such indeed was the case, at least in the air, but then he grasped at the practical excuse – the French could not send in their ground troops immediately, since this would compromise the element of surprise. 'Amit, in line with his directives from Ben-Gurion and Dayan, then suggested that at least the air operations would take place simultaneously. And there things stood for the time being.[75]

Nevertheless, 'Amit met again that day with the Musketeer planning team. Gazin (having been briefed, apparently by Challe and Martin) made a new, improved offer: D-day would mark the start of an Israeli ground strike and Israeli and French air operations. On D+1, the French would keep up their air raids, from bases in Israel and from their aircraft carriers. On D+2 the French would drop their paratroopers and land their marines, and start moving against Qantara. It was better than the previous French plan, but still 'Amit could not accept it.[76]

However, Challe and Martin, excited about this new possibility of breaking the deadlock, but unable to reveal to the Israelis in Paris what lay behind the new idea, asked 'Amit to stay on until political approval could be obtained for Challe's ideas. Nahmias told 'Amit what little he knew about behind-the-scenes activity. On October 17, 'Amit met again with Gazin, and later on with General Paul Ely, the Chief of Staff. Neither French officer knew how much information their Israeli guest had. Ely informed 'Amit that he had reached the conclusion that a simultaneous land operation was an impossibility, but refused to elaborate. 'Amit put two and two together and reached his own conclusion: that a clear-cut political decision was needed before any joint military planning could take place. He therefore declined further French hospitality and returned to Israel. He could not understand why the French were beseeching him to stay on, if they were not prepared to discuss a simultaneous ground offensive; all he knew was that he had been given no mandate to discuss anything else.

On October 18, back in Israel, 'Amit briefed Ben-Gurion about his Paris talks, still with no knowledge about what had transpired at the same time at Chequers and Matignon. Nor was he aware of the exchange of cables between France and Israel, which had decided the Prime Minister and the Chief of Staff to fly to Paris and work things out themselves. Objectively, the situation was complicated. On the French side only Challe and Martin, as well as Bourgès-Maunoury in Paris – and on the Israeli side only Dayan, Peres and Ben-Gurion – knew the whole story. Not even the British knew everything. Those who were privy to all the details of the collusion had to keep up a pretence of secrets and lies both internally and of course externally.[77]

The concluding conference to work out the details of the tripartite coalition was held at Sèvres, a suburb of Paris, from 22–24 October 1956. This was basically an Israeli-French meeting, which was attended by the heads of both countries; the British joined in from time to time at a more junior level. At the end of the conference, an agreement was signed that formed the basis for the tripartite war against Egypt.

A Reluctant Coalition

"Obviously, We and the French See Eye-to-Eye"

France's dependence on a British decision, and Israel's dependence on both Western powers, in effect left to British Prime Minister Eden the decision about whether to launch a war against Egypt. Eden paid a high price for agreeing, however reluctantly, to involve Israel in the scheme. Essentially, this price took the form of the ramifications of Britain's failure to respect its formal commitments – principally to Jordan, though also to Iraq – but, perhaps equally important, it involved also a certain change in Eden's attitude towards Israel. During October, Israel and Britain tested each other, politically and militarily. Both Eden and Ben-Gurion tried to rethink the opinion they held of each other. These complex interrelationships, compounded by grave national concerns and mutual suspicions – which are the theme of this chapter – brought about Ben-Gurion's determination at the Sèvres conference to ensure that no joint operation against Egypt would take place unless the British first committed themselves not to come to Jordan's defence and attack Israel should hostilities erupt on Israel's eastern border.

On 27 July 1956, immediately after the Suez Crisis broke out, the British Prime Minister appointed a small ministerial committee to co-ordinate Britain's response to Nasser's move – the so-called "Egypt Committee" – somewhat in the nature of a war cabinet. This committee was in effect the top governmental organ in charge of conducting British policy during the crisis, although central decisions were brought for Cabinet approval. The committee members were Eden's senior ministers. As primary task, Eden directed the group to formulate the essentials and a timetable for a military operation against Egypt.[1]

Generally speaking, the committee members tended to support Eden's approach. Only Defence Secretary Sir Walter Monckton objected, arguing that Britain should not use force in the Suez before non-military options had been fully explored. Despite his minority position, his reservations carried weight. After all, the Ministers of War (i.e.,

Army) and Air, and the First Lord of the Admiralty, who were not Cabinet members, answered to him. He would have direct responsibility for preparing for war. The fact that Eden did not remove him, despite his reservations, was a major reason for the slow pace of planning and preparations. Monckton finally resigned (his portfolio, not his Cabinet membership) on 18 October 1956; he was replaced by Minister of War Anthony Head, who throughout had been wholly in favour of using force against Egypt.[2]

The unrelenting pressure exerted by US President Eisenhower and Secretary of State Dulles placed Eden in a serious quandary. Also, as time went by, British public opinion and Parliament were becoming less supportive of using force in the Suez. Eden was embarrassed by the disclosure that altogether only 5 per cent of the Canal Company's revenues found their way to British bank accounts. Nevertheless, despite the nationalisation, the revenues which flowed to banks in Paris and London could be easily confiscated. Eden, however, was determined to resolve the issue by military force.

At the UN Security Council, the Soviet Union vetoed a British and French draft resolution calling for military action against Egypt. The West, though, did not put up a united front against the USSR. The Americans even expressed their satisfaction following the adoption, in mid-October, of a lukewarm resolution consisting mainly of a call for further diplomatic efforts. Indeed, Washington was all in favour of continued peaceful efforts. Nasser's assumption – that Western willingness to remove him would decline with time – began to look increasingly prescient.[3]

Eden, however, was not displeased with the Security Council resolution. On the contrary, this was the opportunity he had been looking for. Now the time was ripe for decision. Without consulting either the Cabinet or his own creation, the Egypt Committee, Eden decided in mid-October to collaborate with France – even if this entailed co-operation with Israel as well. On October 15 he visited Paris secretly and finalised an agreement with the French for a joint operation to include Israel. Eden shared his thinking with a small group of very senior or close ministers – Macmillan, Lloyd and Head – and occasionally also with Monckton and Minister of State for Foreign Affairs Anthony Nutting, despite their objections to the use of military force against Egypt. As of mid-October, then, Britain was ready to take part in a joint move with France and Israel. Against this background, however, the Jordan problem assumed major proportions.[4]

"A Strong Israel Will Conduct Itself Better"

The "Israeli" aspect of the Suez Crisis was not raised as an issue in Britain for the first time in October: already in early August Harold Macmillan had suggested sounding out Israel on possible military collaboration against Egypt. Macmillan thought an Israeli connection could be doubly fruitful. To begin with, there was the tactical sphere. Independently of ideas which originated in France, Macmillan, at the very outset of the crisis, had put forward options which were to materialise ten weeks later as the French-British-Israeli "conspiracy". The Chancellor of the Exchequer thought it desirable for the Western powers to push the Egyptian Army eastward, into the Sinai, and blow up the Canal bridges behind it. Israel could then deal with the trapped corps. In this Macmillan had the backing of the Chiefs of Staff Committee, which proposed an Israeli parachute drop near the Canal a few days before the Anglo-French operation. Should the Israelis appear to be attacking Egypt, Macmillan argued, the advantages of collaboration with them would outweigh any disadvantage. Victory would be achieved more readily, and Britain could set up an alternative government in Cairo, with no possible interference by the Egyptian Army. But more important, Israeli intervention would provide Britain with a wonderful *casus belli*.

Second, at the broader international level, Macmillan contemplated a new order in the Middle East. Like Ben-Gurion, he saw the Suez Crisis as an opportunity to change regimes and revise boundaries throughout the region. In his view, a British display of force and Israeli involvement would persuade the parties to the Arab-Israeli conflict to seek a British-sponsored resolution, which would restore Britain's dominant position in this vital area.[5]

Macmillan had put forward his ideas twice: on August 2, before the Egypt Committee, and the next day at the meeting of an inter-departmental civil service committee established to handle the pragmatics of crisis management. On August 5, Macmillan had told Churchill that "it won't work without Israel", and a couple of days letter he sent Eden a memo in the same vein. Thus Harold Macmillan, a senior minister and a future Prime Minister, from the start supported the military's view that collaboration with Israel would be advantageous; Eden, though, refused to consider this notion until mid-October, and the military was not ordered to plan for such an eventuality.[6]

On the Opposition side, Labour's young leader, Hugh Gaitskell, argued that the best response to Nasser would be to give Israel immediate large-scale military assistance, as the French were doing. Initially, Eden rejected this idea, too. In his books, the fear of appearing as an enemy of the Arabs carried significant weight. Still, the British Prime Minister believed that he could use force against Egypt without losing the support of most Arab nations – or at least Jordan, Iraq and the Gulf Emirates. A possible joint operation with Israel was certain to raise difficult problems for Britain. This concern was to preoccupy him even after he had made up his mind to use Israel's services. Eden therefore made a point of ensuring that collaboration with Israel was covered by a fig leaf in order to minimise the damage which would certainly be done to Britain's position in the Arab world by the attack on Egypt.[7]

Still, at least in his close circle Eden did not deny that Britain and Israel did have common interests. His decision in favour of collaboration with Israel also was based on his perception that the two countries had a common enemy and that "a strong Israel will conduct itself better . . . arms means control." What did he mean by "better conduct"? Two interpretations suggest themselves. One was the spirit which permeated his November 1955 Guildhall Address (and which also informed the Anglo-American Alpha and Omega plans): there Eden in effect demanded that Israel "constrict" its borders so that Britain could improve its relations with the Arab world. Israel's withdrawal from territories it had conquered in 1948 might terminate the Arab-Israeli conflict, a development which would relieve Britain of its difficulties in trying to maintain ties with Israel and the Arabs simultaneously: by compelling Israel to concede land, Britain would greatly enhance its position in the Arab world. Perhaps, though, what Eden had in mind was that Israel would give Britain clandestine support in its campaign against Nasser. Since late July 1956, when the Suez Crisis broke out, Eden seems to have been increasingly inclined towards the latter option. Nevertheless, it was clear from the start that any Israeli collaboration with Britain would have to overcome the contradictions inherent in Britain's special position in the Middle East.[8]

A series of developments – American refusal to join with Britain and France militarily against Egypt, the failure of these two powers to enlist UN support for a move against Egypt, and the fact that Nasser did not provide any pretext for such a move (beyond the very act of nationalisation, which became less acute as time wore by) – combined to convince Eden that he had no choice but to accept the notion of an "Israeli pretext", which had been brought up independently by Macmillan and the French. The question facing Eden by mid-October was not if but how to co-ordinate his moves with Israel. On the eve of the tripartite conference at Sèvres, Eden was troubled by several Israel-related problems: the American aspect – Israel insisted on American approval for the operation, which Eden knew would be impossible; the Jordanian aspect – Britain would not be able to honour its commitment to protect Jordan from Israel, if it went to war alongside Israel; the general Arab aspect – concern for Britain's position in the Arab World made it imperative to disguise and deny any collusion with Israel, even where it existed. Eden and Lloyd appear to have genuinely believed that they could portray their country as the preserver of international order, seeking to deliver the Arabs; and the domestic aspect – opinion in Britain was growing stronger against the use of military force at Suez or in the Middle East in general (even against Israel). As a consequence of all these, Eden embarked on a road which was to come close to breaking the rules of democratic play, so cherished by Britain.[9] However he looked at it, Eden could not launch a belligerent move against Egypt without a cogent, convincing reason. In this context Israel grew in importance, as the provider of the only possible pretext.

Eden, like many of his senior ministers, saw the Suez Crisis as an existential threat to Britain, and therefore was willing to do almost anything to bring down Nasser and his regime. Macmillan, in his role as chief supporter of collaboration with Israel, wrote to Eden in late August 1956, at the conclusion of a report on the economic implications of the Suez Crisis: "The conclusion is clear-cut – without oil, the United Kingdom and Western Europe are doomed."[10]

Will Britain Fight Alongside or Against Israel?

While the "Israeli problem" was worrying the British government, the "British problem" was vexing the Israelis. It had been an issue of major concern for Israel almost from the moment that talks began with the French on a possible joint war against Egypt. There were other worries as well: air cover, the IDF's ability to take on the Egyptian Army, and whether Israel should play the aggressor for Britain and France. But overriding all these, Israel's paramount concern was Britain: would it fight alongside or against Israel? Even after he had made up his mind to go to Paris, Ben-Gurion made it clear, on any number of occasions, that his main reservation about the "pretext move" was related to his total mistrust of the British. It was not just a matter of emotions, even bearing in mind that he himself had led the struggle to expel the British from Palestine in the previous decade. There was a more concrete foundation for his suspicions.[11]

France took considerable pains to allay Israel's fears, while at the same time getting Britain to change its hostile attitude towards Israel. Mollet did not confine his efforts only to sending cables, congratulatory and otherwise. On October 21, Challe and Mangin arrived in Israel, purportedly to accompany the Israeli delegation on their way to Paris, but in fact to soften up Ben-Gurion. Immediately upon landing, they met with

Dayan and Peres at the Chief of Staff's office. There the Frenchmen outlined the new "Chequers scheme", to which the British had already agreed (see chapter 6). Challe informed his hosts that the first session at Sèvres had been scheduled for the next day, at 11 a.m., and then wanted to discuss military details of the new plan. Dayan's response was that he could make no commitments, because "tomorrow the PM will move in and will personally run everything". He added that there was no argument about the need for the meeting – they would leave that evening – but Israel was still very much concerned about British policy in this crisis.[12]

The "British problem", as viewed by Israel, consisted of several fundamental issues which had been brewing during the months preceding the Sinai War. First and foremost, there was Britain's policy towards Jordan during 1956, and the role reserved for Iraq in that policy. Indeed, it is impossible to understand the tripartite move against Egypt in October 1956, without taking into account developments in the Kingdom of Jordan. Affecting as they did both Israel and Britain, these developments naturally also affected the relations between those two countries. Nasser's profound hostility towards the pro-Britain Hashemite regimes in Jordan and Iraq was a key factor in the "Jordan crisis", which had preceded the Suez Crisis by several months. That crisis threatened to draw both Israel and Britain into war – but on that occasion, on opposite sides.

On 1 March 1956, Jordanian Prime Minister Samir el-Rifa'i gave General Sir John Glubb, the long-time commanding officer of the Arab Legion (the Jordanian army), two hours to leave the country. The order came from King Hussein. Eden's immediate intervention helped, but only marginally: Glubb Pasha was allowed 24 hours instead of two. Both Eden and Lloyd saw this move within the context of Nasser's anti-British efforts throughout the Middle East. As a matter of fact, on the day Glubb was dismissed, Selwyn Lloyd, the British Foreign Secretary, was in Cairo, on a visit to Nasser. The Egyptian President repeated to him that only the dissolution of the Baghdad Pact could bring about an improvement in the relations between their two nations. Nor did Nasser hide from Lloyd his satisfaction with Hussein's move, though he denied responsibility for it. Lloyd left Egypt for Bahrain, where he was greeted by anti-Britain demonstrations – at Nasser's instigation, he thought.[13]

Be that as it may, Glubb's dismissal and its aftermath had a cumulative impact. Eden and Lloyd took it very hard, speaking of it as the culmination of Nasser's provocations against Britain. Their immediate reaction was to order all British officers to leave Jordan, and even to threaten Hussein with the unilateral cancellation of the Anglo-Jordanian mutual defence agreement. They would have acted, had not

Glubb himself asked them to "understand the boy's [King Hussein] desire to be rid of him". Glubb advised against bringing matters to a head; send no more angry cables, he urged, let the dust settle, and only then decide on British policy *vis-à-vis* Jordan. He was supported by the British Ambassador to Amman, Charles Duke, who proposed that the whole affair be considered a personal matter against Glubb.[14]

Eden therefore confined his reaction to a request to King Hussein to relieve British officers of their command posts in the Arab Legion, while the Foreign Office began to formulate a new long-term policy aimed at improving Britain's standing in Jordan. To that end, the idea was broached to make use of the Hashemite regime in Iraq, then Britain's most stable foothold in the Middle East. Iraq and Jordan shared a long border, their sovereigns were scions of the same dynasty, and Eden was a close personal friend of Iraqi Prime Minister Nuri el-Sa'id. Thus, Iraq was ideally placed to promote British interests in Jordan. A joint Iraqi-Jordanian front, according to the devisors of this policy, could effectively block Nasser's growing influence in the Middle East.[15]

As for Eden, he could no longer regard Jordan as a secure British foothold – which only made him angrier with Nasser, who he blamed for the Jordan débacle. Yet there was a glaring contradiction between Eden's vehement statements when Glubb had been sacked, and the sober policy forced on him by the Cabinet and the Foreign Office (in part, because of crises at the time in Cyprus and Bahrain, which impinged on Britain's ability to react vigorously to developments in Jordan). This contradiction did not escape the notice of both the press and the parliamentary opposition; as a matter of fact, they had a field day. The still-fresh memories of these events must have affected Eden's reactions towards Egypt when, a few months later, the Suez Crisis broke out. This time around, he was determined to have his way with Nasser.[16]

"Jordan Is Unstable and May Break Up"

The need for an Iraq–Jordan front became even more acute when Egypt, Syria and Saudi Arabia renewed their offer to Jordan (originally given in January 1956) to fill Britain's place, should it renege on its obligation to defend Jordan. Britain's policy towards Jordan now strove to achieve two goals: obtain Iraqi assistance in curbing Nasser's growing influence in Amman, and reassure Hussein that Britain stood by its commitment to Jordan's defence – even against an Israeli attack. Nor did it take long before Britain was called on to practice what it preached. In September 1956 the situation along the Israel–Jordan border deteriorated rapidly: Egypt-controlled *fedayeen* raided Israel, Israel retaliated with increasingly massive attacks against Jordanian military and police targets, and

King Hussein asked for help. First he turned to Nasser, but Nasser was in no position to help anyone – he was making his own preparation for an expected Anglo-French attack. Then, in mid-September, Hussein asked Iraq to station a division of its army in Jordan. This request was grounded in the joint military consultations which had been under way between the two countries since March 1956, with British encouragement.

The Jordanian monarch chose to turn to Iraq, rather than Britain (which would have been obligated to attack Israel, under the terms of its pact with Jordan) because of the sharp anti-Western atmosphere then prevailing in the Arab world, as a side-effect of the Suez Crisis. Still, Britain was encouraged, promising Hussein that if he asked for Iraqi help, he could also rely on RAF squadrons then stationed in Jordan. An Iraqi deployment in Jordan was thus obviously a British interest.[17]

Israel viewed developments along its eastern frontier as totally dependent on Britain's will. As the Israelis saw it, moreover, there was a direct linkage between those events and the emerging tripartite collaboration against Egypt. On September 27, in his briefing to the St. Germain delegation, Ben-Gurion said: "We shall not participate [in a war against Egypt] if it is not done with British consent, and this consent must also apply to our self-defence against Jordan and Iraq, should they attack us. For our part, we shall undertake not to attack Jordan or Syria." In the absence of such reassurances, Israel could not sit idly by as Iraqi troops moved into Jordan; Iraq, in fact, was the only Arab confrontation state which had not signed an armistice agreement with Israel, so that formally a full-fledged state of war existed between the two countries. As the Director-General of the Prime Minister's Office, Teddy Kollek, told US Ambassador to Israel Edward Lawson, Israel would have to take over Jordanian territory, "should one Iraqi soldier move into Jordan".[18]

Israel was also preparing itself for another eventuality: Jordan's complete dissolution, which would enable Israel to occupy part of its territory (at least the West Bank). Ambassador Lawson invited himself to Ben-Gurion on October 1, in order to try and allay his fears. Much to his surprise, he heard from the Prime Minister that in his view, "which is also the view in England, Jordan is unstable and may break up. So long as it is still there, we shall respect our armistice agreement and do it no harm . . . As for the Iraqi Army: If this army does not cross the River Jordan – we shall do nothing. But if they do move in west of the Jordan – this will be a problem for us, because there is no armistice agreement with Iraq, and we shall not tolerate an enemy on our doorstep." As far as Israel was concerned, Jordan could be divided between Iraq, to the east of the Jordan River, and Israel to the west.[19] Although both Jordan and Iraq were Israel's enemies, Hashemite Iraq had become more moderate in the wake of the shift in Jordan, and drawn closer to Britain.

Still, the main problem remained Britain. Israeli reaction to developments in Jordan was dependent upon London's policy. The concern in Israel was that the British (with American encouragement), more than either Hussein or el-Sa'id, would ensure an Iraqi troop deployment in Jordan in order to thwart Egyptian influence in the Kingdom. If so, Britain would certainly do everything in its power to prevent an Israeli reaction. Against this background, Israel followed with some trepidation as Iraq massed troops in the H-3 area (on the old Baghdad–Haifa road, near the Iraqi-Jordanian border) – one brigade on the move, one division in readiness. It became urgent to neutralise the British danger. Ben-Gurion asked the Foreign Ministry to query the French as to what they would have done, in Israel's place, to forestall unwelcome developments on the eastern frontier: would they go to war with Iraq, move into Jordan and immediately generate a confrontation with Britain?[20] We have no evidence of a French reply.

Israel knew that Britain was determined to protect its interests in Jordan other than by verbal means. The best way to neutralise this threat was to link the joint move against Egypt with a British commitment not to attack Israel on its eastern border. Thus Israel had a clear-cut interest, on the eve of the Sèvres conference, in a tripartite war against Egypt.[21]

Cordage

Israeli suspicions were indeed well-founded. Britain had developed an operational plan aimed at Israel. Following the March 1956 events in Jordan, London decided to defend Hussein's regime in the face of a possible Israeli attack. One element in this policy was, as described above, to support an Iraq–Jordan axis. The other, military in character, was code-named Cordage. This plan, in its general outline, had its genesis in January 1956, for somewhat different reasons. Glubb Pasha, as Sir John was known, who was then still a central figure in Jordan, proposed that in case of an Israeli attack on Egypt (which, it will be recalled, seemed imminent at the time), the Arab Legion should move into Israeli territory in order to force a cease-fire. The British Foreign Office laughed off this notion; an Israeli counter-attack would tear the Legion to pieces. Eden instructed his diplomats to inform Glubb that his idea was unacceptable. However, he did not prevent British planners from developing a better strategy. The result, in late January, was the Cordage Plan, developed by Britain's Joint Planning Committee, which called for the British to attack on Israel in order to protect Jordan. Priorities were set for the British armed forces: neutralise the Israel Air

Force on the ground; bomb ground forces from the air; raid vital instal-
lations on Israel's Mediterranean coast from the sea; and impose a
six-month naval blockade on Israel.[22]

During the major flare-up on the Israel–Jordan border in September
1956, the British Foreign Office gave Israel an explicit warning: Britain
was ready to move at a moment's notice to fulfil its pact with Jordan; as
for Cordage, although the British, needless to say, did not disclose the
plan's existence to Israel, their behaviour suggests that they assumed
Israeli knowledge of it. Hence Ben-Gurion's directive to the St. Germain
delegation in late September to obtain a British undertaking not to attack
Israel. Still, the warning did have its effect: Israeli reprisals in this period
were more restrained than what past patterns might have suggested.[23]

There is no doubt that the Israeli leadership grasped that the
proposals Peres brought from France on September 25, for tripartite co-
operation in a war against Nasser, could also help neutralise the British
threat. It bears noting that other options were also considered. For
example, the IDF proposed that in case of a British offensive, Israel
should not confine itself to defence, but should dispatch the Navy to hit
the British naval base in Malta. Until mid-October, indeed, the British
feared an Israeli air raid on their Cyprus bases.[24]

Cordage was not cancelled with Glubb's dismissal. On the contrary,
it assumed even greater importance, as Britain's position in Jordan
became more tenuous. Not even the Suez Crisis caused the plan's immediate shelving, a fact which completely confused British officers in the
Middle East. On 10 October 1956, just before the Chequers conference
which marked such a significant turning point in Britain's attitude
towards Israel, as described in chapter 6, and one day before Israel's
largest retaliatory raid against Jordan, the Chairman of the Joint Chiefs
of Staff Committee, Air Marshall Pierson Dixon, asked the Cabinet to
decide whether Britain should operate against Israel, or Egypt. To do
both together, he explained, was virtually impossible. This may have
been another factor in shaping Eden's mid-October decision to hook up
with Israel against Egypt, rather than with Jordan against Israel.[25]

Underlying this confusion there seems to have been a fundamental
misunderstanding, due to conflicting perceptions. Iraq was regarded by
Israel as an extremist confrontation state, the only participant in the
Arab-Israeli war of 1948 which refused to sign an armistice agreement;
yet to Britain this same Iraq was moderate, the most stable Arab nation
in fact. It was to Iraq that the British turned as the linchpin of their efforts
to pacify the Middle East, so that they could concentrate on establishing
their series of anti-Soviet alliances. Moving even a symbolic Iraqi force
into Jordan was regarded by the British as an anodyne, which could
even allow Hussein to curb the Egyptian-inspired perpetrators of

terrorism against Israel – that is to say, they expected Israel to welcome such a move. But there was no intimate exchange of views between Israel and Britain at the time, and the Israelis' suspicions caused them to misinterpret British moves and intentions in the region.

"The Best of British Hypocrisy"

When Eden and Lloyd met with Mollet and Pineau in Paris, on October 16, they agreed on the "Israeli pretext" idea. In exchange, the French requested from Eden – and received – a written promise that Britain would not attack Israel. Although not completely clear-cut, this assurance made it possible for the French to propose the pretext scheme to Israel: a tripartite action by France, Britain and Israel following a solo Israeli strike.[26]

Before noon on October 16, when British intentions were already clear following the Chequers meeting a couple of days before, and the meeting at the Matignon Palace was well under way, Yosef Nahmias, the head of the Ministry of Defence mission in Paris, had a surprise visit. A high-ranking delegation showed up on his doorstep: Challe, Thomas, Mangin and Martin. His four distinguished guests handed Nahmias an official invitation from Mollet to Ben-Gurion to come to Paris in order to discuss a move which would be satisfactory to all three participants. This was an extraordinarily unusual procedure. Four senior officials in the French defence establishment submit an invitation from their Prime Minister to the Israeli Prime Minister, which they choose to convey to the senior representative of Israel's Defence Ministry. Where were the embassies and the Foreign Ministries? What had become of diplomatic conventions?

Even the direct link already established between the offices of the two Prime Ministers was ignored. It would be difficult to find more overwhelming evidence of the fact that it was the leaderships of the two defence establishments, the French and the Israeli, that called the shots in the run-up to the joint war.[27]

Yet before the French invitation reached Israel, a similar proposal was sent from there to Paris. Earlier on the 16th, Peres received a cable sent by Nahmias a day earlier, which outlined the Chequers agreement and the "Israeli pretext" notion. Peres became worried that "Ben-Gurion in his wrath will back out completely, without carefully examining the prospects". Again he needed Dayan to rescue their joint plan. On that day the Chief of Staff was visiting Southern Command, where Plan Kadesh 1 was finally approved, as described later on. Peres wrote an add-on note to Nahmias's cable, and went to meet with the Prime Minister.

In his note he wrote: "In a telephone conversation, conducted perforce with hints and circumlocutions, the Chief of Staff asked me to tell you that:

A. He does not overrate Egyptian danger in the air, and thinks that if no alternative presents itself, we can handle it ourselves. Still, he thinks we should ask for French participation right from the start, with their aircraft or pilots, in destroying Egypt's air force.

B. He does not object to the new possibility [i.e. an Israeli pretext for Britain and France] . . . but he thinks the following questions must be clarified at once: When will [the Anglo-French forces] intervene? Where? How?

If their intervention will be guaranteed 24 hours after the start of ground operations on Egyptian territory, he thinks it's highly advantageous.

Ben-Gurion, as expected, was furious. As Peres noted, "He saw this proposal as the best of British hypocrisy . . . The desire to do harm to Israel showed more strongly than any determination to eliminate Egypt's dictator."[28]

On the same night, Dayan met with Peres to discuss the pretext idea, so that they could "adopt a position which [they] will subsequently preach to the Old Man". They decided that Nahmias should be instructed to clarify in Paris the following points, which, they hoped, they could use in their efforts to persuade Ben-Gurion:

1. The entire move ought to be agreed upon in a signed agreement following direct negotiations between the three participants. At the same time, their contacts could be clandestine, and "assume the character of an orchestrated intrigue, which will look different on the outside".
2. Britain should recognise in principle Israel's freedom to retaliate against Jordan with full-scale war, if the latter were to attack Israel or otherwise interfere with the prosecution of its war against Egypt. Israel must be satisfied that Britain's true intention is to remove Nasser and destroy the Egyptian Army – and would not suddenly turn on Israel, or pressure it to act in a manner not agreed upon in advance.
3. "An agreement between the participants about dividing the spoils of victory should be made in advance – Israel will insist on annexing territories up to the Rafah-Abu Agueila-el Tur line, perhaps even up to the Canal".

Dayan and Peres both knew only too well what was bothering the Prime

Minister, but in fact he had no intention of blocking further negotiations. While the two were talking, Ben-Gurion called Peres and instructed him to send a cable to Nahmias, saying that "We are willing to co-operate with France and England . . . Willing also to examine a joint operation with France alone, provided England does not interfere. We object to the idea of France and England moving in to separate between the two sides."[29]

At this stage, then, Ben-Gurion gave his consent to the framework, but not to its contents. When he found out, shortly afterwards, that a meeting between the Prime Ministers of France and Britain was then taking place in Paris, he sent Nahmias another cable: "Regarding meeting between English and French leaders in Paris, you must contact French at once and ask them whether it is possible to make it a tripartite meeting. Israeli representatives are willing to come at once, under conditions of full secrecy. The level of Israeli representation will be similar to that of the English and French. You must make every effort to contact them at once and cable an answer home at once." The urgency of such a meeting, in Ben-Gurion's view, is apparent from the fact that the expression "at once" was repeated four times in this short message. It seems, therefore, that the Israeli Prime Minister, until then so reserved, was actually the first to propose a tripartite meeting. It was noted in the diary kept by the Chief of Staff's Bureau that "Now Shimon Peres can breathe again. The door remains open; the embers of hope are still smouldering, they should be fanned with new fire."[30]

Thus France and Israel had agreed on the need for a meeting even before all the cables between Jerusalem and Paris reached their destinations. All that remained was to set the date for the three-way meeting and find a way around the pretext disagreement. The French decided to place the ball in Israel's court. Pineau and Bourgès-Maunoury invited Nahmias to a meeting on the evening of this eventful October 16 and pointed out to him that there was no option but the "pretext plan" – the British would have it no other way, and without the British there would be no war. At the same time, they tried to reassure him that no harm would befall Israel as a result – not even at the hands of Britain.

Israel's Entrance Fee

On October 17, Israel received Mollet's official invitation, accompanied by a report about his meeting with the British the previous day. Ben-Gurion, after a brief consultation, accepted the invitation, while reiterating his objection to the Anglo-French pretext idea.[31]

Dayan, having had the time to consider the Anglo-French idea (which was not new to him anyway, having been raised already in St. Germain), now sought to win Ben-Gurion's approval for it. As the Chief of Staff saw it, the two Western powers did not really need Israel's military force, but "we are in a permanent state of war with Nasser . . . We have no difficulty in finding a pretext for war . . . And if indeed it is the pretext that will make the British co-operate with us, we must be willing to pay the price required". Dayan suggested a policy of "threat/payment", as he put it, *vis-à-vis* Britain. The threat would be an Israel move into Jordan, in order to deter Iraq from doing the same, or to come to an arrangement with Iraq on Jordan's partition. The payment would be "our entrance fee for entering an anti-Nasser alliance, namely producing a pretext for war". Dayan came equipped with an argument he knew would get Ben-Gurion's full attention: "If the French honour their word and secure the seas for us, and if the British place aircraft carriers in Haifa to provide AA defence, and if they undertake definitely to join in the conflict, and at a specified time, he [Moshe Dayan] would accept this suggestion. But Ben-Gurion, as was his wont, showed no sign of having been persuaded.

Dayan now resorted to his last argument. He reminded the Prime Minister: "You, Ben-Gurion, said that we will go to war all alone, with no-one's help, if we receive arms and have a Western ally. Now we have all these, and moreover we have the West fighting with us, alongside us, assisting us with equipment, with air cover, and finally in the assault. How can we reconcile our willingness to go it alone with our refusal to do so under more auspicious circumstances, with almost total political guarantees?" Ben-Gurion did not reply to this; his direct reaction to Dayan's argument would be heard later on, at Sèvres. Knowing the "Old Man" as intimately as they did, Dayan and Peres interpreted his very silence to mean that the thesis they had entertained since the spring of 1956 – that Ben-Gurion would be willing to go to war if a suitable ally were found – was vindicated.[32]

On October 18, Israel received Mollet's reply to Ben-Gurion's cable. The French Prime Minister reiterated his invitation to Ben-Gurion to meet in Paris, despite his views about the Anglo-French plan. Ben-Gurion replied that he would arrive with a small delegation on Sunday, October 21. He then immediately convened a consultation. It was decided that Ben-Gurion would take with Dayan and Peres, and in France they would be joined by Nahmias and his designated successor, Asher Ben-Nathan. Others in the delegation would be Ben-Gurion's aide and Military Secretary, Colonel Nehemia Argov; Dayan's Chief of Bureau, Lt.-Colonel Mordechai Bar-On; and Ben-Gurion's personal physician, Dr Baruch Padeh. It was further agreed that the whole episode would be kept secret, even from the Cabinet.[33]

"Four Jeeps Raising a Lot of Dust"

As for the military, Dayan informed his second-in-command General 'Amit, Air Force Chief Colonel Dan Tolkovsky, and the latter's deputy, Colonel Shlomo Lahat, who had already been appointed to liaise with the French Air Force. He asked these officers to provide the delegations with data to support the Anglo-French pretext plan. Dayan told them that he was certain the French would not agree to a simultaneous attack. Consequently, Israel must insist that the French undertake to solve its air defence problems during the period in which the IDF would be fighting alone. The French had already made it clear that if they would not be able to assist Israel directly, they would place at its disposal aircraft and pilots to be used at the IDF's discretion.

Tolkovsky and Lahat did not protest these instructions, even though the inference was obvious: the Israeli Air Force was unable to protect Israel's air-space. Dayan went on to prepare the three officers for the next stage, if the pretext idea were to be adopted: "If we agree with the West on their proposal, we shall have to revise our own plans." Yet he hastened to reassure them that this plan was also advantageous to Israel: "If Britain's problem is that we should first reach the Canal, and only then they will attack, we could make a run for the Canal with a small force, very fast, rather than stretch long lines as we intended. Instead, we shall push first into Gaza or El-'Arish, and settle our immediate border problems. Beyond this, near the Canal we will introduce a *casus belli* only, not actual forces, and if four jeeps were to scurry around there, raising a lot of dust, this should be enough, and we can do this at once, on D+24 [hours], that is, we could bring forward the British and French Air Forces' move against Egypt, and meanwhile we will arrange the rest of our plans to suit ourselves." Evidently Dayan was fully aware, even before going to Sèvres, that there was no option but to provide Britain and France with the pretext they desired.[34]

"A New Map of the Orient"

On October 21, the day the Israeli delegation was due to leave for Sèvres, Dayan made Israel's central problem quite clear to the French: concern about Britain's ambiguous policy in the Middle East. General Challe, who had come to Israel again in order to escort the delegation to Paris, told Dayan at the very outset of their discussion: "In view of the situation which exists now, no positive neutrality is possible and there are only two options: Britain either goes along with us [France and Israel], or against us." To which Dayan replied: "When we talked about positive neutrality, we were talking about the eastern front. There we demanded one of the following: (a) A complete *status quo*, with no Iraqi regiment and no British lies and machinations; (b) Should Jordan attack us (including *fedayeen*), or should Iraq move into Jordan, Britain undertakes not to help the Arabs when Israel retaliates. And meanwhile, they [the British] are already putting changes into effect, are conspiring against us, and in the document they gave us they speak only about not assisting Iraq and Syria, but do not mention Jordan."

Challe replied that the whole thing could amount to "no more than an air raid on Israel", and Dayan had to explain to him that Israel did not take kindly to air raids on itself. The French general also expounded his views on the changes he thought were forthcoming in Jordan; all the British want, he explained, is for a token Iraqi force to enter Jordan and thwart its defection to Nasser's camp. Dayan said he found this difficult to understand: "If the idea is to eliminate Nasser, once there is no Nasser the English will not need a token Iraqi company to prevent Jordan's defection to Nasser's camp . . . The whole story about Egyptian influence in Jordan is a fib. The truth is that Jordan is falling apart and the English have reached the conclusion that Jordan should be written off as an independent country, and Iraq should take its place. The danger is that they will draw us a new map of the orient while we are busy with Egypt."

The French delegation argued that the British were in any event interested in an Iraqi move into Jordan (this was Eden's wish, not Nuri el-Sa'id's), and that they, the French, would also oversee such a move. Dayan was far from agreeable, particularly after he heard Mangin comment that "during the talks [at Chequers and Matignon] Eden was quite indifferent to any possibility of change in [Israel's] borders with Egypt. But he would jump as though bitten by a snake whenever such a possibility was raised with reference to Jordan." Now the French pulled out a new card: "To a certain extent, France could give Israel real guarantees against British intervention, since we are going to send French squadrons to Israel as soon as operations start, and it is not likely that Britain will move against them." Furthermore, once the hostilities with Egypt were ended, Israel could, if it wished, redeploy its forces on its eastern front. It was probably this argument, more than any other, that convinced Dayan. Still, as he had taken care to declare when the meeting began, the decision was not his to make.[35]

"We Can Give You Every Guarantee"

On the evening of October 21 the Israeli delegation gathered in Peres' office at the Defence Ministry in Tel Aviv, proceeding from there to Hazor air base in the north of the country. Dayan used the time to brief

Ben-Gurion about his talks with the French emissaries that morning, and about Britain's posture. Ben-Gurion was furious. "Why then are we going? I'm afraid this will only spoil our relations with France." Dayan was not surprised by this reaction; he knew patience would be needed. He realised that the direction was favourable and Ben-Gurion was only trying to improve Israel's bargaining position – until then, Ben-Gurion had negotiated with the French through Peres and Dayan – particularly regarding the Jordan problem, which bothered him most.[36]

Ben-Gurion was still hesitant even as he was flying to France. In the plane he told Challe and Mangin that "If you intend to offer us the British proposal, then the only positive outcome of my visiting France will be that I will have the opportunity to meet your Prime Minister." As far as we know, he did not, on this occasion, engage them in discussion about the British idea. His approach stemmed not only from moral indignation at the pretext scheme, but also from concern about the British refusal to make any commitment with respect to Jordan. With this problem still pending, the Israeli delegation arrived in Paris on the morning of Monday, October 22. The diary of the Chief of Staff's Bureau summarises the situation upon their arrival, prior to the start of the talks: "We must obtain an authoritative commitment from England that there will be no change on Israel's eastern border during the operation against Egypt, and that if Jordan attacks, or Iraq moves into Jordan and Israel fights and occupies some of their territory, England will not come to their assistance."[37]

The venue of the secret conference, Sèvres, was a quiet, well-to-do suburb of Paris. The villa in which the meetings were held belonged to the Bonnier de la Chapelle family, which had maintained close ties with the French Resistance during World War II. As an 18-year-old student the family's only son, acting on the order of the Resistance, had murdered Admiral Darlan, the commander of Algeria on behalf of the Vichy government, and had been executed by the Vichy authorities. Indeed, most of the French leadership of 1956 was associated with the Resistance, and in some way the spirit and daring of that earlier period pervaded the proceedings at the home of the Bonnier de la Chapelle family more than a decade later.

Ben-Gurion emphasised already in the opening session at Sèvres (in which no British representative was present) that nothing would be achieved unless Britain dealt honestly and in good faith – but he also made perfectly clear his scepticism in this regard. He went on to outline to the French a "fantastic" scenario, as he dubbed it himself, for a new order in the Middle East under the auspices of the Western powers. With Nasser's regime crushed and Jordan dissolved, new boundaries could be drawn. Among other things, Ben-Gurion wanted to divide

Jordan between Iraq and Israel. Did he wish to postpone the imminent war? For patently, such a proposal would require quite some time to gestate. Or perhaps he wanted to intimate to the French that the pretext move must be regarded as part and parcel of an overall Western alignment in the Middle East – an alignment which would be binding for Britain as well? Probably it was the latter. In any event, Ben-Gurion noted in his diary that night that his plan was "in doubt, since it requires first of all good will and loyalty from Britain".[38]

The French were sympathetic. Pineau explained, "We had not decided to approach you with this concrete proposal we are discussing today until we were quite certain that we could give you every guarantee you asked of us regarding British policy." In his view, Eden's guarantees were quite satisfactory, and the opportunity for a joint operation against Nasser should not be missed just because of the Jordan–Iraq problem. Pineau asked the Israelis to be patient and not try to sort out all problems at once, even if the Jordan issue "will not be resolved on this occasion". The French Foreign Minister explained that just as Israel had "a British problem", so Britain had "an Israeli problem" – London feared an Israeli move against Jordan, and also realised that France could go it alone with Israel, leaving the British out. He added that "if Eden were to agree that France go it alone it would be highly significant, it would be Eden's political suicide, he would appear to his government as indecisive, standing idly by while the French are moving in. It is no wonder then that Eden hit the ceiling when he heard about a possible French move with Israel alone. It seems to me that, in a way, it was one of our best means for putting pressure on him to make Britain join in."[39]

On that same October 21, general elections took place in Jordan, and Nasser's supporters emerged strengthened. This lent further urgency to the next day's talks at Sèvres. Already during the first session some participants pointed out that Britain's position in Jordan might be affected by the election results. Now, Dayan told the conference, Iraq could no longer move in. Ben-Gurion explained that, generally speaking, he would not like to see Britain withdraw completely from the Middle East. He announced that following the Jordanian elections, it was easier for him to promise that Israel would not attack Jordan – "if only [Eden] agrees to go with us against Nasser."

The discussion kept reverting to the question of the mutual guarantees Britain and Israel should give each other. It looked as if the entire pretext plan would unravel unless Israel's "British problem" were solved. Everyone agreed that without direct negotiations with a British representative it would be impossible to accept the misleadingly simple formulation proposed with respect to Jordan: Israel would not initiate an attack on Jordan, but would reserve the right to counter-attack – with no British intervention – should Jordan attack Israel. Without that agreement, Israel and France could not proceed towards the desired conclusion.[40]

"We Shall Take Jerusalem and Not Return it Ever"

On the evening of October 22, British Foreign Secretary Selwyn Lloyd turned up at Sèvres. The French were taken aback; they had expected anyone but Lloyd, since they knew the depth of his objections to collaboration with Israel. Nevertheless, Eden made his Foreign Secretary go to Sèvres, as he wanted to bring him closer to the joint move and distance him from the damaging influence exercised by Nutting and Shuckburgh at Whitehall. The French saw it as a bad omen; they suspected that if Eden sent either Lloyd or Nutting, this would spell the end of the joint move.[41]

Lloyd's arrival spoiled much of the spirit of willingness to reach accommodation that had prevailed until then between the two delegations, French and Israeli. Lloyd's very presence irritated the Israelis, and the French mistrusted him. Consequently, only a general discussion was possible, without elaboration. Still, Lloyd made himself very clear to the Israelis with regard to Jordan and Iraq: Britain "will not tolerate an Israeli attack on Jordan, but will try to prevent any Jordanian attack on Israel, and if [Israel] is attacked nonetheless and reacts, they [the British] will not intervene." It was also made clear that British forces already stationed in Jordan – in Amman and Aqaba – would not move out of their camps.

Lloyd himself, according to his biographer, was uncomfortable at the meeting, since the British level of representation was lower than that of Israel and France. The atmosphere in the room seemed charged by the disgust Lloyd felt towards all the others present. Thus, in his memoirs the British Foreign Minister saw fit to take note of an Israeli officer (apparently Bar-On) who was sound asleep in his chair during the meeting. British historian Keith Kyle, who knew Lloyd personally, told the present author that "Lloyd didn't like foreigners in general".

Still, he had delivered the goods as far as the Israelis were concerned, and from that moment the only question left concerned the practicalities of the joint operation. Lloyd left Sèvres with a promise to present Israel's position to the Cabinet; Pineau then announced that he was going to London as well, since he did not trust Lloyd to convey the Israeli position persuasively to Eden. Nonetheless, the meeting with Lloyd opened the way to a concrete discussion of the pretext scheme.[42]

Throughout the following day, October 23, additional and more reliable news streamed in about the new situation in Jordan – the ascendancy of pro-Nasser forces there. Ben-Gurion became more relaxed: "It is better to face Jordan alone than Jordan and Britain." Indeed, these developments seemed to strengthen the British motivation to move against Nasser, which was a boon to the Israeli interest. Meanwhile, until Pineau's scheduled departure for London that evening, the discussion focused on the pretext move and how to implement it. This question, too, as related below, involved disagreements with Britain, and Pineau wished to arrive at a joint French-Israeli position before leaving for London. With the eastern front problem now safely out of the way, negotiations could proceed between France and Israel about the western theatre.[43]

Following Pineau's return from London, on the 24th, with an answer which was satisfactory to the Israelis, Peres suggested that the British be told outright, so as to leave no room for doubt, that "if Jordan dares to attack we shall take [East] Jerusalem . . . and not return it, ever". Ben-Gurion agreed that Israel should again make it clear to the British that it insisted on complete freedom of action against Jordan. Bearing in mind that all these concerns had already been put to Lloyd, and that Pineau had already brought back a satisfactory reply, the Israelis' attitude is a good measure of the suspicion and mistrust they continued to harbour against Britain.

In the final discussion before the agreement was signed, on October 24 in the afternoon, two relatively junior British representatives were present: Patrick Dean, a senior Foreign Office official who was the chairman of the Joint Intelligence Committee, and Donald Logan, Lloyd's junior private secretary, who had been at Sèvres a couple of days earlier with the Foreign Secretary. Before taking pen in hand to sign, Ben-Gurion again reminded all and sundry that the meaning of Lloyd's undertaking was that Britain would not abide by its defence pact with Jordan, should Jordan attack Israel. The British delegates agreed that this indeed was the spirit of Lloyd's commitment, but hastened to add that they had not been authorised officially to declare that Britain was no longer standing behind its defence pact with Jordan. Pineau immediately realised that this could bring down the entire edifice he had worked so hard to construct, and interjected: "I wish to remind [everyone] that this was one of the first conditions France put to England when collaboration with Israel was originally raised."

Because of the junior level of British representation, it was not possible to bring the matter to an orderly conclusion. Dean hinted that he and his colleague were willing to take the risk and acknowledge that Britain would not use force on Jordan's behalf; in other words, it was clear to him that Britain was willing to abandon its commitment to

Jordan. Logan commented (in a whisper, noted Bar-On, who took the minutes for the Israeli side) that the Israelis overestimated the Arab Legion.[44]

Under the circumstances, and since the pact which concluded the conference required ratification by the governments involved – in particular, Dean's signature required a corroborating signature by Eden – Ben-Gurion asked that Britain's commitment be incorporated into the agreement itself. He could not be satisfied with verbal understandings, he said, and wanted an explicit undertaking, ratified in the form of a signed agreement, by the British government. What Ben-Gurion wanted was the insertion of a clause in which Britain would undertake not to honour its defence pact with Jordan, should that country (or Iraq, through Jordanian territory) attack Israel. His demand was accepted, and Article 5 in the Sèvres Protocol states that Israel undertakes not to attack Jordan "during the period of operations against Egypt", and adds: "But in the event that during the same period Jordan should attack Israel, the British Government undertakes not to come to the aid of Jordan."[45]

On October 26, when preparations for war were already in full swing, Asher Ben-Nathan arrived in Israel with France's and Britain's final letters of ratification. Eden, however, had addressed his letter of ratification only to Mollet (so as not to expose the Anglo-Israeli connection), and the French Prime Minister then forwarded a copy to Ben-Gurion. Despite this diplomatic snub, it was final confirmation that Britain had lifted its threat to attack Israel from the east. Plan Cordage was called off, at least for the time being – even though Musketeer leaders were not informed of this fact, as related above, because of the heavy cloak of secrecy imposed by the British Cabinet on this "Israeli connection".[46]

8

Decision at Sèvres

Not If, But How

In order to understand the tripartite military move against Egypt, it is necessary to return to the Sèvres conference and its military give-and-take. On the face of it, Sèvres was the field of the politicians: Mollet and Pineau for France, Lloyd for Britain, Ben-Gurion for Israel. In fact, it was personnel of the military in France and Israel who not only brought the conference about but also masterminded the agreement.

Several times the conference was on the brink of collapse. For example, Ben-Gurion at one point already made up his mind to leave Sèvres, because no common ground could be achieved regarding the time interval between Israel's intended act of provocation and the start of the Anglo-French move; he felt Israel would remain exposed too long. At that stage, Peres and Mangin conspired to invent a mechanical problem with the presidential DC-4 plane put at the disposal of the Israeli delegation, and informed Ben-Gurion that he would not be able to leave before the 25th. Having been compelled to stay, Ben-Gurion decided he might as well go on with the conference, while at the same time Dayan and Challe hammered out the plan which would eventually break the deadlock.[1]

As we saw, early on during the conference it became clear that Britain was willing to undertake a non-intervention posture with regard to Jordan. This effectively resolved the pre-eminent question; a joint move was in fact feasible. It remained to decide the concrete details of its implementation. The political questions were serious, but it soon transpired that all three parties were eager to act, indicating that the differences were reconcilable. Ben-Gurion noted at the outset of the meeting that he had moral qualms about placing Israel in the role of the aggressor, but during the proceedings he did not raise the issue concretely. In fact, he made sophisticated use of the moral argument in order to extract more promises and additional aid from the French.

The entire pretext scheme was far from palatable to Ben-Gurion. It will be recalled that according to this scenario, worked out in advance of Sèvres, Israel was to make a significant military move close to the Suez Canal, and then accede to an Anglo-French demand to withdraw from the Canal Zone, allowing those Western powers to intervene as peacemakers; in effect, they, too, would operate against Egypt, since it was assumed from the start (rightly) that Nasser would reject a demand to withdraw his forces from sovereign Egyptian territory.

Ben-Gurion's distress over this point was genuine, but it did not hold up the talks. The Israelis who were at Sèvres and afterwards wrote memoirs, tend to represent the pretext problem and Ben-Gurion's objections to it as a major issue. Notwithstanding, two things stand out in retrospect: first, his anger never made Ben-Gurion stop the proceedings; and second, as soon as the agreement was signed, Ben-Gurion's anger evaporated completely. Evidently, then, this question assumed major proportions only after the fact, when the time came to paint the picture for public consumption. During the Sèvres conference itself, other matters exercised Ben-Gurion and Dayan much more.[2]

Not least was their concern the fact that in the original Anglo-French scenario, Israel would have to wait for 48 hours after the start of its campaign for Anglo-French intervention in the air. In other words, Israel would remain with no real air cover during the first stage of the war. It should be recalled that air raids on population centres were a real nightmare for Ben-Gurion, who refused throughout to go to war without military support from one of the powers, particularly in the air.[3]

The argument over the pretext idea, then, focused not on the scheme as such, but on the timetable, specifically how long Israel would have to wait after perpetrating its act of provocation for the European powers to intervene. On the one hand, it was necessary to address and allay Ben-Gurion's fears; on the other the conference had to draft a scenario which would allow Britain to claim "plausible deniability" in the face of possible charges of collusion with Israel. Any exposure of that collaboration was unthinkable for Eden, whose domestic position was already tenuous.

The result was that a conceptual and operational gap opened up between Britain and Israel, which the French alone could bridge, as Dayan and Peres realised only too well. Already during the flight to Sèvres they had tried to explain to Challe and Mangin the nature of Ben-Gurion's worries and propose ways for Mollet to help overcome them.[4]

In order to arrive at a formula which would satisfy all parties, the following conditions were necessary:

1. An Israeli operation which would generate an immediate threat to the Suez Canal, in the shortest time possible, thus reducing the time

interval, so critical in Israeli eyes, until the start of the Anglo-French operation.

2. British consent to minimise that interval.
3. A reasonable commitment by the two powers to provide Israel with active military assistance, particularly in the air but also on the sea.
4. To these provisos was added, during the discussions, the question of the payment demanded by Israel for furnishing the European powers with the pretext they wanted: their readiness to allow Israel a free hand in the Sinai, in pursuit of objectives the Israelis set for themselves, without any direct linkage to the Suez crisis.

During the conference, it emerged that (a) Israel would not launch forces west of the Suez Canal; (b) the French could not and would not co-ordinate their moves with Israel; (c) the French were ready to assist Israel, with "not too large" a force, in taking El-'Arish, the chief provincial town in Sinai, in return for an Israeli provocation at the Canal.[5]

"Go to War, Just Like That?"

Military issues were raised already during the first session at Sèvres, on October 22. Most of that meeting was devoted to clarifying the parties' positions, with the French representing the British position in the initial stage of the meeting. Having agreed that Britain must commit itself not to intervene on Israel's eastern frontier should hostilities erupt with Jordan, the French and the Israelis turned to the modalities of a joint attack on Egypt. Naturally, Ben-Gurion immediately raised the central military problem as he saw it, and which would remain the focal point of discussions during the following days: "In our present situation (things may change during the next six months) the Egyptians can launch a massive bombing raid against Tel Aviv in eight minutes . . . How could we face such havoc and destruction during all these days we shall have to wait for the Anglo-French intervention?" Ben-Gurion, who did not believe that the Israel Air Force could defend the country, added, in support of his argument, that it would take the IDF's advance forces four to six days to reach the Canal – far too long a period for Israel to stand alone.[6]

Bourgès-Maunoury tried to address this issue directly. First of all, he argued, Israel would receive significant naval and aerial support. Bearing in mind the capabilities of Egyptian pilots, it seemed to him that Ben-Gurion's fears for Tel Aviv were exaggerated. Moreover, the French Defence Minister explained, "we are talking about 28 hours of Israeli exposure, not four days". Even the British were talking about an interval of 36 hours, and "we (the French) are still arguing the point with them".[7]

Bourgès-Maunoury could talk about hours rather than Ben-Gurion's days because the French assumed that Israel's act of provocation would be swift and limited in scope. Generally speaking, he told the Israelis, the move should be only symbolic, and as such it can be accomplished rapidly: "There will be no journalists there, and Israel will always be able to announce that its forces are already near the Canal [even if they are nowhere near it], so as to trigger the political plan [an Anglo-French ultimatum to both sides to withdraw from the Canal Zone], and subsequently the military one." Israel could prevaricate, the French held, since no one could prove otherwise.

Ben-Gurion next broached the danger of Eastern Bloc "volunteers", who would enhance the quality of the Egyptian forces, and implored the French to launch an "unqualified joint operation". Israel's problem, he explained, was not a technical one; we fear a heavy loss of human life. But the French remained adamant: you will come to no harm during the first 24 hours. Ben-Gurion now played his moral card, the pretext idea: "Go to war, just like that, out of the blue – I will not be able to do it." But he immediately returned to what was, for him, the crux: "Militarily we are not adequately prepared today."[8]

Mollet and Pineau tried their hand at persuasion, but Ben-Gurion would not budge. Now Bourgès-Maunoury put forward what sounded very much like a threat:

> France is already now almost at the limit of its capabilities, in terms of mobilisation for war . . . In addition to what we need in Algeria . . . we are already doing our utmost to maintain the effort, and it is doubtful whether we can keep it up for more than another ten days. Also, morale in the divisions whose duty was extended beyond the conscription limit is not too high, all the more so because the troops are now beginning to get the feeling that the entire call-up, the entire effort, was in vain. If we do not use them now, we may face a collapse of discipline . . . The beginning of November seems to me to be the limit. Later on we will be able to support Israel, and we will do so, with equipment, with arms, with small units etc., but we cannot maintain the entire order of battle for long.

The message was clear: France would pull out of the joint war. Ben-Gurion was not impressed; he was willing to go to war the next day, if England and France took care of the air and sea, "even if Israel will be required to provide the bulk of the ground forces". Thus, when British Foreign Secretary Selwyn Lloyd arrived at Sèvres, on the evening of October 22, he found Israel and France deadlocked over the military question.[9]

The French placed Lloyd in another room and continued the discussion with the Israelis, ignoring the Foreign Secretary. They did not wish to start talks with Lloyd, who they knew was hostile to Israel, before reaching a constructive conclusion with Ben-Gurion. It was Dayan who saved the day.

Having stood aside until then, the Israeli Chief of Staff now took the floor in order to propose, "by Ben-Gurion's leave", a compromise. In the evening hours of D-Day, Israel would mount a long-range raid somewhere near the Suez Canal. Britain and France would conclude their political manoeuvres during the night and attack the next morning. If so, the political pretext would have to be broader than originally proposed. That is, rather than issue an ultimatum to both sides (and await the required amount of time), the two powers would announce that in view of the deterioration of the situation into a state of war, they had decided to seize and secure the Canal.[10]

Pineau accepted Dayan's idea in principle, since it included the pretext required by Britain and France. Still, the French Foreign Minister thought it would take at least 24 hours before the senior members of the two Cabinets, the French and British, could meet – at first separately and then together – "so as not to put the face of collusion on it". Only then would they issue an ultimatum, which would also be time-consuming. Dayan clung to what seemed to him, at the moment, to be the last chance to save the joint move (with Lloyd still waiting in the next room). He asked Ben-Gurion, in Hebrew: "Is it really important to you who will bomb Egyptian airfields? For the first night's raids we have sufficient force." Ben-Gurion allowed him to proceed. Dayan then put forward a compromise proposal, emphasising that it was his idea and not Ben-Gurion's, although it represented the "red line" beyond which the Israeli Prime Minister would not go:

> It is also possible that Israel, helped by French squadrons (with Israeli markings, apparently) will conduct during the first night massive bombings of Egyptian airfields. England will move in the next day at dawn (an interval of 12 hours). At any rate, England must make the interval between the start of operations and its own move much shorter. This interval is highly dangerous for Israel, and I could not recommend that we put at risk our army and our cities because of Britain's subtle gentlemanly considerations, which we find questionable anyway.[11]

Dayan was trying to play both sides against the middle. On the one hand, an air campaign of the kind he proposed could not have been carried out by the Israel Air Force, in its condition at the time, without massive French support (albeit in disguise). On the other hand, Dayan did not take the Egyptian air threat as seriously as Ben-Gurion did. He tried to make a case which both the French and Ben-Gurion would find reasonable.[12]

Minister of Defence Bourgès-Maunoury hastened to agree that it was possible to reduce the time until the Anglo-French entered the fray.

Monday, October 29, 7 p.m.

With this glimmer of mutual understanding, the French delegation moved to the next room, where Selwyn Lloyd was waiting impatiently. The Israelis followed shortly. At the outset the discussion threatened to ruin the entire conference. In the interval before the Israelis entered, the French apparently brought Lloyd up to date, but with the three sides present he continued to insist on the pretext scenario as originally agreed upon between Britain and France, before the latest discussions with the Israelis: Israel should launch an all-out war against Egypt and prosecute it alone for 72 hours. An Anglo-French condemnation of both sides would then be issued, together with an ultimatum, and only after its rejection by Egypt would the aerial campaign begin.

Ben-Gurion in his response did not address the issues, since he had already made his position crystal clear. He was furious with Britain in general and Lloyd in particular, outraged by the Foreign Secretary's attitude and manner. Ben-Gurion rejected outright everything Lloyd said, asking, "Why should we undertake an operation for which we are going to be condemned?" Still, Ben-Gurion did not want to end matters here. Aware of Lloyd's commitment regarding Jordan, he forsook his moral indignation and reverted to military affairs – more specifically, to the proposal raised by Dayan a short while earlier.[13]

Now it was timetables all over again. Lloyd said that if Israel undertook a major operation in the vicinity of the Canal, it was possible to consider shortening the time interval to 36, even 24 hours (rather than 72 as before). At the same time, he explained that he had been authorised to propose a joint operation only on the basis of an ultimatum issued 48 hours after the start of the Israeli action. Although ruling out French air support for Israel launched from Cyprus, he hinted that Britain would be ready to ignore such an operation if launched from Israeli territory. Despite his political reluctance, Lloyd proved well-versed in the military issues and even sought to make contributions of his own in this sphere.[14]

By the end of the first day of the Sèvres conference, only one thing was actually agreed to: with Lloyd's consent, it was decided that Israel would commence hostilities on Monday, October 29, at 7 p.m. GMT (5 p.m. Israel time). This was not to change. In addition, Dayan had succeeded in making his plan the basis for further negotiations, Lloyd promising to sound it out in London. Pineau met with Dayan early the next day, took notes and then went to London himself, after Lloyd: the French had little faith in Lloyd's willingness or ability to persuade Eden.[15]

"I Think I Should Go to Hollywood"

On Tuesday, October 23, Israeli and French military leaders met in Mangin's home. In this session there was no need to preach to the converted. All the participants were wholeheartedly involved in an effort to develop a plan which would be acceptable to both Ben-Gurion and Eden. They realised that all their military planning now hinged, frustratingly, on political decisions. Their brief was to come up with a military plan which would address both Britain's political needs and Israel's fears.

Challe sounded an optimistic note: "I have turned these things over in my mind all night, and I think I have found a new plan for a political scenario which will satisfy all and meet everybody's conditions". Dayan replied: "When this operation is over, I think I should go to Hollywood to write scenarios." Challe: "We shall all be going to Hollywood together."[16]

Dayan put to Challe two essential questions from Israel's point of view: How large a force could the allies field on the day after Israel began its operations? How soon could their entire land force join in? Challe then presented the plan he had worked out during the night. The French general had been the key figure in the British-French-Israeli triangle, and his plan represented the culmination of his efforts during the previous months, even taking into account the previous day's talks at Sèvres and Dayan's ideas. The fundamental conditions, as Challe understood them, were as follows:

Complete secrecy – for both the Israelis and the British – was a *sine qua non*. Ben-Gurion's concerns (which Challe thought were exaggerated) about the Egyptian air threat should be addressed. And the allies' entry into the war should be delayed by at least 24 hours, in order to satisfy the British. It was impossible, Challe explained, to conclude in one night all the moves necessary for the political scenario.

What Challe proposed, then, was that an incident be staged on the Israeli-Egyptian border. The following day, the Cabinets in Paris and London would convene to consider the situation in the Middle East. While they were in session, Israel would stage a fake air raid on Beersheba (Challe, who was perfectly serious, wanted aircraft to overfly the city as some buildings were blown up on the ground below, giving the impression of bombing from the air) and immediately blame Egypt for the attack. Israel would then declare war while the two Cabinets were still in session. By midnight, both Britain and France would issue ultimatums, differently phrased for each side. Israel would be required to keep clear of the Canal, Egypt to withdraw its forces from the Canal Zone. The two powers would also condemn Egypt for "attacking" a civilian population. Since Israel would not be condemned as an aggressor, the French could more conveniently help defend its air space.[17]

Dayan rejected the idea. Personally, he felt comfortable with it, but he knew that Ben-Gurion would never accept it; furthermore, Egypt and the UN would have little difficulty exposing the hoax. Dayan was trying to anticipate Ben-Gurion's objections, since it was the Prime Minister who had to be persuaded. He repeated Ben-Gurion's "war out of the blue" argument, as put forward the previous day, and tried to explain to his hosts the problems Ben-Gurion faced at home. The government and the Knesset, which were completely in the dark about the present move, would not understand the change in Ben-Gurion's position, since he had earlier objected to an Israeli-initiated war. Furthermore, there was no chance for a military move based on a lie. Dayan again raised the problem Ben-Gurion was having with Britain and France playing Hamlet to Israel's Claudius. Dayan believed that Ben-Gurion understood that not all of Israel's demands would be met, and therefore, besides making Israel's responsibility for the outbreak of war as vague as possible, the Prime Minister should be given a more reasonable timetable for the entry of Anglo-French forces into the fray.

Here the Israeli Chief of Staff again suggested a military solution which he thought should please everyone: "Israel will be willing to drop a force from the air even without any bombing of Beersheba. Israel will even be willing to instigate a dogfight above the Canal, if the British will insist on one. We need no further pretext." Challe was taken aback: "You are talking about a much more serious act of aggression than anything I proposed to you." Dayan explained: "I intend to retaliate for a real situation we are facing on our borders daily. We cannot invent a reality which does not actually exist."

Challe seems to have accepted Dayan's logic, which was based on the Middle Eastern facts of life, as well as full knowledge of the IDF's capabilities and operational plans, and most importantly, of Ben-Gurion's character and attitude. Without withdrawing completely his own ideas, Challe agreed to support this plan.[18]

The "Dayan Plan"

At the Sèvres villa that afternoon, the military personnel briefed the politicians on the results of their earlier meeting. Challe presented his ideas, which were promptly rejected by both Ben-Gurion and Pineau, who explained that what the British wanted was a military move involving the Canal directly. Then Dayan introduced his ideas, which were accepted in principle. Ben-Gurion authorised Pineau to represent Israel in Britain on the basis of the "Dayan Plan", emphasising that a parachute drop near the Canal was not essential for Israel, but would be carried out nonetheless for the benefit of the Western allies. Most of that session consisted of joint efforts by Dayan (using notes scribbled in Hebrew) and the French to convince Ben-Gurion that the air power which the French would place at Israel's disposal should be sufficient to eliminate any real threat by the Egyptian Air Force against Israeli cities. The French also realised that, apart from Ben-Gurion's genuine fears, there was also his acute mistrust of the British, which served only to aggravate his worries. And there was still the timetable problem to resolve.[19]

During the meeting, Dayan proposed to Ben-Gurion (in a note, of which the French were not aware) the following compromise: Accept Lloyd's minimal timetable of 36 hours. That is, if hostilities commenced on Monday afternoon (October 29), the British air offensive would be launched on Wednesday morning (October 31). The French would provide Israel with pilots for its Mystère fighters (Israel had 60 such aircraft, but could use only 12, because of a lack of pilots and other problems) and a fully operational Mystère squadron of their own. On the first day the Israel Air Force would concentrate its efforts on attacking air and ground bases in Egypt, in order to forestall an expected Egyptian counter-offensive. French aircraft carriers would enter Haifa harbour and the waters off Tel Aviv by stealth before the beginning of hostilities, and the next day the British would join the war.

After the joint session with the French, Ben-Gurion convened the Israeli team and allowed Dayan to present his ideas on air cover, within the framework of the already accepted pretext plan. For tactical negotiating reasons, it was decided that for the time being this would be presented as Dayan's private idea rather than Ben-Gurion's position.[20]

Dayan then returned alone to meet with the French team. Having explained Ben-Gurion's problem – his refusal to put Israeli cities at risk of air attack without serious means of defence – Dayan asked the French to reconsider the possibility of an independent operation of their own if the British should renege on the agreement or if Nasser were to accept the ultimatum. He also presented a few additions to his plan. The French accepted Dayan's general outline, but stressed that they anticipated difficulties from the British, who they thought would be happy to seize on any pretext to beat a dignified retreat from the whole affair – French, and especially Israeli, suspicions of Britain would persist even during the war itself. The French also proposed to station in Israel a squadron of F-84 fighter-bombers, which would greatly improve their ability to defend Israeli airspace. Nevertheless, the question of France going it alone, without Britain, remained moot. Pineau took down Dayan's additions, explaining that these would serve him as "credentials" in his talks with Eden, scheduled for that night. Essentially, the French were unwilling to go to war without Britain.[21]

It was a queer discussion, in which the Israeli put forward ideas and the French played the role of the British, trying to anticipate their reactions. One thing was clear: the decision would be made in London. On October 24, Pineau explained to Ben-Gurion: "We have brought the British from complete to partial misunderstanding." Ben-Gurion: "The conclusion is then that there is a chance that they may be brought to full understanding."

The Israeli Chief of Staff was losing his patience. He slipped a note to his aide Bar-On: "All these new proposals [e.g. Challe's ideas] are just unnecessary humbug." Even Ben-Gurion's attitude looked strange to Dayan: "Did he go cold on the whole thing, or is it just a trick?" The next day, when Ben-Gurion put some questions to him, Dayan retorted: "Are these issues to be addressed, or just nuisance questions?"[22]

"Israel's Suez Canal Is the Straits of Tiran"

While all these ambiguities were being sorted out, it remained clear that following the Anglo-French invasion of Egypt, Israel would be able to pursue its own interests in Sinai. The French had no objection to extensive Israeli operations there, and the two British emissaries, Dean and Logan, while pointing out that they did not expect Israel to annex Sinai after the war, nevertheless hinted (or so the Israeli team understood) that they "would not object to minor border adjustments we may effect during the campaign". On the morning of the 24th, before their final talks with the allies, Dayan outlined to Ben-Gurion and Peres what was to gell into operational plan Kadesh 2 – Israel's part in the Sinai War.

Israel would dispatch a minimal force to the vicinity of the Canal Zone, just enough to abide by the agreement with the British. Dayan was prepared to send even one squad, although he added realistically that "we shall not get away with less than a battalion". Should the British demand an entire brigade, Israeli forces could seize an airfield by a parachute drop and then land the rest of the force in aircraft. At any rate, the IDF would have to open a communications line to the "pretext force" near the Canal in order to reinforce and supply it.

The conquest of Rafah and El-'Arish, as envisaged by Dayan, would

be postponed to a later stage, "even two days after the start of the
Franco-British bombardment. We will only go to Rafah after the
Egyptians have heard about what is going on at the Canal." Dayan estimated that it would take the Egyptians 36 to 48 hours to understand
what was afoot, after the Israeli provocation and the Anglo-French ultimatum and the onset of the Allies' bombing of the Canal Zone. In any
event, there was no need to hurry, he believed. Israel's only first-stage
commitment was "to create a threat to the Canal". The "pretext move"
would be launched in the Mitla Pass and be supported by a thrust
through central Sinai; subsequently, two efforts would be initiated
which were solely in Israel's interest: towards Rafah and El-'Arish, and
towards Sharm el-Sheikh. Dayan noted that it would be better to engage
the bulk of the Egyptian Army in the Sinai only after the allies had begun
their invasion of the Canal Zone. At that stage, the Egyptians would stop
sending reinforcements to the east and concentrate on the Canal.

Israel's air defences were to consist of six jet fighter squadrons
(French, Israeli and mixed), Israeli Air Force prop fighters and two
French vessels, armed with anti-aircraft guns, anchored off Haifa and
Tel Aviv. "In this new constellation," Dayan said, "I doubt whether we
should strive to destroy Egypt's forces." Perhaps it would be better to
try and capture them, so as to improve Israel's bargaining position after
the war.

Ben-Gurion accepted this plan, but added that the IDF should also
plan for the conquest of the Gaza Strip, El-'Arish and the oil fields in
western Sinai. He also raised the question of superpower reaction. As a
matter of fact, Ben-Gurion broached this question several times during
the Sèvres conference, but it was never seriously discussed, beyond a
bland French assessment to the effect that the Soviet Union, being preoccupied with the crisis in Eastern Europe (particularly Hungary), would
not intervene in the Middle East. Finally, the Israeli team agreed not to
provide the French, much less the British, with operational details about
the IDF's moves in the Sinai; they would have to be satisfied with the
pretext move Israel was going to execute for their benefit.[23]

During the afternoon of October 24, Pineau returned from London
and the French-Israeli forum reconvened. The understanding achieved
with Eden dovetailed well with the plan outlined by Dayan to Ben-
Gurion in the Israeli team's private consultations. The British demanded
an Israeli operation near the Canal. It would be best if Israel sent a ship
there, but it was up to the Israelis to decide what form their provocation
would take, and the British did not insist on a maritime strike. Still, they
insisted on an Israeli operation bearing the character of a major offensive, and as near to the Canal as possible. A commando raid would not
do. Pineau then added, much to Ben-Gurion's astonishment, that all of

Israel's retaliatory raids so far had not provided Britain with a proper excuse to intervene – therefore, a much larger operation was needed. As far as Pineau could understand, it was not the number of troops that counted; the main thing was the mode of the operation and "the noise it will make". The British undertook to commence their air campaign on Wednesday, October 31, at approximately 4 a.m. local time.

They also agreed to create a situation in which Nasser would be unable to claim that he would accept the ultimatum. Any Egyptian attack, whether on Israeli forces or even along the Israeli border, would be considered a violation of the ultimatum. This would include a demand to both sides to pull back their forces 10 miles from the Canal – manifestly a condition the Egyptians would be unable to accept. And if all this were not enough, the Western powers would also demand that their forces be allowed to occupy the Canal Zone. This would go right to the heart of the Suez crisis, and Nasser would certainly refuse. The British would use the word "appeal" rather than "ultimatum", so as not to wound Israel's feelings. Britain accepted that the French Air Force, including F-84 aircraft, would assist in Israel's defence, "but they will be happier if, during the first day, these will bear the markings of the Israel Air Force."

Pineau concluded, "to my mind the agreement so far coincides with Dayan's proposal, and it is not a bad agreement." Thus the moment of decision seemed to have arrived, and Ben-Gurion was inclined to accept Pineau's ideas. Precisely on that account, however, the Israeli delegation was struck by a fit of nerves. Dayan and Peres, in particular, tried to seize the moment to introduce some improvements. In front of an amazed high-level French delegation (Pineau, Bourgès-Maunoury, Challe and Thomas), the Israelis broke into a heated and lengthy exchange in Hebrew. Dayan's main concern was the reference to a cease-fire in the ultimatum, which could conceivably leave Israel with only its pretext move in the Sinai – without having achieved any of its own objectives. This time, it was Ben-Gurion's turn to pacify his colleagues: "Lloyd wants us to have a small unit near the Canal already in the first stage of the operation. This can only be done with a parachute drop. The question is, what will become of that unit if the ceasefire comes into effect within 24 hours of the ultimatum?" That is to say, the pretext move would work as a *casus belli* for Israel as well, allowing it to further its own interests in the Sinai. However, the fear was that if a ceasefire were to be achieved immediately after the ultimatum, or even shortly after the Allied bombing of the Canal Zone, Israel would not be able to realise its war goals: to devastate the Egyptian Army and capture the Straits of Tiran.

Even though Pineau did not speak Hebrew, he seemed to grasp the gist of the Israelis' internal debate: "The reply to the ultimatum," he said, "should be a declaration of willingness to comply, which is not the same as *immediate* compliance." Thomas added: "The language of the ultimatum will not be relevant to Israel anyway, because its forces will not be within 10 miles of the Canal." In addition, Pineau noted, the ultimatum speaks of a bilateral cease-fire. Under the conditions set for the Egyptians, there was no chance of their agreeing to a cease-fire. Dayan remained recalcitrant, but Ben-Gurion cut in and announced that he accepted Pineau's proposals.

At this stage Eden's delegates, Dean and Logan, arrived at Sèvres. The French went out to receive them and probably brought them up to date; we do not know what was discussed between them. The Israeli delegation used the opportunity for a brief consultation, in which it was decided to provide the allies, after all, with an outline of Israel's war objectives in the Sinai, so as to prevent any misunderstanding during the war.

In the concluding session, on the afternoon of October 24, Dayan's plan was effectively adopted, though with a British modification in the form of a demand for "a real war-like act" near the Suez Canal. It was emphasised, regarding the Anglo-French air campaign against Egypt, that it would "take place on Wednesday morning. The actual time will be decided on by the military staffs, taking into account tactical circumstances". It was also agreed that the cease-fire would have to be mutual: so long as Egypt did not accept it, it was not binding on Israel.

In this meeting, Ben-Gurion and Dayan clarified two matters regarding Israel's independent interests in the war against Egypt. Ben-Gurion: "Israel's Suez Canal is the Straits of Tiran . . . we intend to occupy the Straits of Tiran and safeguard freedom of navigation to and from Eilat." Patrick Dean of the British Foreign Office (and MI6) asked: "Who will seize the Straits?" Ben-Gurion: "Us! And we intend to stay there for good." Dean: "Did you not think of seizing the Straits as part of the original plan?" Ben-Gurion: "We certainly did. We thought about it a lot. We have much experience in these territories, some thirty-five centuries of it, since we came out of Egypt." Donald Logan joked, "But then you did not travel in command cars." Dayan: "That's why we didn't manage it in 24 hours." On a more serious note, Dayan told the British representatives: "Did I understand correctly that you require our army to stop 10 miles from the Canal, and when hostilities stop this will be our front line, and between ourselves and the Canal there will be your troops?" Dean: "Indeed, this is what Article 2 of the proposed agreement says." Ben-Gurion: "We have troubles with the Egyptian Army in Sinai. Do you want them in England?" Logan: "We shall leave this worry for you." Ben-Gurion and Dayan regarded the entire Sinai

Peninsula, apart from the Suez Canal, as an Israeli objective. They did not want British troops in the Sinai. Apparently the British delegates understood this.[24]

Israel Will Do What England Wants

Ben-Gurion now tried to postpone D-day by 24 hours, but Dayan stated that he could meet the proposed timetable. The Israelis also informed their partners that they were not going to make a formal declaration of war against Egypt. As Ben-Gurion put it, "You have ambassadors in Cairo, you can afford diplomatic niceties." On the other hand, Ben-Gurion undertook to make a public statement to the effect that his troops had taken up positions near the Suez Canal. Logan requested that Israel launch its troops sufficiently deep so "that we can reasonably claim that there is a threat to the Canal". Dayan promised to honour this request, although he refused to reveal how the IDF would implement the pretext move; he also asked Ben-Gurion and Peres – in Hebrew – not to elaborate on this. Dean, however, insisted on knowing the ways and means, and Ben-Gurion explained that Israel would do what England wanted: station paratroopers near the Canal. Dean requested more extensive operations which could be construed as provocative: a ship in the Canal, a dogfight above the Canal, call-up of reserves prior to D-day. The first two demands were rejected, with French support. As for the last, Israel would have to call up its reserves anyway before D-day, and the mass character of the mobilisation would ensure its quick discovery. In the end, the British had no conception of the tactics Israel planned to use in its pretext attack, but they let the matter ride.

Before the three parties got down to drafting the agreement, Ben-Gurion concluded the proceedings by saying (in paraphrase): What I wanted to explain both to you Englishmen and to my French friends is this. Israel would never have resorted to war in order to obtain freedom of navigation in the Suez Canal, but we are willing to fight over the Straits of Eilat, in order to uphold the international principle of freedom of navigation. I would not fight for the Suez, but the Eilat problem is much more essential to us.

The agreement was signed by Ben-Gurion, Dean and Pineau, pending ratification by their respective governments. In a separate, bilateral agreement, France undertook to provide Israel with air defence during October 29–31, by means of aircraft and warships. This addendum was signed by Bourgès-Maunoury for France; the author found no Israeli signature on this document, and the British were kept in the dark about this agreement. Late on October 24, the Israeli delegation went home.[25]

A Heavy Atmosphere of Uncertainty

From the start of the joint planning with the French, the British took control of the operational plan against Egypt, codenamed Musketeer. The operation's commander was British, General Sir Charles Keightley, and directly under him were three British Task Force commanders (air, land and sea). All four officers had French deputies whose independence was limited. This basic situation, compounded by British hesitations, dragged out the planning, and plans had to be changed from time to time due to the international situation, weather, and so forth. Four different operational plans were drawn up for Musketeer between August and October of 1956, but at the critical moment there was no agreed plan and the Allied commanders had to improvise. The situation when the decision to wage a joint campaign was finally made, at Sèvres, was that the time frame to launch the Musketeer forces (the time needed from receiving the order to setting out), according to the latest operational plan (the "Winter Plan"), stood at 14 days – compared to 11 days on October 21. Besides the need to dispel possible notions of a collusion, the forces were no longer as ready as they had been at the beginning of October, and precautions had to be taken for winter weather. In short, by the time of the Sèvres accord the Allies could not have moved before November 6 or 7, with the actual Anglo-French landing (N-day) taking place about a week after the Israeli provocation.[26]

During October, a heavy atmosphere of uncertainty pervaded the British forces which were to play the leading role in Musketeer. Reserves had to be discharged, under the assumption that the new timetable would leave sufficient time for recall. The recall itself was done reluctantly, because of the growing restiveness of reservists who were mobilised only to be kept idle, and the trade unions were complaining that civilian vessels were being commandeered by the military indefinitely without explanation. Admiral Sir Guy Grantham, Commander-in-Chief Mediterranean, had some harsh things to say about the decline in morale; after writing to London on October 6, he was summoned for discussions with the Chiefs of Staff, who were also worried. The general feeling was that the Suez plans were no longer real; and the French, as will be recalled, had also lost their patience.[27]

As a matter of fact, the military was not fully aware of the real situation. During the second week of the month, the political process began to gather momentum, and consequently Eden decided (without telling the military why) to halt further work on the Winter Plan. On October 19, he decided that Britain should participate in the conference with France and Israel, and immediately an advance group went to Cyprus

– still with no knowledge of the expected D-day – to set up an air command post. It was only on October 22 that General Keightley heard, from French colleagues, that D-day was at hand. This was known to just a few senior French officers, who still had no actual orders, and they shared their knowledge with the British. London still gave no sign, and British officers in the field continued to feel, as Lt.-General Hugh Stockwell, the Land Task Force commander put it, that the entire Suez operation would be called off pretty soon.[28]

Meanwhile, the British Chiefs of Staff had decided to launch an exercise in the Eastern Mediterranean. Code-named "Boathook", it was planned for November 6–9, and in the final week of October Musketeer forces began shipping out of Britain and Malta in order to participate in it. Boathook as such was not carried out, of course, and instead became a fortuitous cover exercise, or a "deception after the fact". As in Israel, officers involved did not know their real mission almost until it began; Exercise Boathook was, as it were, "converted" into Operation Musketeer in midstream – or mid-sea.[29]

Not until October 24, when the Sèvres Conference ended, did Keightley receive the necessary authorisations to commence concrete preparations. He was ordered to co-ordinate his revised plans with the Sèvres timetable (i.e., to launch the first air strike on October 31, 36 hours after Israel attacked Egypt), though still with no knowledge of what had actually been agreed. The next day Keightley informed the various task force commanders that the revised plan of operations was again in force, and that they should prepare themselves for a landing on Egyptian soil within nine days, if not sooner. Keightley ordered his commanders to get ready for action according to version B of the revised plan, which included three stages: an air campaign, including psychological warfare; then a swift takeover of Port Sa'id and Port Fuad, using available forces, in order to establish a beachhead for the main force; and finally, a breakthrough to the south, in order to occupy the entire Canal Zone.

This was a major departure from previous versions, intended to accomplish landing only within 48 hours after the commencement of the aerial stage. This was to involve light infantry (paratroops and commando), with minimal armoured support. Keightley made this swift operation contingent on there being no resistance in Port Sa'id. Should such resistance manifest itself, the only way would be to wait off the Egyptian coast for the main force, in which case there would be no landing before November 6 or 7.

Throughout the planning and execution of Operation Musketeer, British officers seem to have lived in the shadow of one of their famous World War II disasters, the failed Operation Market Garden, launched twelve years earlier to capture the Rhine bridges in the Netherlands. Then, the British plan was far too daring; now, the British were acting not only as though Nasser were another Hitler, but also as though Suez were another Arnhem. This attitude would eventually stifle the entire Operation Musketeer.[30]

Now a scramble began. Staff officers wiped the dust off the revised Musketeer plan, in order to update the timetables for ship movements across the Mediterranean, where forces had already been on the move without any knowledge of their D-day, or of the option to be finally selected. Confusion was great. As a matter of fact, the plan which came into being so soon before the onset of war was remarkably similar to the one presented to the Egypt Committee by the joint planning team and the Chiefs of Staff on July 31, as if nothing had happened in the intervening months.[31]

9

In the Forefront of the Hottest Battle

From the Israeli point of view, the Sinai War was divided into two distinct phases:

1. Israel *vs.* Egypt – from the Israeli invasion of Sinai, on October 29, until Britain and France joined in, on the evening of October 31.
2. The completion of Israel's operations in Sinai under an Anglo-French umbrella – from the night of October 31 to the ceasefire on the night of November 6–7.

The Sinai War, then, began on October 29, at 5 p.m. local time, when Israel dropped a battalion of paratroopers near the Mitla Pass, about 30 miles east of the Suez Canal. This represented the act of provocation, as agreed at Sèvres, which was meant to give Britain and France a pretext to attack Egypt. In the meantime, the other three battalions of the IDF's Paratroop Brigade crossed the border into Sinai and advanced inland in order to reinforce the parachutists or assist their withdrawal, according to need.

The first point to be made in analysing this war is that the Egyptians were taken by surprise. They had expected an Anglo-French military move, but not an Israeli attack. Second, it should be borne in mind that for Israel it was, finally, a war against a single Arab country. Both before and during the fighting Israel was much concerned about possible intervention by Jordan, Syria, or both, since both countries had a mutual defence pact with Egypt. But in the event, this did not materialise.[1]

Next, the IDF enjoyed absolute superiority, particularly on the ground and in the air – not only did it have the advantage of surprise, but the Egyptians had concentrated most of their forces in the Canal Zone itself. In addition, Israel also enjoyed direct and indirect support from French and British forces in the Middle East, as stipulated in the tripartite agreement. The IDF utilised the equivalent of three mixed divisions (infantry and armour) on the Sinai front, plus four independent brigades and support forces: artillery, air force and navy.[2]

The Egyptians had thinned out their forces in Sinai during the Suez Crisis, concentrating them in the Canal Zone instead; Cairo assumed that Israel would not attack while the crisis remained unresolved. On the eve of the Sinai War Egypt deployed two infantry divisions in Sinai, though only one of them was a regular division, complete with supporting forces. It was deployed in the Qseimamjim–Abu Agueila–El-'Arish area. The other division included Palestinian forces organised under the auspices of the Egyptian Army, and it was concentrated in the Gaza Strip, mainly around Rafah. Additional forces, totalling less than a regular brigade, were stationed in various places in southern Sinai.

Egypt's most glaring inferiority in Sinai was in armour, although this was partially offset by a reinforced armoured brigade stationed west of the Canal. The Egyptian troops in Sinai could theoretically draw on support from the country's Air Force, whose operational bases all lay west of the Canal, and from the Navy, particularly along the Mediterranean coast. The problem was that they could not be intensively committed to Sinai, as Egypt awaited an Anglo-French assault on the Suez Canal. Under these favourable circumstances, the IDF's main problems were not the Egyptian Army but the difficult desert terrain and the limited amount of time at its disposal until the UN or the superpowers decided to intervene.[3]

"Withdraw Forward"

To launch the war and furnish France and Britain with a *casus belli*, the IDF's elite force at the time, the 202nd Paratroop Brigade, was chosen; its mission was in fact more political than military. Still, the drop near the Mitla Pass was not altogether without military rationale: the underlying motive was definitely political, but it could nevertheless serve some useful military purposes. A forward position in the heart of Sinai could be used to support a move from the northwest against Egyptian positions controlling the Straits of Tiran, and also pose a direct threat to the Canal Zone, should the need arise. Other immediate military (rather than political) benefits which accrued to Israel from the "pretext" move were of course the French commitment to help defend Israel's air space and territorial waters from the very start of the war, the Anglo-French commitment to launch a bombing campaign against Egypt's air bases 36 hours after the IDF's initial strike, and Britain's commitment not to attack Israel even if it reacted to a perceived threat by Jordan. Indeed, the British warned Jordan not to initiate an offensive against Israel, as it would not be able to count on British support in such a venture. This alone made the Israeli gambit worthwhile, from the military stand-point.[4]

The 890th Paratroop Battalion was, in the event, dropped some 35 miles from the Canal because of a last-minute change of plan. Yet even the original point selected was more than 25 miles from the Canal – well beyond the minimum distance of 10 miles agreed at Sèvres. In his auto-biography, Abba Eban, then Israel's ambassador to the United States and the United Nations, noted dryly with respect to the Anglo-French ultimatum, "Since we were nowhere near the Canal, we would have to withdraw forward in order to obey the ultimatum."[5]

The Sèvres agreement stipulated "a real act of war". The distance of the Israeli forces from the Canal could have jeopardised the entire action, in this respect. Indeed, it later transpired that initially the Egyptians did not view the parachute drop in terms of a full-fledged war. For some hours they thought it was just another retaliatory raid, differing from the many previous operations during the past couple of years only in range.[6]

Following the last-minute change in the site of the drop zone, from the western to the eastern gateway of the Mitla Pass – in the wake of the discovery of what was thought to be an Egyptian force at the western side of the pass, but which afterward turned out to be civilians – Dayan had to make a weighty decision: whether to take the risk and initiate an additional move. This would have placed Israel in a state of full-fledged war with Egypt well in advance of the planned Anglo-French interven-tion. The paratroop battalion had not been sent to fight but only to create an Israeli military presence near the Canal. If now, for example, this isolated force were to do anything beyond digging in – perhaps try to seize control of the Mitla Pass and so draw closer to the Canal – the Egyptians might counter-attack and thus compel the IDF to mount a rescue mission without Anglo-French support.

Dayan decided not to attack the mountain pass for the time being, even though this meant that the paratroop battalion was left in a rather exposed position, at the foothills. The main thing was not to provoke the Egyptians to attack as long as Israel stood alone on the battle front. Until the allies moved in, it was hardly in Israel's political or military interest to become involved in an all-out war. It was better to leave the para-troopers exposed, deep in enemy territory, and keep the Egyptians guessing.[7]

On the other hand, to make the gambit a genuine pretext for war for the allies, the Mitla provocation had to look like the real thing. An imme-diate withdrawal following the drop would have rendered the whole move pointless. The result was that the drop and its immediate aftermath focused the entire attention of Israel's Supreme Command Post (SCP) on the first day of the campaign. The Air Force was ordered to give supreme priority to the defence of the paratroopers and to ensure on-going supplies to their two separate groups – those at the Mitla and those moving inland to link up with them. To execute this, the Air Force kept six pairs of Mystères in rotation above the Mitla Pass – the bulk of the operational Mystère force, which amounted at the time (apart from the French squadrons stationed in Israel, which were not allowed to leave Israeli air space) to only 16 aircraft.

In fact, Israel had 61 Mystères when the war began. However, most of them had just arrived and were not yet serviceable. This was the reason for the French decision to send to Israel, in addition to two squadrons of aircraft, one of Mystères and one of F-84s, only one squadron of Mystère pilots, to fly the Israeli aircraft. The problem was that the Mystère was almost as new to the French as to the Israelis: they, too, had not yet mastered it. So the advantage of having the most advanced jet fighter in the theatre of operations was largely offset. Of 21 Israeli Mystère pilots, only 12 had more than eight hours of flight time on it.[8]

The original idea was for the IDF to complete its "pretext move" by dropping one battalion of paratroopers near the Canal, have the rest of the brigade move on land to join them, and then sit tight and wait for the start of the Anglo-French bombing campaign, scheduled for the early hours of October 31. However, neither the allies nor the IDF followed this plan.

On the morning of October 30, the allies informed Israel that they had decided to postpone their operation by 12 hours (subsequent reports, provided by Israeli liaison officers seconded to Musketeer HQ in Cyprus, quoted even longer delays). As the day wore on, the possibility that the allies would not fulfil the Sèvres agreement loomed as a real possibility to the Israeli leadership.[9]

A totally new situation had developed. Because of this change, it now seemed that Israel would remain alone, in the forefront of the hottest battle (as one Israeli leader once put it), at least one day longer than originally planned. By the morning of October 31, it would no longer be possible to claim that this was only a long-range retaliatory raid and withdraw all the forces back across the border – since by that time, as agreed at Sèvres, an entire Israeli division would have been operating in central Sinai for 24 hours. During the morning of October 30, then, the question facing Dayan was whether to give this division the go-ahead to move, as planned, when his entire concept of the war, which he had so persuasively put forward at Sèvres, seemed to have collapsed.

Ben-Gurion and Dayan instituted throughout a strict policy of compartmentalisation regarding Israel's collaboration with Britain and France, and this was to have far-reaching implications for the fighting in Sinai. Each of the three allies had its own reasons to limit the number of those in the know about their collusion to the barest minimum. In Israel, Dayan knew things which the people who ran actual operations at SCP never dreamed about, although they knew a great deal more than the commanders in the field. Friction is a constant of war between those who direct efforts from behind and the commanders at the front, and in the Sinai War such friction was at its highest.

The IDF's Southern Regional Command (SRG) was never given a full explanation of Israel's central war aim during the first 48 hours, let alone its motives. It therefore put its mind, early on Tuesday, October 30, to the accomplishment of the next aim – defeating Egypt's main forces in the Sinai – while Supreme Command, which knew that it was carrying out basically a political move, was undecided about whether to pursue the original "pretext" gambit. Dayan instructed his forces not to intervene in Sinai, except for the paratroopers' moves, for a period of 48 hours after the original drop. Thinking the order must be a mistake, his subordinates hastened to correct it. The head of Southern Command, Colonel Asaf Simhoni, was not told why he should hold still and found the situation unacceptable. Using his best military judgement – as Dayan had always encouraged IDF officers to do – he committed more troops to Sinai only hours after the parachute drop at the Mitla Pass.

Thus, early on October 30, many hours before the Anglo-French ultimatum was due, the IDF was already fighting in central Sinai. Simhoni, in fact, was doing exactly what the British had asked for at Sèvres, a request Ben-Gurion had rejected out of hand. Now, though, the Prime Minister lay sick in bed in Tel Aviv, having come down with the flu, and Dayan "compassionately" refrained from reporting to him during the first 24 hours (not that Dayan himself was fully informed by Simhoni). Ben-Gurion had no idea, then, that the IDF had in effect given the Anglo-French coalition all that it wanted and more. Not only were there Israeli troops near the Suez Canal, but an entire reinforced division, including two armoured brigades, was fighting openly in the Umm Kataf-Abu Agueila compound in central Sinai. Moreover, it was all proceeding without the allies engaging the Egyptian Air Force, which Ben-Gurion had declared was a *conditio sine qua non* for that kind of operation. In short, Israel moved in too early and then was informed that the British and the French would move late, and began to suspect that they would not move at all.

The SCP assessed that without Anglo-French intervention Egypt might launch a counter-offensive and perhaps be joined by other Arab states. IDF intelligence reported that both Jordan and Syria seemed inclined to accede to Egypt's call to attack Israel from the east. The Israeli evaluation was that military coordination among the three Arab countries would not be effective, but troop movements were detected which made it impossible to rule out a joint Jordanian-Syrian offensive.

In the meantime, the Egyptians were moving reinforcements into Sinai: "Elements from two battalions are moving towards the Mitla, deploying there with armoured forces in readiness to attack", IDF Intelligence reported. Another force, two battalions or perhaps a whole brigade, was on the move from the Canal Zone towards Jabl Libni, on the central route, and a brigade was also making its way on the northern route, from Qantara to El-'Arish. Compounding matters, Israel expected Egyptian aircraft to bomb Tel Aviv and Haifa.[10]

So it was only natural that the Chief of Staff ordered every effort to be made to close the gap between the serious situation that was developing in Sinai, and the new realities arising from the postponement of the Anglo-French campaign. Particularly interesting, in this respect, was the personal dilemma Dayan was facing in his relationship with Ben-Gurion. Prior to the war, he had assured the Prime Minister that Israel would not fight alone against Egypt. Now his chief worry was less the Egyptian Army or the possibility of more Arab states joining in; his major concern was that Ben-Gurion would order an immediate withdrawal, before the war had been decided. Dayan knew that sooner or later political pressures would force Israel to pull back, and his concern was that the ambiguous situation on the morning of October 30 could hasten that conclusion.

During the entire day Dayan refrained from reporting to Ben-Gurion under the pretext that "the Old Man is ill . . . What little strength he has, he devotes to pursuing the political effort, and of course, there is no one else to direct us. We will have to carry the burden ourselves for the time being." Thus did the Chief of Staff exempt himself from reporting to his political superior that the IDF had moved far larger forces than planned into Sinai.

By October 31 the situation had deteriorated further, and Dayan was forced to manoeuvre *vis-à-vis* both Ben-Gurion and the IDF's Supreme Command. For one thing, he took care to report to Ben-Gurion as late in the evening as possible. Still, what he had to report was very serious. Even before they met, Dayan sent word to Ben-Gurion, through the latter's adjutant, that he considered the allies' postponement of their campaign a severe blow to Israel and that he proposed informing them that Israel was considering a pullback of the paratroopers to a more convenient line of defence – more distant from the Canal, of course.[11]

In their meeting, held at Ben-Gurion's residence in Tel Aviv, Dayan apprised him formally of the Anglo-French delay and about the preparations he had made "to pull back Arik [Sharon, commander of the 202nd Paratroop Brigade] and stabilise a new line from Nahl to El-'Arish." Ben-Gurion, though, went further, demanding "to pull [the paratroopers] back right away, tonight, in order not to remain in a difficult situation yet another day [beyond what was planned]. We made our commitment to [the British and the French] and abided by it, and we no longer have to remain in such forward positions."

This was in effect what Dayan had already instructed his staff officers to prepare for, but he was still reluctant. "Advancing to the rear" ran deeply against his grain. He tried to persuade Ben-Gurion: "If after all the British go ahead [with their bombing campaign], it will be a pity to give up this position, which is so important for the continuation of war in the southern Sinai and the Straits. Besides, it is doubtful whether we can pull them back already today." To this Ben-Gurion found no answer. Dayan's virtual disappearance during the first 48 hours of the war had, therefore, proved useful: he achieved Ben-Gurion's support both for withdrawing the paratroopers, should the need arise, or leaving them where they were. Still, it is doubtful whether he could have kept things hidden from Ben-Gurion – who assumed that Dayan was busy running the war and that he had nothing to report on or consult the Prime Minister about – for much longer. Fortunately for Dayan, a few hours after his meeting with Ben-Gurion, British bombers appeared above Egyptian air bases in the Canal Zone. The Anglo-French campaign had begun.[12]

During that day Dayan had to tread very carefully with the SCP and the forces at the front. On October 31, he could no longer give orders to stop any advance westward, prepare the forces for rapid movement the next day, and apart from that, stay put. The postponement of the allies' campaign, on the one hand, and the speed of the IDF's advance in Sinai, on the other hand, combined to create serious problems for the SCP. First and foremost was the need to resupply the fighting forces, a problem made acute by the fact that Israel, unexpectedly, did not have air superiority in Sinai.

In staff discussions it was agreed that the IDF must prepare for immediate further movement as soon as orders were given, but that those orders should be delayed until the allies entered the war. At the same time, it was agreed not to stop moves already under way: the attack on Egypt's strongest positions in Sinai, around Abu Agueila, and the continuing advance of the rest of the 202nd Brigade to link up with its isolated battalion at the Mitla Pass. Completion of these two operations, it was thought, would facilitate subsequent efforts to stabilise a new, improved line of defence in central Sinai, should events warrant this.

The Rift in NATO

On Wednesday, October 31, at 7 p.m. local time, the European allies launched Operation Musketeer and began their bombing campaign against Egypt. For Israel, the war was transformed. Finally, military considerations could be treated as supreme in the conduct of battle and could supersede political strictures. Thus, when fighting was resumed in the pre-dawn hours of Thursday, November 1, it was characterised by *military* collaboration between Israel and France, and indirectly with Britain as well, as related in the following chapters.[13]

At the same time, once it became clear that two members of the tripartite coalition deployed against Egypt were major Western powers, the war's implications transcended the regional arena and sent shockwaves through the entire international system. Not the least of its consequences was the rift it generated in NATO, which had a direct influence on the Cold War. Still, both the United States and the Soviet Union opposed the war, each for its own reasons. The Sinai War was also fought against the background of international developments, which affected the Middle East crisis in varying degrees.

The Soviet invasion of Hungary. On October 23, a popular uprising erupted in Hungary against the Soviet-controlled regime. In response, Soviet troops moved in and occupied the entire country by November 6. As in Poland four months earlier, the Soviets moved swiftly and relentlessly. By the time Israel was completing its moves in Sinai and the British and French were just beginning their landing in Egypt, Moscow was already free to address problems outside its own backyard.

Elections in the United States. The American presidential election campaign reached its peak as the Sinai War began. The fortunes of President Dwight D. Eisenhower, who was seeking a second term, were tied in no small measure to his foreign policy. His approach, however, seemed to clash with that of America's chief NATO allies. Even before the war (and the elections), the President had spoken out strongly against possible hostile aggression in the region. His easy victory on November 6 placed him in a strong position to dictate the course of events. Although Soviet sabre-rattling could not be ignored, it was Washington's reaction that prevailed.

The United Nations. As soon as it transpired that a full-fledged war, at least in regional terms, had erupted, the UN went into high gear. Initially, all the pressure was brought to bear on Israel. But on October 30, while the Security Council was deliberating a motion calling on Israel to cease and desist, Eden told Parliament in London that an ultimatum had been presented to both Israel and Egypt. Both the UN and the US were instantly suspicious. On October 31, when Britain and

France vetoed an American draft resolution in the Security Council calling for an immediate cease-fire, it was clear that some sort of "conspiracy" was afoot. The veto bought some time for Israel and its allies, but from that time the race against the international hourglass, as the Israelis called it, became a dominant factor.

It did not take long for the UN to overcome the obstacle created by the Anglo-French veto. Already on November 1 the General Assembly, which was then holding its regular annual session, began to debate the war in Egypt. It soon adopted a resolution calling on all parties to cease hostilities forthwith and decided to remain in session until the crisis was resolved. (Unlike the Security Council, the General Assembly does not allow the Great Powers the right of veto; on the other hand, it does not have the power to impose sanctions.) The Secretary-General, Dag Hammarskjöld put his personal reputation on the line by suggesting that he would resign should UN efforts to end the fighting fail. On Saturday, November 3, Canadian External Affairs Minister Lester Pearson proposed the establishment of an international force to supervise the Canal and the Israel–Egypt border, maintain the ceasefire (see below) and replace the IDF in areas it now occupied. Pearson's proposal was adopted on November 5, and another Canadian, General E. L. M. Burns, head of the UN Truce Supervision Observation (UNTSO) force in the Middle East, was appointed commander of the new UN Emergency Force (UNEF).

On November 3, Hammarskjöld asked Israel, Britain and France for clear responses to the UN's cease-fire demand. Israel, its forces by then well entrenched in Sinai, which was most susceptible to international pressure, tended to accept a cease-fire, even though it had not yet achieved all its war aims – most notably, its troops had not yet reached the Straits of Tiran. Britain and France, however, played for time, since Musketeer land forces had not yet reached Egyptian shores, meaning that they had as yet gained nothing from a war which was still in progress. Accordingly, London and Paris replied that they would accept a cease-fire, provided Egypt agreed to allow Anglo-French forces to be stationed in the Canal Zone until they could be replaced by UN forces, with the latter to remain there until a solution could be found which would be satisfactory to all parties. Patently, this was completely unacceptable to Nasser.

While all this was going on, Israel was reduced virtually to the position of bystander. Britain and France took the brunt of international pressure and superpower outrage, and this was one of the most important kinds of help they gave Israel in the Sinai War.[14]

On the battle front, the allies' bombing campaign effectively decided the war for Israel. The SCP had not yet abandoned completely the option of a pullback from the Mitla to a more easily defensible line in central Sinai, but once the air campaign began it could begin planning further offensives, to the west and south. By the end of the fighting on November 1, the ground battle was decided to all intents and purposes. Isolated pockets of Egyptian resistance remained (Umm Katf, El-'Arish, Sharm el-Sheikh), but the IDF's ability to eliminate them was more a function of surmounting difficult terrain and, even more, of the Egyptians' ability to evacuate their forces in an orderly fashion – the Anglo-French bombardments had prompted Nasser to order all his troops in Sinai to rush to the defence of the Suez Canal.

The IDF's situation was also eased because French pilots operating from bases in Israel were now free to fly missions over Sinai. They attacked Egyptian ground forces in western Sinai and brought back intelligence information. Communications were still a problem, ruling out the use of French aircraft for close ground support and limiting them to interdiction missions away from the actual fighting zone. But from November 1 onwards, SCP logs are full of information about the doings of "our French".[15]

A Partnership in War:
Israel and France

"This Collaboration was Damaging to the IDF"

Political and military collaboration between France and Israel had begun, as related above, many months prior to the Sinai War. It was in the war, though, that this collaboration reached it peak – generally speaking, in ways that were satisfactory to both sides. Where difficulties emerged they were in part "technical" and in part due to British duplicity, as described in the next chapter. Where full, on-going Franco-Israeli co-operation was concerned, Britain was very much the spanner in the works.

Still, some in Israel tried to play down the role of French (not to mention British) assistance to Israel in the war. In his final report on the war, the commander of the Israel Air Force, Major General Dan Tolkovsky, wrote (about a year after the event) that "although air activity by the enemy was brought to an 'artificial' end by Anglo-French intervention . . . it will be untrue to say that the IDF's success was possible because of the active participation of foreign forces in the Suez/Sinai campaigns. There is no doubt, however, that this participation allowed the Air Force to achieve what it did with minimal losses. And this was the real military achievement of these forces."

General Meir 'Amit, then Chief of Operations, wrote a few years after the war that "collaboration with the French and British was damaging to the IDF, operatively speaking. The IDF was placed under severe constraints: It was ordered not to cross a line passing 10 [miles] from the Suez Canal, it was ordered not to use its air force and armoured forces until a certain date. These restriction tied its hand in a very significant way . . . I would have thanked God if those restraints had not been put on us. Without them, we would have achieved much better results."[1]

This is not the place to discuss the psychology which gave rise to such sentiments at the time, but the material we have today paints a completely different picture. When the war began, on 29 October 1956, Israeli military co-operation with France, and indirectly with Britain, had already assumed a distinct operational character. In part, this co-operation was handled in Israel through the French air squadrons stationed there as well as via land and sea liaison officers, and in part through the joint Anglo-French HQ in Cyprus. The focal point was Israel's Supreme Command Post (SCP) in Ramla, near Tel Aviv, where the French military mission, headed by Colonel Jean Simon, was also based. From time to time General André Martin flew in, acting in his dual capacity as personal representative to both French Chief of Staff General Ely and to Admiral Barjot, France's senior officer at Musketeer HQ.

For Israel, the chief liaison officers were Lt.-Colonel Shlomo Gazit in Israel and Colonel Yuval Ne'eman (and afterward Lt.-Colonel Yosef Kedar) in Cyprus. In effect, Shimon Peres also took an active part in the liaison operation, since he continued to be in charge of handling arms supplies during the war, and also because of his special ties with the French. Occasionally, Colonel Nehemia Argov would join in, as Ben-Gurion's personal representative. In Paris, Yosef Nahmias and his designated successor as head of the Defence Ministry mission, Asher Ben-Nathan, and with them the military attaché, Colonel Emanuel Nishri, kept in touch with Challe and Mangin. Personal contacts, then, played a major role in the management of the military collaboration during the war – although it should be borne in mind that this collaboration usually took the form of coordination and direct or indirect support, rather than actual joint operations.[2]

Liaison in Cyprus

The joint Supreme Headquarters for Musketeer was located in Cyprus, and it was only natural for an Israeli delegation to be present there. As soon as the war started, Dayan sent deputy chief of intelligence Colonel Yuval Ne'eman and Lt.-Colonel Yosef Kedar, from the air force, to Cyprus. En route to Cyprus Ne'eman flew into Israel on October 29 from Paris, where he had headed Israel's delegation to the joint planning staff with the French. Before proceeding to Cyprus he met with the French and British military attachés in Israel and urged them to pressure their respective governments to issue the Anglo-French ultimatum, which Israel was waiting for anxiously ever since its paratroopers crossed the border. The attachés, until then victims of a thorough deception campaign conducted by both Israel and their own governments, now heard from Ne'eman a truthful exposition of the situation, at least as it stood in the field, "emphasising our proximity to the Canal." All other military attachés in Israel received written notification. As the diary entry of Dayan's chief of bureau for that evening notes, "Moshe [Dayan] gives a green light to send to the attachés notices prepared in advance about our performance [*sic*] at the Mitla Pass at 7 p.m."

Ne'eman did not, however, explain to the attachés the story behind Israel's gambit, hoping that they would both convey their astonishment to their respective capitals. The British attaché swallowed the bait. He immediately informed the ambassador, John Nicholls, who had as little knowledge of the Sèvres agreement as the attaché did, and the latter sent an urgent cable to London reporting Ne'eman's statement verbatim.

The reaction that night in the Chief of Staff's bureau, following the announcement of the Anglo-French ultimatum, was that the French attaché had grasped the issue at once, whereas his British counterpart "understood nothing and remained confused till the end". In any event, even after the tripartite war started, military liaison was not handled by the attachés stationed in Israel. On October 30, Ne'eman met twice with the two attachés, but once the ultimatum had been issued, that same night, responsibility for liaison with them shifted from the Chief of Staff's bureau to the IDF Spokesman, where it rightfully belonged. Ordinarily, liaison with military attachés is maintained through diplomatic channels, and these channels, as we saw, had nothing to do with the entire operation, which was handled by the defence establishments in France and Israel. The only exceptions to this rule were French Foreign Minister Pineau, the French ambassador in Israel Pierre Gilbert, and Israel's military attaché in Paris Emanuel Nishri, who had been let in on the "conspiracy" on a personal basis.[3]

It was also on the night of October 30 that Dayan briefed Ne'eman on his mission in Cyprus. As a general rule, Ne'eman should have kept in mind that the IDF's objective was to occupy all of Sinai, other than the Canal Zone, and urge the allies to internationalise the Zone. He added that "[i]t is important to us that the French [rather than the British] control the east bank of the Canal." Dayan authorised Ne'eman to promise the French any assistance the IDF could give them east of the Suez Canal: "We shall put at their disposal more bases, hospitals, convalescence facilities." On the other hand, Dayan issued no instructions for liaising with the British – it went without saying that this would be engineered by the French. As a matter of fact, Ne'eman went to Cyprus more as an observer than as a full-fledged liaison officer. Liaison was handled by Dayan in Israel, through IDF officers and members of the French mission in the country.[4]

Ne'eman's first report from Cyprus reached Israel on the afternoon of October 31: no one had expected him there, and in general, "they are not fighting here yet [for Israel, the war was already two days old]." After some legwork, Ne'eman managed to find Martin and Barjot (the latter was the senior French officer in the Musketeer command structure, under the British General Keightley) in the joint HQ near Episkopi. He found "Barjot scared stiff of the British – what will he do if they don't want [Israel] in." Ne'eman was in fact persuaded to go into hiding, for the time being, on the Akrotiri base, where the French were stationed, until they could obtain British permission for his very presence on the island. This location made it impossible for Ne'eman to maintain regular communications with the French HQ; Martin had to shuttle back and forth between Barjot and Ne'eman.

Eventually the French were able to persuade Keightley that operational and technical coordination with Israel was a must. It was then agreed that the British "know nothing" about the presence of an Israeli mission in Cyprus, and Ne'eman ruefully reported, "All kinds of Englishmen told me (quietly): 'It never crossed my mind that we would be allies, but I must say I'm delighted.' As for myself, I was less than delighted about their dubious fair play."[5]

Initially, Ne'eman stayed in touch with the Israeli SCP through French Colonels Simon (French liaison officer at the SCP) and Perdrizet (at Israel Air Force HQ). These two officers, as well as some others, were constantly on the move between Ramla and Cyprus, on a daily shuttle which operated throughout the war. Not until the night of October 31 was a radio link established between the mission in Cyprus and the SCP at Ramla.[6]

On November 2, Ne'eman entrusted his business in Cyprus to Yosef Kedar and flew with Martin to Israel, there to supervise the liaison operation at its chief location. The Cyprus mission functioned until the end of the war, and an Israeli courier flew back and forth daily on the French shuttle. The major achievement of the Israeli liaison mission in Cyprus was the coordination of Operation Tushiyah ("resourcefulness"), in which 65 Egyptian Jews were smuggled out of Port Sa'id on November 18–19. An Israeli team wearing French uniforms went to Port Sa'id and took out those members of the Jewish community who wished to go to Israel. They were transported, again with French assistance, in an Israel Navy vessel.[7]

French Air Support

As related above, three French air squadrons were stationed at Israeli air bases, their main mission being to defend the country's air space. In addition, though, the squadrons, together with other units of the French Air Force that were based in Israel, provided direct air support to Israeli ground troops, flew interdiction missions, served for transport, attacked targets in Egypt proper, and supplied intelligence. The French missions were flown from three Israeli air bases – Ramat David in the north and Lod and Kfar Syrkin in the centre – and from British bases in Cyprus.[8]

In the sphere of air transport, the French carried out air drops for Israeli troops in Sinai, and transport from France and Cyprus to Israeli air bases for both the IDF and the French forces in Israel. When operating over Sinai, French transport aircraft usually carried navigators from Israel Air Force Transport Squadron 103, who helped locate and co-ordinate with ground forces.

However, communication between Cyprus and Israel was unstable at best, and the French had to work hard to avoid overt coordination which might give away their collaboration with Israel. The result was a number of unco-ordinated missions, particularly air drops. General Brohon, Musketeer's senior French Air Force officer, later claimed that the British deliberately jammed radio communications between Ramla and Cyprus. We have no corroborating evidence of this, and Israel Air Force historians maintain that it was the French, to achieve deniability, who refrained from using their channels to Cyprus, falsely claiming that their equipment was out of order. Be this as it may, on quite a few occasions during the war French aircraft entered Israeli air space unexpectedly, and it was only sheer luck that they were not intercepted by Israeli planes. Due to the confusion much equipment was delivered to unscheduled sites, where no one knew what to do with it (in one case, a French paratroopers force even landed at Lod). On November 4, the IDF's 202nd Paratroop Brigade reported unidentified aircraft approaching its positions near the Mitla Pass in western Sinai. However, it soon emerged that this was not an Egyptian bombing raid but the French, who had arrived unannounced to drop supplies, including C rations with bottles of wine – unheard of in the Israeli army.[9]

Some of the problems were resolved by the daily shuttle flight operated by the French between Israel and Cyprus. At one stage there was talk of cancelling these flights, but the French liaison mission in Israel protested, and the DC-3 kept flying, taking to Cyprus a French courier, the executive officer of the French mission, with a written report on the status of the French forces in Israel. He was accompanied by an Israel Air Force officer, equipped with a daily report about the IDF's air and ground situation, a meteorological report, a list of requested targets for air strikes in Sinai and in Egypt proper, a report of his own about the status of French forces in Israel (delivered to French HQ on Cyprus), and requests for intelligence information. On the return flight he carried back similar information, although this usually proved disappointing in both quantity and in quality. Mostly it was air intelligence about Egypt,

including aerial photographs, obtained by French and British reconnaissance missions. The French refused to provide Israel with
intelligence about Syria and Saudi Arabia, despite repeated requests.[10]

The Israel Air Force was unable to persuade the French on Cyprus of
the need to establish a common radio frequency for Musketeer aircraft
and its own, or even a common frequency for messages of distress. For
emergencies there was an agreed procedure for British and French
aircraft to land in Israel, but nothing had been agreed for search-and-
rescue operations in Sinai. The result was that in Sinai, particularly over
the western part of the peninsula, Israeli aircraft (including French
planes based in Israel) and Musketeer aircraft operated simultaneously
but without communication or coordination.

French Naval Support

French naval support to Israel was fraught with even more mishaps and
misunderstandings than the situation in the air. Whereas in the air there
had at least been orderly advance joint planning, all the joint naval operations were last-minute improvisations. As a result, Israeli expectations
were constantly frustrated. Furthermore, if in the air there was no direct
contact with the British this was not the case at sea. The chaotic, unco-
ordinated situation caused at least one direct collision, brought about
by lack of coordination in the air and the absence of preparations for
orderly naval coordination between Israeli and Musketeer forces.

Small wonder, then, that all the naval operations which involved
some contact between Israeli and Anglo-French forces remain contro-
versial to this day: the French bombardment of Rafah, the capture of the
Egyptian destroyer *Ibrahim el-Awwal*, and an Israeli air strike against the
British destroyer *HMS Crane* off Sharm el-Sheikh.

On Monday, October 29, in the afternoon, hours before the start of
hostilities, Dayan informed the French that Israeli support for their
forces at the Canal, if required (as described below) would be contingent upon Israel's receiving significant French naval support. At 1:45
p.m. he summoned a meeting to discuss this issue, with Ne'eman and
Gazit of the Israeli liaison team, Israel Navy commander Admiral
Tankus, and liaison officer Commander Zvi Kenan. France was represented by Colonel Simon and Captain Guerrin, commanding officer of
the French flotilla which had arrived, as agreed at Sèvres, to help
provide anti-aircraft cover for Israel's cities.

Guerrin had his orders cut out for him: under Operation Archer
(codename for French naval support for Israel) two of his destroyers,
Surcouf and *Cressant*, were to patrol off Haifa, while another, *Beauvet*,
would do the same off Tel Aviv. They were to co-ordinate their moves

with the Israeli craft executing the same mission, namely, the destroyers *Eilat* and *Jaffa* and the frigate *Miznak*. The French informed Israel that early on October 31, when Anglo-French air raids against Egypt were to start, they would reassign two of their destroyers to escort French convoys on their way to Egypt, leaving only the *Cressant* in Israeli territorial waters. Guerrin himself was on board the frigate *Guerarre*, which sailed between Cyprus and Haifa, to handle operational naval liaison with the IDF.[11]

It soon turned out that orders handed down in accordance with Sèvres were not enough for the French seamen (who, of course, were in the dark about the collusion); they claimed they needed further authorisation. The French flag officer asked Dayan to make a formal request for anti-aircraft defence to the French Navy. This was certainly a bizarre request, since the entire issue had been decided at the highest possible level. Dayan thought the reason was French reluctance to give written orders to their units in Israel, lest the British discover France's "off-limits" assignment. This may have been part of the reason, but not all of it. To maintain internal compartmentalisation between the two French operations, codenamed "700" (Musketeer) and "750" (assistance to Israel), the heads of the French forces dispatched to Israel, both navy and air force, were not apprised of their real missions. They received their orders only after reaching Israel, and even then were told nothing about the political background. At the same time, they were directed to co-ordinate naval support (down to the minutest details) and air support (more generally) with Musketeer HQ in Cyprus, prior to implementation. Thus, in addition to the cross-purposes between Britain and France the operation was further hampered by internal secrecy between the French forces.[12]

Dayan could not care less for such niceties. He instructed Ne'eman to prepare at once the formal request which the French wanted, while Kenan was put in charge of liaison between the French flotilla and the Israeli navy and air force. Dayan explained that Guerrin's forces must be at full alert as of the next day (October 30) and suggested that "the sailors be allowed an off-duty evening in Haifa, they should have some entertainment, because tomorrow they may well have their hands full."

Dayan proceeded to discuss naval support for Israeli operations in Sinai, and for starters asked for artillery support in the IDF's attack on Rafah, on the northern Sinai coast. He reminded his interlocutor that this was not some spur-of-the-moment plan concocted by General Beaufre (second-in-command in the Musketeer ground force), as Captain Guerrin thought: "It was agreed to by Generals Challe and Martin, we were promised execution . . . The entire operational plan is based on it . . . We [furthermore] intend to ask for more support as we go along on the Mediterranean coast." Much to Dayan's surprise, the French had received no orders on this point. It was agreed that they would begin planning their support and meanwhile send an officer to Barjot in Cyprus to get specific orders. It turned out that the French had in mind much less support than Dayan expected. In support of the attack on Rafah, for instance, they proposed using 10 tons of shells. Dayan asked for 20, otherwise "the whole thing will not be worth its while." Israeli naval experts told Dayan that while the quantity cited by the French was serious, it would not produce a real "softening up" of Rafah. Aware that bombardment from the sea would have limited effect anyway, Dayan ordered Israeli aircraft to take part in support of the planned attack on Rafah, in bombing and in psychological warfare, using a DC-3 equipped with loudspeakers. In fact, operational expectations of the French naval bombardment were never very high: for Dayan, it was more of a test case to discover the extent of French willingness to support Israel, as well as establishing a precedent which could be used should the need arise.[13]

On October 31, Ne'eman discussed this problem in Cyprus with Martin. The latter was all too anxious to meet any Israeli demand, in view of the fact that the allies had violated the Sèvres agreement by failing to launch the air campaign against Egypt that morning (see below). Martin accepted Dayan's request to intensify the Rafah bombardment, but he also made it clear that once their own sea-borne operations commenced the French might find it difficult to supply additional naval support (except in the Straits of Tiran, should this be required). The French also made their support at Rafah conditional on an escort of two Israeli destroyers for the cruiser which would carry out the bombardment, and on Israel's withdrawing its request for French support in its attack on El-'Arish, even though this had already been agreed on.

"The Camps Area Became an Inferno"

Under the original plan, the French were to shell Rafah during the night of October 31–November 1, and El-'Arish the following night, November 1–2. However, the British put back the start of their air operations by nearly 24 hours, until the evening of October 31, causing a parallel delay in the operational timetable of Israel's 77th Division, which was to operate in northern Sinai. The French were now concerned that an attack by their naval forces on El-'Arish during the night of November 1–2 would interfere with Operation Musketeer itself. During the night originally scheduled for their shelling of Rafah (October 31–November 1), the allies' air raids on Egypt were supposed to be in full swing. At that stage, Musketeer HQ intended to have all its available forces engaged in movement towards Egypt. France's Admiral Lancelot, the deputy commander of the Naval Task Force of Musketeer, having consulted with his British superior, Admiral Durnford-Slater, therefore agreed to make his cruiser *George Laique* available to French-Israeli collaboration for 40 hours only, from October 31 to November 2.[14]

This cruiser reached Haifa in the afternoon of October 31 and then moved south under cover of darkness. Beginning at midnight, the French bombarded military camps around the town of Rafah, which straddles the border between the Gaza Strip and Sinai proper, for four hours. Dayan was an eye-witness to the attack, and his aide Bar-On noted in his diary: "The camps area became an inferno. But because of little experience [with international joint operations] there were long pauses between successive barrages, and between the last one (which was rather unimpressive) and the actual assault." The French, in turn, claimed that the breaks were intended to allow Israeli aircraft to provide their own support, which somehow failed to materialise. Although it had meagre results in terms of combat effectiveness, the French bombardment of Rafah should be judged by its contribution to Israel's confidence, as a concrete indication of French willingness to help. It was no mere whim on Dayan's part to have invested so much time in coordinating this single action. Finally, the bombardment did in fact hasten the fairly rapid collapse (within 9–10 hours) of Egyptian positions in and around Rafah.[15]

Admiral Barjot, too, thought that although the barrage was unimpressive it helped the IDF overcome the Rafah obstacle fairly quickly, thus indirectly supporting Anglo-French moves in the northern part of the Canal. He went even further, arguing that the bombardment had made a strong impression on other Arab states (meaning Syria and Jordan), who remained on the sidelines despite their mutual defence treaties with Egypt. In general, Admiral Barjot, the deputy allied commander-in-chief, regarded Israeli efforts in Sinai, particularly along the northern route, as an integral part of the campaign for Port Sa'id, Port Fuad, and the entire Suez Canal Zone. Dayan too was thinking, before the war, about the military and political benefits that would accrue to Israel from the spread of rumours about active French support for Israel's offensive.[16] The contribution of the naval shelling the ground battle at Rafah reinforced the IDF's plan to mount a similar operation in support of the attack on El-'Arish during the night of November 1–2. Since the French had already explained that they could not participate, the assignment fell to the Israel Navy. However, by the time its vessels reached effective range El-'Arish was already in Israeli hands, and the shelling did not take place.[17]

Who Captured the *Ibrahim el-Awwal*?

Early on Wednesday morning, October 31, an Egyptian destroyer, the *Ibrahim el-Awwal*, was captured off the Israeli coast. In terms of impact on the progress of the war as a whole, this was a very minor event. Its significance lies in its embodiment of the military collaboration between Israel and France, despite the controversies which would inevitably arise about the relative contributions of each (see below). The event also boosted morale in the Israel Navy and among the general public. An indication of its relatively minor significance can be found in the somewhat indifferent manner with which it was noted at the time by Israel's High Command. It was to assume broader proportions only after the war.[18]

According to Israeli sources, the following picture emerges: the first siting of the Egyptian destroyer was made at 2:45 a.m. on October 31. The vessel appeared on naval radar screens at Haifa, but was not identified as hostile. At 3:30 a.m., however, the ship, which turned out to be the *Ibrahim el-Awwal*, opened fire on Haifa, shooting more than 200 shells which hit the harbour area but without causing much damage. Having completed its barrage, the vessel started withdrawing northward. At this stage, Israel Navy HQ ordered the destroyers *Jaffa* and *Eilat* and the frigate *Miznak*, which were patrolling the coastline, to make full speed for Haifa and give chase.

Then, according to Israeli sources, the Egyptian vessel encountered the French destroyer *Cressant*, which was at anchor inside Haifa harbour on an "anti-aircraft mission only". The sources shed no light on how the Egyptians, who never entered the harbour area, were supposed to have "encountered" the French, who never left it. Be that as it may, at 3:39 a.m. the French destroyer opened fire, shooting "altogether 64 shells, originally intended for anti-aircraft, on a flat trajectory." This report does not specify whether the French action damaged the *Ibrahim el-Awwal*. Not until 5:30 a.m. did the Israeli vessels begin to fire on the Egyptian destroyer, which by now was some 25–30 nautical miles west of Haifa.

There were four American ships near the Egyptian destroyer (they had been sent by prior arrangement to evacuate American nationals from Israel and from Gaza), which complicated the situation. The Egyptian destroyer was hit, however, and lost speed. An Israeli DC-3 illuminated the scene, and at 6:40 a.m. two Israeli Ouragan fighter-bombers joined the attack. At the same time, French Mystère jet fighters were launched to provide air cover, in case enemy fighters intervened. At 7:10 the Egyptian captain ordered the white flag raised (he never explained why he had not scuttled his ship), and 30 minutes later the ship was captured. It was subsequently repaired and joined the Israel Navy fleet under a new name, *Haifa*.

As naval encounters go, it was a fairly short battle. The Egyptian ship approached Haifa without escort; facing superior forces, it stood little chance of accomplishing its mission and withdrawing safely. It was reported to the IDF's Supreme Command Post during the morning that the destroyer had surrendered to a joint (naval and aerial) Israeli operation and was "in tow". The report did not mention the French.[19]

French sources paint a totally different picture. They say that on the night of October 30–31 the French destroyer *Cressant* was on patrol off Haifa harbour. Its mission was to provide anti-aircraft defence and to intercept any unidentified vessel. The *Cressant* was equipped with various types of armament, not all of it for anti-aircraft purposes. The French claimed to have sited the *Ibrahim el-Awwal* already at 2:30 a.m. and noted that it opened fire at 3:30. The object of the attack, though, was not Haifa harbour but the *Cressant* itself, they claimed, but the Egyptians overshot them (perhaps they were aiming for Haifa?), and the *Cressant* sustained no damage.[20]

The French immediately returned fire and gave pursuit, and the Egyptian destroyer withdrew. Among other weapons, the French fired four surface-to-surface missiles, and called on the Israel Navy to join in, since they knew some of its vessels were patrolling the area. At a distance of about 10 km from Haifa, the French captain, Bois, stopped, and then turned back towards the harbour. He later explained that there was a problem with the ship's engine, and also that his mission was to defend Haifa, not to give chase on the high sea. He was right: that was the task of the Israel Navy, which had indeed prepared for it – except that the Israelis identified the destroyer as hostile only after it had opened fire.

The French naval historian Philip Masson cites another, more complex, reason for Bois's surprising withdrawal: the American presence in the area was potentially embarrassing to the French. They did not wish to reveal their collaboration with the Israelis to the US Sixth Fleet, which was closely monitoring the war (this indeed was a cause of much consternation to both France and Britain, as well as to Israel). Therefore Bois was ordered to make for Haifa with all speed and to explain his presence there, should the Americans inquire, as a need for repairs. Still, the French captain himself probably did not know the reason for this disgraceful order.[21]

Although seeking to hide their involvement from the Sixth Fleet, the French still wanted to prove to the Israelis that it was they who had captured the Egyptian destroyer. In his final report, Bois explicitly took credit for its surrender. The French even sent a technical officer, Captain

Caupin, to examine hit marks on the Egyptian vessel; not surprisingly, his conclusions supported Bois's version of events. Caupin explained that the missiles fired by the *Cressant* were armed with fragmentation warheads, which on impact scatter dozens of pieces of shrapnel. It was just such fragments which had punctured numerous holes in the destroyer's fuel tanks, causing the ship to run out of fuel and stop. The point was that Israel had no such missiles. Caupin added that the Israeli ships had been completely ineffective, and had the Egyptians sent a faster ship the results would have been very different.

Years after the war, Dayan came out in support of the French version. He agreed that it was the French who had first identified the Egyptian destroyers: "Israel Navy ships on patrol along the Israeli coast never detected it. . . . The French destroyer which was stationed that night off Haifa harbour [that is, not "anchored in the harbour," as his own navy had claimed] was first to spot the *Ibrahim el-Awwal* and open fire . . . but it did not give chase. The Egyptian destroyer's captain began a rapid withdrawal." In order not to rob the IDF of all credit, Dayan pointed out that the Egyptians hoisted the white flag after the follow-up operation by the Israeli navy and air force.

It is difficult to know where the truth lies in this debate, but the main point is not who hit the *Ibrahim el-Awwal*. What is significant is that both in the air and on the sea French support lent Israel both mental confidence and material reinforcement. Incidentally, within Israel a debate also sprang up, between the navy and the air force, over who should have credit for the capture of the Egyptian destroyer. Both branches apparently felt an overwhelming need to beef up the list of their achievements in the Sinai War.[22]

"The French Government Must Know Nothing"

The possibility of the IDF's actually reaching the Suez Canal itself was raised on several occasions in the discussions between Israel and France during October, both at St. Germain and Sèvres, and in between. Although the Israelis made it clear that they had no interest in reaching the Canal, the French kept bringing up the idea, particularly in discussions between military representatives.

One of Yuval Ne'eman's chief tasks in Cyprus was to ensure that no clashes would take place between the IDF and French or British forces, due to misunderstanding. Two areas of potential danger in this respect stood out from the start – the Suez Canal and the Straits of Tiran. A combination of circumstances – the IDF was already active in the straits, Anglo-French forces were set to operate there, and the absence of real communications between the IDF and Musketeer HQ – added up to "an accident waiting to happen" on land, sea or in the air. On the morning of October 29, only hours before Israel's H-hour, the French liaison officer to the ground forces, Colonel Simon, gave Dayan an outline of the Musketeer ground forces' battle plan. Simon told Dayan that General Beaufre was worried about the pace of British preparations and that he expected Israeli pressure to spur the British to action. In fact, Beaufre asked that the IDF destroy the Egyptian forces in Sinai before the French landing at Port Fuad, scheduled for November 6 or 8, so that the northern Sinai coast would be clear of enemy forces. Beaufre's worries were prompted by the fact that the area assigned to the forces under his direct command (Musketeer's Force A), on the eastern bank of the Canal, was too narrow for effective deployment.

Thus Beaufre brought up a possible French-Israeli operation which went well beyond the Sèvres agreement. His approach was a purely military one: he had always regarded French military assistance to Israel as part of the master plan for war against Egypt (which in turn was part of the master plan for war in Algeria). He took the view that any move in support of Israel came at the expense of forces intended for war against Egypt, and therefore, like his colleague Admiral Barjot, he tended to regard the IDF, in effect, as part of the French forces deployed against Egypt. In his memoirs he would comment on the absurdity of the IDF's using three divisions to attack a single Egyptian division (in fact, the Egyptians had two divisions in Sinai, though one of them, the Palestinian National Guard in Gaza, was a relatively inferior fighting force). Instead, he thought, the IDF should have been used in support of his forces, who fought the bulk of the Egyptian Army. Another concern of the French general was that Egyptian forces pushed westward by the IDF would link up with the units engaged against his troops at Ismai'lia and Qantara. The allies had hoped that at the time of their landing, Israel and Egypt would still be locked in battle, with the Egyptian Army having been driven eastward into Sinai, there to become an Israeli problem. However, such hopes were dashed when it became clear that the allied landing would not take place before November 5, at the earliest.

Beaufre also claims to have raised the idea of a joint French-Israeli operation, without the British, already in early October. In his scenario, the Israelis were to attack first and give the French a pretext for intervention. As we saw, such ideas were in effect put forward already at St. Germain, in late September, though Beaufre did not know it at the time.

Indeed, Beaufre's protestations make sense. Leaving aside the apologetic note which permeates his memoirs, the French could in fact have expected, as they went to war, much more than they were to get from the IDF, which enjoyed both clear superiority over the Egyptians in

Sinai and extensive Anglo-French support. Dayan, in fact, believed that Israel could take advantage of the French need for assistance and its acceptance of Beaufre's requests to advance its own interests. As we saw, for example, he enlisted French naval artillery support as a condition for the progress of his troops along the northern Sinai coast. Still, during the first few days of war, there was no reason to expect genuine co-operation in this spirit.[23]

With the delay in the commencement of the allies' operations, the Israeli SCP became increasingly concerned about the presence near the Canal of the small IDF unit, which had little capability to defend itself. Therefore, the SCP decided, during the evening of October 30, to examine the possibility of air strikes against the Canal bridges and thus prevent the Egyptians from moving reinforcements into Sinai. Such an operation would have meant trespassing into an area reserved for Anglo-French operations, and the IDF had to reconsider Beaufre's offer of co-operation, made a day earlier.

For a start, Ne'eman, in Cyprus, tried to sound out the French on an IDF strike against the bridges, using French aircraft stationed in Israel (and bearing Israeli insignia). The French, who had already expressed an interest in getting Israeli support near the Canal, did not explicitly object but made it clear that the bridges were not on their target list. It should be borne in mind that for both Britain and France the main objective was to seize possession of the Canal and reopen it at once; hitting the bridges would block the waterway. Besides, they would have liked to see more Egyptian forces moving away from their intended combat zone. If the IDF could draw Egyptian forces into Sinai, this would facilitate the allies' situation in the Canal Zone. Britain and France, then, did not especially care whether the Egyptians moved east; however, they had a vested interest in not letting them move back to the Canal.

Accordingly, they explained to Ne'eman that IDF operations in "their" area would require careful coordination, but in principle, if Israel wished, it could deal with the Canal bridges later on – after the Egyptians were beaten. For Israel, though, the idea was to destroy the bridges in order to help bring about an Egyptian defeat in the first place. Moreover, at this stage the French did nothing to further the necessary coordination. Even the next day, when, as we saw, they were more willing to meet Israeli demands due to the delay in the start of the air campaign (in breach of Sèvres) the French did not accept Ne'eman's suggestion – it was put on ice for the time being. Still, he found some hope in French willingness to consider the possibility that Israel would capture the harbour of Port Taufiq, at the southern entrance to the Canal (opposite Suez City); although far from the initial Anglo-French combat zone, Port Taufiq, which connects the Suez Canal with the Gulf of Suez, was an important strategic site for the Israelis. Thus Ne'eman quoted Martin as saying that "[we may regard] ourselves free to take Port Taufiq as well, if we are interested."[24]

In retrospect, it seems that it was not Israel's pre-war distress – its being barred from using the Canal – that made the French willing to consider a joint operation to occupy the entire Canal Zone, but rather the IDF's successes during the first few days of the fighting. Observing the weakness of the Egyptian Army in Sinai (especially the ineffectiveness of the Egyptian Air Force) following four days of allied air strikes, beginning October 31, and of IDF advances, the French apparently decided to re-examine the possibility of making use of the Israeli forces near the Canal, which by now had been reinforced. On Friday, November 2, Martin flew to Israel with Ne'eman. In a meeting with senior Israeli officers at the SCP in Ramla they discussed ways in which the IDF presence near the Suez Canal could facilitate the French landing there. When Dayan returned to Ramla from Sinai, his first reaction to these ideas was not to exceed the 10–mile limit imposed by the ultimatum. However, once the French reach the Canal "we will send out patrols to make contact with them."[25]

Dayan then convened the General Staff and told them that the French would like to see the IDF at the Canal by Monday (November 5), to support them at Port Sa'id and Qantara. Afterward, as far as the French were concerned, said Dayan, Israel could do as it pleased in the Sinai. It was not clear whether France would politically endorse an Israeli occupation of part of the Canal, but "the French are even prepared to see us taking Port Taufiq." Dayan explained that this port was important for Israel because "we have no other route along the Suez, and we have no water in that area."

Dayan then approached the Prime Minister. Ben-Gurion hesitated: he still wanted no direct Israeli involvement in the Anglo-French war against Egypt, and now he stressed that Israel ought to do nothing in the Canal Zone which would be directly linked to the Suez Crisis. In general, Dayan and Ben-Gurion both preferred at this stage to dissociate Israel's operations in Sinai from the Anglo-French operation. Israel had upheld its obligations, had given its allies a pretext for war, and should now be left to take care of its own interests in Sinai. Still, occupying Port Taufiq could be regarded as a move which was not too obviously connected with events in the Canal Zone. Ben-Gurion thus agreed that Dayan should examine this possibility, and Dayan concluded: "We would prefer it this way: the [UN General] Assembly meets in New York, while Uri [Colonel Ben-Ari, CO 7th Armoured Brigade] and Arik [Lt.-Colonel Sharon, CO 202nd Paratroop Brigade] meet on the Suez Canal."[26]

During the night of November 2–3, Dayan and his deputy, Meir 'Amit, debated between them the Port Taufiq idea. Dayan was greatly impressed by the swift advance of the 27th Armoured Brigade towards Qantara. With Anglo-French forces advancing on the Canal, El-Tur on the southwestern Sinai coast falling into Israeli hands that evening and his troops ready to take Sharm el-Sheikh, he thought it would be advisable to take Port Taufiq as well, and thus base supply lines on two harbours: Eilat and Port Taufiq. It was decided that the task would be given to the 7th Armoured Brigade and Sharon's paratroopers, who were still positioned near the Mitla Pass. Dayan talked it over with Ben-Gurion again and obtained his permission to conquer Port Taufiq (only).[27]

A further discussion with the French on this issue was encouraging. On Saturday night, November 3, Dayan met with Colonel Simon, who brought with him a further elaboration on Martin's ideas of the previous day. As a matter of fact, Simon preferred to talk about Qantara rather than Port Taufiq, having received from Martin and Barjot instructions which left him little room for independent decision. It turned out that the French were in a difficult position, in view of UN demands for a cease-fire, on the one hand, and British insistence on sticking with the original plan and not landing until November 6, on the other hand. The French wanted to attack at once, and were even reconsidering the possibility of going it alone – though this was more bark than potential bite. As in the past, there was again a role for Israel in such a plan: Martin and Barjot requested that the IDF support a French landing at Port Sa'id by taking eastern Qantara (on the Canal proper). The French were perfectly aware that this was a major departure from the Sèvres agreement: "Israel has the right to say no," Simon told Dayan.

The French were eager to start: air strikes on Sunday morning (November 4), and a landing at midday. His superiors, said Simon, knew that the IDF preferred night attacks, and were therefore willing to postpone their landing till sundown. Without Israel, they would be hard-put to accomplish this. An embarrassed Simon told Dayan that it was all hush-hush: the French government must know nothing about it, to say nothing of the British. Of course, he added, the IDF will clear out of Qantara as soon as French troops reach it. He went on to explain that the idea of Israeli support for a French landing in Egypt was conceived by Barjot, in order, as he believed, to make it easier for his government to reach a decision, if and when the question should arise. Therefore, a departure from the Sèvres agreement could hardly be discussed openly. Barjot was even willing to lend the IDF French uniforms for the mission. Dayan rejected the whole idea out of hand.[28]

Accepting the French plan would have turned the attack on Port

Taufiq, already approved by Ben-Gurion, into a full-scale Israeli war for the entire Suez Canal Zone. Dayan tried to help Simon work out a more realistic plan, which stood some chance of getting Ben-Gurion's approval. First of all, he pointed out, it should be remembered that the Anglo-French ultimatum, which required Israel to keep a distance of 10 miles from the Canal, was still formally in effect. It would be highly embarrassing if the British, ostensibly trying to prevent an Israeli capture of the Canal, were to find Israeli troops already there. Second, the French government obviously did not want Israeli participation in the occupation of the Canal Zone, even on the east bank. Consequently, said Dayan, such a move would also embarrass the French.

As a more practical way out, Dayan asked Simon to consider a possible landing by the French (and the British too, if they wished) at El-'Arish, already in Israeli hands, and a move to the Canal from there. "Anyway, the French may move forces on all our routes, any place they choose." But if they insisted on their plan of an Israeli attack on the Canal itself (with or without the French), Israel would even agree to a daylight attack – on two conditions: massive air support and coordination with Britain. Dayan did not want to create a situation in which "the English reach Qantara before the French and open fire on us at 200 metres range, and then claim we did not let them know we were there in the first place."

Dayan demanded official liaison, including liaison officers on the ground. Simon hesitated. It was finally agreed that the IDF would be ready to assist the French even if they landed on November 6, but under Dayan's two conditions. They would also be able to evacuate their wounded to Israel, on any route controlled by the IDF. Dayan then went to Tel Aviv to consult with Ben-Gurion, and Simon flew to Cyprus, to talk things over with Barjot.

By now Ben-Gurion was "in a contrary state of mind", according to Dayan. He heard him out on the details of the new French idea, but his part of the discussion consisted mainly of reminiscing about his stay at Qantara with the Jewish Battalion in World War I. Finally Ben-Gurion approved Dayan's plan, with all its qualifications. The General Staff instructed the 202nd Paratroop Brigade to prepare to retake the Mitla Pass, from which the brigade had in the meantime withdrawn, in order to facilitate the move to Port Taufiq – the "Israeli objective" in the joint operation with France along the Canal.[29]

Eventually the French decided not to take independent action. Under growing pressures from the UN and the US, the French and British governments reached a compromise to execute the landing on November 5, rather than the 6th. Because of the abridged timetable, Musketeer HQ improvised a fast landing plan, called Telescope. En route to Port Sa'id another change was made, the equally improvised plan Omelette, for a "light" landing (infantry and paratroopers, without heavier support). By this stage, it was obvious that Egyptian resistance would be minimal. Incidentally, these plans were distributed to task force ships by helicopters – a great innovation at the time.[30]

Now the French asked Israel to refrain from any activity at all in the Canal Zone. There was no possibility of approaching closer to the Canal without their approval, and Dayan was forced to back off. This put an end to the Port Taufiq plan.[31]

11

A Partnership in War:
Israel and Britain

The exact scope of the collaboration between Israel and Britain was never clear to either side throughout the entire Suez Crisis and the war itself. It is best characterised as a state of on-going ambiguity, the product of Eden's determination to keep his collusion with Israel secret while realising that he needed Israel to provide the pretext for the war against Nasser he so fervently desired. A similar ambiguity, not to say duplicity, characterised the reluctant military co-operation between the two countries. Eden's political constraints were due mainly to his desire to minimise the potential damage to British interests in the Middle East. While other Arab states might forgive Britain for attacking Egypt, he thought, they would never condone British collaboration with Israel. These hesitations and constraints were the cause of a number of serious military mishaps, including direct collisions between the two ostensible allies.

Deniability at all Costs

Israel's leaders pinned great hopes on the allies' bombing campaign against Egypt, which had been decided at Sèvres, and the higher the hopes, the more intense the disappointment at its postponement. During the night of October 30, anxiety in Israel reached new heights in the wake of intelligence information (albeit not wholly reliable) to the effect that the Egyptians were preparing a massive air raid against population centres in the country. No real effort was made to confirm this report, but in any event Dayan consoled himself with the thought that the allies' campaign, which was to start at the same time, or earlier, would prevent the Egyptians from carrying out their plan.[1]

Then came the news that the campaign would not begin on schedule, and with it came outrage and fear. Dayan summed it up: "Those bastards. They make a political agreement in which one of the main clauses, one we insisted on, was an air strike on Wednesday morning, and here they casually postpone the operation by 12 [hours] with no warning, not even an apology, the bastards."

According to information conveyed by Ne'eman from Martin and Barjot in Cyprus, the postponement was due to a "rebellion" by the British commanding officer of the joint forces, General Keightley, against his own government. Keightley, who had not been informed of the Sèvres agreement, simply refused to attack at first light (on October 31) because he thought it would be wrong from a purely military point of view. His own plan called for a strike at last light. Keightley insisted on his view to the point of willingness to offer his resignation, and would not budge. This information, however, did little to console Ben-Gurion and Dayan. It was all Dayan could do to dissuade the Prime Minister from ordering a general withdrawal.[2]

The French were worried about precisely such an Israeli reaction. Early on Wednesday, October 31, Mangin, the advisor to Defence Minister Bourgès-Maunoury, arrived in Israel. It was not a scheduled visit: Mangin was sent to allay Israeli fears. He explained to the Israelis that there was more to it than Keightley's preference for night bombing. There was also concern about the results of a high altitude reconnaissance flight made by a British Canberra bomber over Egypt during the first night of the war. It was chased by an Egyptian MiG to an altitude of 50,000 feet, and "the Canberra pilot had the feeling that there was a foreign pilot in this MiG, not an Egyptian." The British, said Mangin, were worried about possible encounters with East European pilots, and perhaps feared that their involvement would be uncovered even before the ultimatum was issued. On this, at least, Keightley saw eye to eye with his government.[3]

In fact, the information given the French, and passed on to the Israelis, was far from complete. Had the British informed the Israelis, through the French, what had really transpired that day in Cyprus, Ben-Gurion might have relaxed a little. But the British were too deeply entangled in their own trap of deniability at all costs. As a matter of fact, it is difficult to reconstruct these events even today, because most of the documents involved were destroyed immediately afterwards, and others are still classified more than 40 years later. To this day, Britain is still trying to conceal all evidence of the "Israeli connection". British historian Keith Kyle, who devoted years to uncovering the relevant documents, discovered that an order was given to burn any document, or part of any document, which might indicate that Britain had known in advance of the Israeli offensive on October 29.[4]

Musketeer commanders in the field, much like their IDF counterparts, received no information about the Sèvres agreement. Nevertheless, on

October 28 they were given orders to prepare for their first bombing raid on Egypt before dawn (2:15 a.m. local time) on October 31. No one bothered to explain to them what was behind this order: a political commitment to Israel. Here was the price of compartmentalisation. The next day they were told that the raid might have to be launched even earlier, and preparations were speeded up.

On October 29 two Canberra squadrons, one in Cyprus and one in Malta, were ready to lift off at 6 hours' notice, and H-hour had not yet been changed. The first targets were to be the Radio Cairo broadcasting station and four air bases, including Cairo West, where the (for Israel) fearsome Il-28s were based. Time was therefore of the essence, and Air Marshal Barnett, commander of the Allied Air Task Force, sent reconnaissance missions over Egypt, though these could have been quite compromising. All the same, by October 31, Musketeer forces were authorised only to continue with the execution of the Boathook deception manoeuvre, which had begun on the morning of October 29 with ship movements from Malta to the eastern Mediterranean.[5]

Throughout October 30, British pilots remained on alert, with no certainty that they would finally attack. The only hint that reached Cyprus from London was that the final go-ahead might be given only after the mission had been launched and the planes were airborne – which did little for morale. During the day Egyptian radar indeed identified British aircraft involved in photo-reconnaissance missions over Egypt, and jet fighters were scrambled to intercept them. In the afternoon, Keightley was ordered to move the first strike, which had been planned for night-time, to a later, daylight hour. Apparently London did not want its strike to follow so closely on the heels of the ultimatum, which had been issued on Tuesday, October 30, at 6 p.m. local time, Barnett urged Keightley to appeal to the Chiefs of Staff in London: a daylight raid could put his aircraft at risk. Both officers, as mentioned above, were unaware of Sèvres.[6]

Keightley's request was discussed in London during the night of October 30–31, at a meeting between Eden and his inner Cabinet circle and the Chiefs of Staff. As a matter of fact, since the British government did want to put as much time as possible between the ultimatum and the commencement of hostilities, Keightley's request was a godsend – not rebellion, as the French thought.

The strike was postponed by several hours for political reasons, and then by several more for operational reasons. A few ministers, says Kyle, noted ironically noted that there was no sign so far that Israel had attacked Egypt from the air. In the end, Keightley was ordered to launch his first strike at night, but also to be ready for immediate action against Egypt, "if Israel suffers serious air attack that morning [by Egyptian

Ilyushins]". Thus, the start of the air campaign was delayed by 12 hours altogether.[7]

Kyle summed up the entire episode thus: "The cover story had to fit not only here and now but also the history books of tomorrow." For the sake of deniability, Eden was ready to renege on his agreement with Israel, although not totally. As noted above, plans would have been changed had Israel been attacked from the air. This Ben-Gurion and Dayan did not know, however, nor did the French; though it stands to reason that they should have been aware of the preparations, which were made in their presence in Cyprus. In the final analysis, the Musketeer command structure gave the British the final word in the air, as in all other spheres of military activity.[8]

Ne'eman tried to protest to the French ("I cried havoc") and hold them accountable, in the absence of any direct link with the British, for the delay. He also demanded that the French vessels on anti-aircraft duties along the Israeli coast, which had been pulled out that day, return immediately. The French replied that they had left one ship at Haifa and could not provide any more, since these ships were needed to escort the convoys moving towards Egypt. Ne'eman tried to argue that, if push came to shove, it was better to leave the convoys exposed rather than Israel's cities, but this argument somehow failed to convince Barjot. He promised to look into it, but seems to have done nothing further in the matter.[9]

In reply to Ne'eman's request for intelligence information, the French told him that Egypt's 1st Armoured Brigade had crossed the Canal eastwards, and that the French were even ready – in the light of Israel's disappointment – to consider the possibility of using their squadrons to attack Egyptian armour, even in advance of the overt allied strike. But it was clear that within the Sèvres framework, and under the constraints of the Musketeer command structure, this was as impossible as it had been for the French to make General Keightley attack on the morning of October 31.

The French, as we saw, were willing to go out of their way to please Israel so that it would not renege on its commitments, but there was little they could do. As a gesture of conciliation, Martin put at Ne'eman's disposal a special aircraft so that he could shuttle between Cyprus and Israel as he wished. Some gestures were also made, as mentioned above, to accommodate Israel's requests for naval support in its movements along the Sinai coast. But committing French aircraft based in Israel (even camouflaged) before Britain and France officially started their war, would have blown the cover off Eden's pretence that the European powers were intervening in order to secure the Suez Canal from the ravages of an Egyptian-Israeli war.[10]

On October 31 during the night, Ne'eman told Dayan that the British intended to land at Port Sa'id only on November 6. He thought that in this matter, too, there was serious disagreement between the generals in the theatre of operations and the government in London, as well as between the British and the French. Ne'eman said that the French wanted to land as early as November 3 and that "Martin is blowing his top and bombarding Paris with cables". He even ventured the opinion that British generals lacked "operational discipline". But the Israeli liaison officer could not have known the scale of the dilemmas facing the British command in view of the on-going ambiguities surrounding Musketeer; or that these British generals were even less well-informed than Martin, or himself, as to what underlay the equivocal instructions they were receiving from Eden through the Chiefs of Staff in London. Ne'eman never dreamed that the decision to land on November 6 was actually an improvement, since in the original timetable it had been set for November 8.[11]

While Wednesday, October 31, was the most difficult day in the Sinai War for Israel, it had actually enjoyed the assurance of full Anglo-French air backing. As, however, the Egyptians mounted no significant air attack on Israel, allied intervention was unnecessary, and Israel's leaders could not know that such a contingency had existed. As for the IDF, its commanders knew that the French were willing to commit their forces should the need arise – which it did not, because the Egyptians were apparently too concerned about the British and the French to launch their air force against Israel. Still, the very knowledge that the French were on standby alert helped ease Ben-Gurion's mind. As for his generals, and Dayan first and foremost, they saw no reason to halt IDF penetrations into Sinai on October 31.[12]

Britain and Israel – Allies or Adversaries?

As noted in the previous chapter, France and Israel discussed a possible joint operation in the Suez Canal Zone. Israel was willing, but the French eventually dropped the idea, though the reason had little to do with purely military considerations: Britain had pressured France to avoid any overt military collaboration with Israel. As the British saw the situation, Israel had done its part and helped foment a war for the two European powers; now, though, it was no longer a desirable ally and the British insisted that the French no longer involve it in their operations. The embarrassed General Martin not only had to terminate any discussion about possible Israeli moves along the Canal, but also sought, on November 3, to enter into an understanding with the IDF whereby "the partnership between Israel and the allies is now liquidated, [Israel] having done its part, so that there is no reason now to continue with military coordination."[13]

This was not a significant problem for the IDF, provided the allies continued, as agreed at Sèvres, to support its advance towards Sharm el-Sheikh, which was anyway nearing completion. Politically, too, such an understanding did not pose a serious political problem for Israel. Ben-Gurion and Dayan were quite willing to cease hostilities even before the Musketeer landing took place. This would certainly have pleased the British, who could then proceed without being accused of collaboration with Israel, and perhaps also without having to face continually mounting pressures.

In view of this, the IDF was not surprised to hear Ambassador Abba Eban announce at the UN on the evening of November 4 (New York time; early November 5 in Israel) that Israel was prepared for a cease-fire, provided the Egyptians agreed as well. This should not be construed to imply that there was close coordination between Israel's defence and diplomatic establishments – on the contrary. Behind Eban's statement one can more readily find the foreign ministries of the two European allies, which throughout did not take part in the real decision-making process. Eban, who faced heavy pressure in the UN, asked Foreign Minister Golda Meir to find out whether her French and British counterparts assented to an Israeli declaration that it would accept a cease-fire. Meir, who knew most of the collusion story, spoke to the two ambassadors in Israel. She knew they were unaware of the secret agreements, but it is not clear whether she assumed they would consult with their respective ministers, who were in the know, and whether she herself consulted with Ben-Gurion beforehand.

Be that as it may, both Whitehall and Quai d'Orsay responded affirmatively to her question.

Militarily, however, the situation was far more complicated. Egypt's acceptance of a ceasefire along with Israel would have placed Britain and France in an untenable position: the Anglo-French pretext for war would disappear even before the first British or French soldier had set foot on Egyptian soil. Egypt, indeed, agreed to the ceasefire, and now Mollet and Eden found that they still needed Israeli support, after all. On November 4, Abel Thomas, Director-General of the French Defence Ministry, called his Israeli counterpart Shimon Peres to protest Israel's willingness to accept a ceasefire. Then the minister himself, Bourgès-Maunoury, called Peres, with whom he had close personal relationship, to tell him that Israel's decision was tantamount to a betrayal of France, and had radically changed the situation. Britain, though, even at this difficult moment, kept its silence. Deniability was to be maintained at all costs.

Defending Israel's position, Peres cited the postponement of the Anglo-French invasion of Egypt, and particularly Martin's November 3 declaration on the end of military collaboration. Still, it was clear that Eban's statement would damage French interests, and this was the last thing Ben-Gurion and Dayan wanted at the time. Frantic political negotiations with the French produced a new formulation for Israel's agreement to a ceasefire, which in practice would mean a 12-hour delay in its commencement and give Musketeer forces enough time to make their landing at Port Sa'id and Port Fuad.

That same night, November 4, New York time, Eban explained to the UN that his previous statement had been misconstrued—he had only meant to describe the situation in the war zone. At the same time, Britain and France informed Hammarskjöld that they continued to think their intervention would be necessary in order to prevent the escalation of Israeli-Egyptian hostilities. It was essential, given the new military situation in Sinai, that Israeli troops withdraw at once. Ben-Gurion reacted furiously – he thought the British were serious and would influence French thinking as well – and the French tried to explain that they meant withdrawal only from the Canal Zone. Even at the height of the collusion, then, Israeli mistrust of Britain reached new heights.

As Secretary-General Hammarskjöld demanded Israel's unconditional agreement to the ceasefire, Britain and France brought forward their D-day for landing in Egypt by 24 hours. Israel finally accepted the ceasefire late on November 5, local time, having accomplished all its objectives in Sinai, other than the occupation of the tiny islands of Tiran and Sanafir on the approaches to the Straits of Tiran. By then, the Anglo-French invasion was already under way, and the allies no longer needed the "Israeli pretext". In the final analysis, Israel preferred the buffer between its forces and the Egyptian Army to consist of Anglo-French, rather than UN troops (according to Lester Pearson's proposal, adopted that day by the General Assembly).[14]

Dayan and his aide Bar-On, furious about the British attitude and the French willingness to toe Eden's line in this respect, noted in conclusion of the ceasefire affair: "What pleas and remonstrations could not accomplish [namely, bringing Musketeer D-day forward] this bold, merciless and impartial diplomatic move did [i.e., Israel's unilateral agreement to a ceasefire]. The shameless Britishers, who stuck by their rigidly frozen plan like a blinkered horse, now lost their aplomb and were forced to bring their landing forward by a whole day, when they suddenly realised they needed Israel even after they thought they could drop it by the sidelines." This was not a completely accurate representation of the facts, but it certainly reflected Israeli feelings about the British, even before hostilities ended.[15]

"Israel Is Trying to Make Up a Story"

This was an acrimonious final chord to a series of events which left Israel at a complete loss in terms of understanding British policy in the Suez Crisis. It did not escape Israel's notice, for instance, that even during the war, British propaganda broadcasts to the Middle East continued to strike a blatantly anti-Israel (and anti-Zionist) note.[16]

Before the war, Britain had worked hard to lay the foundations for a new relationship with the Arab world. London's propaganda even suggested that it was in fact Nasser who was in collusion with Israel. During the war Ambassador Nicholls, in Tel Aviv, raised the idea of seizing the opportunity to effect a rapprochement with Israel and bolstering British influence there, but Whitehall would have none of it. Nicholls was warned to tone down his understanding for Israel's problems. He tried to explain that Israel was worried about Soviet inroads in Syria, but London replied that Israel was "trying to make up a story" and that no Israeli troop movements would be tolerated, even if they were "intended to save the region from Communism. In such an eventuality, it is better that Iraq [an Arab state and loyal to Britain] take action."

The official in charge of London's reactions was Donald Logan, a private secretary to Selwyn Lloyd, and one of the very few in Britain who knew about Sèvres, having accompanied Lloyd there (chapter 8). Even Eden himself protested, arguing that there was no comparison between Israeli and Communist actions, but the Foreign Office stuck by its guns. The situation in Egypt was clearly going to end in disaster, public opinion was furious, and Whitehall carried the day. The general atmosphere was hardly conducive to collaboration with Israel, which was consistently denied after the war as well. On 22 November 1956, the British government insisted, in response to a query in Parliament, that there had been no contacts, direct or in writing, between Britain and Israel about the situation in the Middle East.[17]

British-Israeli political antipathy was mirrored in the military sphere. Agreements reached between the two countries before the war were qualified and adversarial. Britain could *not* help Jordan if it initiated war against Israel, and Israel for its part would *not* attack Jordan if Britain agreed *not* to intervene. For the British, even during the Sinai War, Israel remained an "enemy by official definition". In various Musketeer operational orders, as well as in intelligence reviews, Israel and Egypt could both be found under the "enemies" category.[18]

The British were regularly informed by the French about IDF moves and, more important, intentions. It stands to reason that the detailed daily report sent through the Israeli liaison officer in Cyprus was also given, in whole or in part, to the British. But this was not enough. The Royal Navy was instructed to monitor and observe Israeli actions. In fact, Franco-Israeli collaboration could not be easily concealed from the British. There was no hiding the fact that two French fighter squadrons had landed in Cyprus, taken off again and never returned, or that a large-scale daily airlift by French transport planes was under way between Cyprus and Israel. And some French operations – such as the bombardment of Rafah by a French cruiser described in chapter 10 – were undertaken in direct consultation with the British command at Cyprus. Still, it seems that while a few British officers were in the know, others were kept in the dark. According to Dayan, Martin later told him that "the English [in Cyprus] asked if it was true that Israel was going to take over all of Sinai and when he said it was true, general apoplexy broke out there."[19]

Search and Rescue

Although the British refused in principle to have any contact with Israel, such contact did take place, by necessity. Already on the first day of hostilities, Britain asked Israel to provide humanitarian aid in the efforts to locate an Egyptian civilian aircraft which had been lost over the eastern Mediterranean early on Monday, October 29, not far from the Israeli coast. The request followed an Egyptian appeal to Britain itself, on a similar basis. The Israel Navy joined in the search.

The Israel Air Force (IAF) knew nothing of the navy's involvement. Thus, after discovering the search flotilla, late on Monday night, it asked the Supreme Command Post (SCP) to call in the navy to engage it. The air force, however, or at least its top command, knew very well what the ships were looking for. During the night of October 28–29, two Egyptian aircraft had taken off from Syria for Egypt. One of them was carrying Egypt's Chief of General Staff, Field Marshal 'Amer, on his way home from a series of meetings in Jordan and Syria. Israeli intelligence got word of the flight, and the air force tried to intercept his plane. Due to an error (which is still the subject of acrimonious debate between some ex-IAF officers), the wrong plane was shot down, killing several officers and civilians. 'Amer reached Cairo safely.[20]

On November 3, the Egyptians shot down a British plane, whose pilot bailed out and landed near Qantara. The British scrambled a search-and-rescue task force, and a unit from the IDF's 27th Armoured Brigade in the area tried to assist. But HQ at Cyprus instructed the task force not to allow the Israelis to participate, since this could have been interpreted as collaboration. According to Barnett, the task force commander needed no such warning, since for all he knew the Israelis were as much his enemies as the Egyptians. Indeed, Musketeer forces had no liaison arrangements with the Israelis for such eventualities. But to be on the safe side, British aircraft circled the area to keep Israeli troops at bay. The rescue itself was performed by helicopter – perhaps the first of its kind.[21]

Britain continued to ignore the fact that Israel was its ally. An internal British report on a successful French strike against the Luxor air base, on November 4, omitted to mention that the attacking aircraft, F-84s, had lifted off and returned to an Israeli air base. Furthermore, the entire strike was an Israeli idea and approved by Musketeer HQ in Cyprus.

Israel, as related above, was greatly concerned about Egyptian Il-28 bombers, the only type of aircraft in Egypt's hands capable of raiding Israeli cities. These bombers had been hastily evacuated from their regular base, Cairo West, to remote Luxor. A first raid on Luxor, executed by British bombers from high altitude, was largely ineffective. Major General Dan Tolkovsky, the commander of the IAF, kept up steady pressure on the French to eliminate the Il-28s and provided them with the necessary intelligence. A first raid by French F-84 fighter-bombers took off from Israel's Lod air base on November 4 at 6 a.m. Again success was only partial, and the French agreed to launch another strike in the afternoon. Altogether, eighteen Il-28s were destroyed on the ground; the Egyptians then evacuated the rest to Saudi Arabia.[22]

The Road to Sharm el-Sheikh

A key Israeli objective of the war was to remove Egypt's naval blockade on the Straits of Tiran, which meant in effect eliminating the Egyptian presence along the entire southeastern Sinai coast, down to and including the Egyptian base at Sharm el-Sheikh, near the tip of the peninsula. The attacking force was to proceed by land south from Eilat, and because it would be exposed and vulnerable during the several days of its advance its departure was dependent on the removal of any threat from the air – in other words, on the start of the allies' air campaign. Advance elements of the force, the 9th Mechanised Brigade, had crossed the border into the Sinai already on October 31, but then came an order to stay put, which was rescinded only 12 hours later.[23]

Early on November 1 the brigade set out in full force, but during the morning its orders were to refrain from advancing at full speed. There was some reason for optimism that morning, which had been conspicuously absent from the SCP during the previous day. Still, there was still uncertainty about the effectiveness of the allies' air campaign.[24] On the other hand, the SCP was aware that Sharm el-Sheikh must be conquered as soon as possible, and not only because of "the international hourglass". Dayan could not tell his immediate subordinates who headed the SCP, General 'Amit and Colonels Narkis and Gavish, that the allies had agreed at Sèvres to an Israeli takeover of the Straits. Consequently, the three senior officers were worried that the allies would try to occupy the site commanding the waterway themselves, before Israel could get there.

On November 2, Israeli intelligence reported intensive allied activity in the Straits area. An Egyptian frigate under way from Suez to Sharm el-Sheikh was sunk. At noon it was reported that "the British intend to bombard Sharm el-Sheikh from the sea". The 9th Mechanised Brigade was instructed to send a small unit towards Sharm el-Sheikh at once and stake Israel's claim to the Straits of Tiran.[25]

At the same time, more encouraging reports were coming in about the success of both allied air strikes against Egyptian air bases and French interdiction missions in Sinai proper. Thus, at midday on Thursday, November 1, it was agreed that the 9th Mechanised Brigade would prepare for rapid movement the next morning – it was now 24 hours behind schedule. On this front, as in northern Sinai, decisions could now be made according to a purely military rationale. Still, compartmentalisation was a bane. It was typical of the entire conduct of the war that the desire to capture Sharm el-Sheikh as soon as possible resulted both from Britain's tacit support of such a move, which made it possible for Israel to ignore mounting pressures from the UN – a fact known only to Ben-Gurion, Dayan and Peres – and from the concern at the SCP, which feared that Britain might try to take control of the Straits for itself. It should be pointed out, in this respect, that Dayan was only infrequently at the SCP: his style of command was to be with the troops at the front, so that the overall prosecution of the war was entrusted primarily to his second-in-command, Major General 'Amit, who knew some, but not all the politics of the situation.[26]

Israel consistently rejected any collaboration with Britain and France regarding the Straits of Tiran. As already related, the Israeli leaders had demanded, and received, assurances that control of the waterway would be considered a purely Israeli interest. Dayan therefore had to support SCP policy on this matter, even though he knew that his lieutenants' concerns were exaggerated.

On the afternoon of November 1, Colonel Ne'eman, Israel's liaison officer at allied headquarters, sent a message from Cyprus: "The English propose bombardment at the Straits. Should we agree?" Dayan replied, "We will get along without it." Yet, in order not to sound too harsh, he added: "We will be ready [to accept], provided it is closely co-ordinated with our forces" – a condition which necessitated direct military co-operation between Britain and Israel. Needless to say, the British withdrew their offer.[27] During the evening of November 1, intelligence reported that the Egyptians in Sharm el Sheikh had been ordered to evacuate, and later on the SCP was informed that withdrawal had begun towards Suez, along the southwestern Sinai coast. Clearly, speed was of the essence, and all the more so because the SCP was still unclear about British intentions for the Straits and whether they could be taken without resistance.

The 9th Brigade's progress on Friday, November 2, was much slower than anticipated, because of the difficult terrain. On Saturday there was real fear at the SCP that the Straits would not be taken before international pressure forced Israel to accept a ceasefire. The air force was sent in strength (fighting in northern Sinai having all but ended) to support the advance of the 9th Brigade.[28]

On Sunday morning, November 4, there was renewed concern about a possible British attempt to seize the Straits of Tiran: "The English claim that their forces at 'Aqaba [in Jordan] were left without supplies, and therefore they should open up the Straits," Israeli intelligence reported. "It is not clear what's behind this." The next day it transpired that the British had in fact bombarded Sharm el-Sheikh and other positions in the area over the previous days, and now Dayan himself was worried: "The British have an interest in freedom of navigation in the Straits to 'Aqaba, and they may make troubles and use force to prevent an 'Israeli Gibraltar' [at Sharm el-Sheikh] . . . The British may be interested in having their forces hold this place, or at least leave it empty, so they could demand that we remove our forces. We must be well prepared for the eventuality of [British] occupation by airdrop or landing." Dayan did not put it beyond the British to renege on the Sèvres agreement, but his order was "not to provoke the British even if they land a force there . . . Even if they bomb the area we must not return fire . . . Our way to overcome the English will be to have ships moving through the Straits . . . to make the sea there come alive."[29]

In the meantime, the 9th Brigade had overcome the hardest part of its route – until then it had been considered impassable – and now sped south. The terrain was easier and the Egyptians had withdrawn their forces from Ras Nasrani, commanding the narrowest part of the Straits, south as far as Sharm el-Sheikh, which was now cut off. By the afternoon of November 4, the 9th Brigade was in control of Ras Nasrani and had halted 3 miles north of the main Egyptian positions at Sharm el-Sheikh. A night assault failed because of the weariness of the attacking force and the strong resistance offered by the defenders. It was then decided to attack again at first light. By this time, it was known that the allies were going to land at the northern approaches of the Suez Canal, so that Israel did not feel unduly pressured by time.[30]

Early on Monday, November 5, the Israeli forces attacked Sharm el-Sheikh again. It took three attempts, but by 9:45 a.m. the 9th Mechanised Brigade completed the conquest of the entire area. The commanding officer cabled the SCP: "Sharm el-Sheikh in my hands. All is well and done, praise the Lord, creator of the universe." The SCP replied prosaically that he should also take the two islands controlling the Straits from the east, Tiran and Sanafir – which he accomplished the next day, November 6. For Israel, the Sinai War was over.[31]

HMS *Crane*

In the absence of any direct military liaison between British and Israeli forces, friction was inevitable in such a compact theatre. Some instances were related above, but the most serious case occurred on the afternoon of November 3. At 4 p.m. (local time) Israeli planes attacked the British frigate HMS *Crane*, inflicting light damage. The whole affair was hushed up – neither Israel nor Britain had any interest in making it public, and the details are still a matter of controversy. According to the IAF, the attack on the frigate, which had SCP authorisation, was due to mistaken identity. The vessel sustained only light damage because the rockets that were used were not armour-piercing type. The *Crane* afterward left the area.[32]

Combining material from all possible sources, the following picture emerges: On November 2, concerned that a ceasefire might be imposed on Israel at any moment, and with the 9th Brigade just beginning its advance south, the SCP ordered the air force to attack any vessel that might interfere with the brigade column, and any Egyptian positions along its route.

On the same day intensive Egyptian activity took place in the Gulf of Eilat, consisting mainly of the evacuation of troops to Saudi Arabia, on the opposite shore. A mixed Anglo-French flotilla, under British command, was also operating in the gulf as part of Operation Toreador, which had been mounted to support the main Musketeer effort from the south – its primary task was to intercept Egyptian reinforcements moving to the Canal Zone or to the Straits of Tiran. Already on October 30, Toreador ships beat the IDF to the draw, sinking an Egyptian troop carrier which was sailing from Suez to Sharm el-Sheikh. The IDF was less than pleased at this – its fears about the British intention to seize the Straits seemed to be confirmed.

Once the British found out that Israel was actually moving to take control of the Straits, Toreador command was ordered not to interfere. The Israeli operation, Toreador command was told by British HQ on Cyprus, would take some pressure off the Musketeer forces further north. But Israel knew nothing of this directive, and Dayan, as noted above, gave orders regarding a possible British effort against Sharm el-Sheikh. With the normal fog of war made even thicker by unclear intentions, mutual suspicions and proximity of operations, a clash was virtually inevitable.[33]

On Saturday afternoon, November 3, the IAF reported sinking several ships. At first there was concern at the SCP that they were French; then it was suggested that they were Egyptian. However, that night it became known that no ship had been sunk but that one ship had been hit – though it was neither French nor Egyptian, but British (HMS *Crane*). The British, it was further reported, claimed that their vessel had not been damaged and had shot down one of the attacking Mystères.[34]

A flurry of denials followed. The IAF denied that one of its aircraft had been shot down. The Foreign Ministry denied that anything at all had happened. Dayan feigned innocence: "It is doubtful whether we shall ever discover the truth. Neither side's debriefing could be sufficiently accurate in these conditions of altitude, range and speed, and for aircraft operating in areas they barely know."[35]

On November 5, the *Crane*'s captain made his report. He said he was attacked off Ras Nasrani. Three sorties were made against him, causing small damage. His ship returned fire, and one of the attacking planes was shot down. Only he thought his attackers were Egyptians.[36]

On November 2, about 24 hours before the air strike against the *Crane*, an Israeli Mystère was shot down above Ras Nasrani. The pilot, Major Benjamin Peled (later the commander of the IAF), claimed he was hit by Egyptian anti-aircraft fire from Ras Nasrani. Bearing in mind the proximity in time, British identification problems (the British also fired on Ras Nasrani that day), and Israel's haste to issue a sweeping denial about the attack on the British frigate the next day, we cannot rule out the possibility that the attack was Israeli retaliation for the plane shot down the day before, and that the only Israeli Mystère lost during the war was brought down by British, not Egyptian, fire. Whatever the truth, the IAF was careful to avoid similar incidents during the next few days; no one wanted to confront the British military. The situation was sufficiently complicated without that.

On Wednesday, November 7, the IDF was busy consolidating its positions in Sinai. Its orders from Dayan were to be on the alert for a possible Arab attack from east or west, as well as for possible intervention by external forces. First on that day's list of priorities was preparedness for air strikes, either Soviet or British, in view of the IDF's assessment that, hostilities in the region having ceased entirely early that day, the British might try to appease the Arabs at Israel's expense, and in view of a threatening letter sent to Ben-Gurion by Soviet Prime Minister

Bulganin. In the event, political pressures forced the subsequent withdrawal of both Israeli and Anglo-French forces from Egyptian territory.[37]

12

In Retrospect

The Sinai War was the culmination of a lengthy process, which had its genesis in the Israeli leadership's assessment that a "second round" against the Arab states was all but inevitable, and culminated in Israel's war against Egypt, launched on 29 October 1956. Concretely, the process began shortly after the end of Israel's War of Independence, with the failure of the Lausanne peace conference in 1949. This book deals mainly with the period of 1955–6, which marked a watershed, following which events unfolded in a totally new way. Most important, from 1955 onwards a spade was called a spade: Israeli leaders began to talk about initiating a war. At the same time, they recognised the vital need for a close alliance with at least one significant Power in order to pursue their goal.

Preparing for War

When David Ben-Gurion resumed his duties as Minister of Defence in February 1955, the IDF already had a series of "master plans" which conceptualised an Israeli-initiated war. Since late 1953, staff planning in the IDF had led to the conclusion that under the circumstances then prevailing Israel *must* initiate war. The notion that Israel should absorb the first blow, and only then move to the counter-offensive and take the war to enemy territory, was considered unrealistic. Israel was simply too small to sustain such a blow and recover. Hence the idea of a pre-emptive, or preventive blow: if it was clear that an attack was imminent, Israel should take the war initiative and forestall the existential threat.

The Chief of Staff, Lt.-General Moshe Dayan, and the Director-General of the Ministry of Defence Shimon Peres, were the ultimate authors of this conception. However, they did not seek war for its own sake. Their chief, Defence Minister David Ben-Gurion, was still more reluctant. Nevertheless, all three believed that a "second round" was only a matter of time. During 1955–6, it seemed obvious that Israel's

Arab neighbours, led by Egypt, were going to attack Israel sooner or later. Yet, this attitude seems to have been more a state of mind than the result of a systematic evaluation of the situation, and consequently requiring no concrete proof. Nasser's aggressive rhetoric, his huge arms deal with Czechoslovakia and the volatile situation along Israel's border with Egypt, particularly the Gaza Strip boundary, were enough to convince Israel's defence leadership that Nasser was bent on war, even if no actual preparatory moves were identified. It followed, according to this logic, that Israel should initiate the "second round" itself, rather than fall victim to Arab initiative. Moreover, the Israelis felt that even if their dire predictions failed to materialise and a situation should arise in which Israel could make peace with one or more of the Arab states, peace within the 1949 boundaries – leaving Israel without control of most of its water resources and without safe passage through the sea lanes leading to and from its southern port of Eilat – would not be worthwhile. Israel should therefore initiate war as a means to improve its geopolitical position, en route to peace. For the Israeli defence leadership, then, war was a means to an end: a sustainable peace with the Arab world.

The possibility of an Israeli-initiated war was first broached in the Cabinet for open discussion in March–April 1955. In late March, following a particularly shocking terrorist attack, Ben-Gurion submitted a motion which, if implemented, was certain to generate a war: to drive the Egyptians out of the Gaza Strip. He was voted down, but since then Dayan ceaselessly tried to persuade Ben-Gurion, and through him the entire Cabinet, of the need to initiate a war.

From April through September, Dayan tried to implement a policy to escalate what the Israeli defence establishment called "current security" incidents into full-scale war. The volatile mix of "current security" incidents and Israel's fundamental security problems should have yielded the results Dayan was seeking. Basically, it was a simple idea: Israel's reprisal raids for terrorist actions perpetrated by Palestinian infiltrators were aimed at military targets in the countries from which the terrorists had set out. Israeli retaliation grew progressively harsher, even when its ineffectuality was blatant, because Dayan wanted to provoke a military reaction from Egypt, Jordan or Syria. The IDF could then respond even more forcefully, sparking a chain reaction that would inexorably lead to war. The chief target was of course the leader of the Arab world, Egypt.

It soon transpired that things were not quite that simple. Although there is no definite proof for this conclusion, the restrained military reactions by the Arab states in question suggests that they were careful not to be drawn into the dynamics Israel was trying to force on them. At the same time, it should be borne in mind that all efforts to enter into negotiations with these countries also proved futile. They seemed to be biding their time. The end result was that although Israel did not go to war in the spring and summer of 1955, the idea of an initiated war became central to the thinking of the country's decision makers.

In the summer of 1955, Israel channelled its efforts to provoke a war in another direction: the question of freedom of navigation in the Straits of Tiran. Basically, this had been a problem ever since Israel's establishment in 1948, but in the absence of a harbour at Eilat it was more a problem in principle than in actual effect. It was only when Israeli leaders began looking for a *casus belli*, i.e., since early 1955, that the dust was shaken off the old plans to build a harbour at Eilat. In September 1955, Egypt announced new measures to enforce its blockade of the Straits of Tiran, and Ben-Gurion, at that time holding only the defence portfolio, directed the IDF to make plans for breaking the blockade. By late October 1955, Operation Omer to force the Straits of Tiran open was already on the drawing board. Obviously, as Dayan emphasised to Ben-Gurion, its implementation would mean full-scale war. Certainly the Egyptians would react by launching an offensive from northern Sinai and the Gaza Strip at Israel's "soft underbelly" if attacked in southern Sinai. This was equally obvious to the Israeli Cabinet when it decided, in January 1956, not to execute Operation Omer.

Indeed, since the Fall of 1955 the feeling had been that the time was not opportune for an Israeli-initiated war, and that Dayan's cherished project should be postponed. In December, the Cabinet, again headed by Ben-Gurion (since 2 November 1955) instructed the IDF to resume a defensive posture. This turnabout resulted from a new evaluation of the situation, which took into account the alarming information about the Egyptian–Czech arms deal. Ben-Gurion found himself (briefly) in agreement with the "dovish" wing in his Cabinet, led by Foreign Minister Moshe Sharett: Israel must concentrate its efforts on making a "counter-deal" with one of the Western Powers, to offset Egypt's armament efforts. The United States was approached, and also Britain, France and Canada. Needless to say, such efforts would have been frustrated by any war-like activity initiated by Israel. Ben-Gurion reasoned that even if Israel were to start and win a war, it would then face a "third round". Only this time it would have to deal with a well-equipped Egypt, whereas no one would sell arms to an "aggressor" Israel. Thus the Egyptian–Czech deal did not push Israel into war: on the contrary, it put an end, for the time being, to Israel's efforts to bring about war. The course of events which started with the intensification of terrorism in March 1955 seemed to have been halted.

France and Israel

Once arms procurement became the axis around which Israel's defence policy revolved, in late 1955, another issue, already been discussed by Israel policy-makers during earlier stages, came to the fore. Ben-Gurion had made it perfectly clear that he would not agree to an Israeli-initiated war without political and military support by a Western power – preferably the United States, though Britain or France would also do. During the winter and spring of 1956, his wish was coming true, gradually.

By the winter of 1956, an atmosphere of impending war prevailed in Israel. Although there was, again, no concrete evidence for this, the general assumption was that Nasser was readying his country for a war that summer. In this atmosphere, the Ministry of Defence and the IDF received unprecedented powers. While the Foreign Ministry did its utmost to obtain arms and sign a mutual defence pact with the United States, the defence establishment was doing the same *vis-à-vis* France. Where Foreign Minister Moshe Sharett failed, Peres and Dayan succeeded. Even though the reasons for failure in America and success in France had far more to do with the domestic political circumstances in each country than with the comparative skills of the Israeli negotiators, the upshot was that Sharett's political career came to an end, whereas Dayan and Peres emerged even stronger than before.

France was concerned at the time with its – ultimately futile – efforts to suppress the Algerian uprising. The French tended to regard Nasser as the rebels' chief source of support and hence as the major reason for the frustration of their efforts. What Peres proposed to the French defence establishment was an alliance against the source of problems for both countries: Nasser's Egypt. The French bought the idea, and Ben-Gurion gave his go-ahead. In late June of 1956, the intelligence chiefs of the two states signed a first agreement. Initially, both sides viewed it as a purely military matter not requiring ratification by either government, unless and until concrete measures for its implementation were called for.

This was the agreement signed in Vermars, a small town south of Paris, on 26 June 1956, which provided for arms supplies to Israel in unprecedented quantity and quality. France also undertook to support Israel politically in its conflict with the Arab states. In return, Israel agreed to help France in its struggle against Nasser, by providing intelligence and carrying out concrete (mainly covert) operations. For Dayan and Peres, it was worth the risk: if war was inevitable anyway, and an alliance with America was unattainable, then French backing would be more than useful.

As for France, its alliance with Israel must be viewed, like its role in the Suez Crisis which broke out soon afterwards, from the perspective of its war against the Algerian Front de Libération National (FLN). As mentioned above, the French blamed Nasser and his regime for many of their troubles in Algeria; frustrated after three years of fruitless efforts, they sought innovative ideas. In retrospect, the French greatly overestimated Nasser's willingness, or ability, to assist the FLN (just as they underestimated the rebellion's base of popular support in Algeria itself). But as things stood in the summer of 1956, France was prepared to join in an alliance which was sure to undermine its position in the Arab world, for the chance to be rid of Nasser and his regime.

Just before the Suez Crisis broke out, Israel was beginning to enjoy the first fruits of its new alliance. In secret (as the French insisted), arms shipments were arriving in Israel: new aircraft, tanks and artillery pieces. With the Czech–Egyptian arms deal counterbalanced, Israel was again considering a war of its choosing, though this time the timetable would be French. It was estimated, in the early summer of 1956, that the refurbished IDF would be ready for war in a year's time, at the earliest. But the realities of the situation dictated their own timetable.

The other components of the Vermars agreement, which were of equal importance, had to do with concrete military collaboration. There was the intelligence aspect, according to which the respective intelligence services started exchanging information on topics of mutual interest, primarily Nasser's Egypt. Even more important was the issue of operational collaboration and the creation of a liaison apparatus for joint military planning. Within this framework, procedures were developed to obtain mutual approval, from the lowest planning echelon to the highest political level. The joint planning, which began well before the Suez Crisis, showed that France wanted Israel to pull its chestnuts out of the fire, at least as far as covert operations against Egypt were concerned.

It should be emphasised that it was clear all along to Ben-Gurion, Dayan and Peres that the alliance with France could well drag Israel into a war with Egypt that would be initiated by the French – Israel being just a part of an overall French war effort. They were not daunted, though, since the alliance changed the arms balance, which had previously made Israel postpone its own war against Egypt. Furthermore, they believed that by providing France with the assistance it required, Israel could realise its own best-case scenario: defeat Egypt and eliminate its war capabilities, and perhaps negotiate a settlement from a position of strength.

In any event, a joint French-Israeli planning staff was already operating in Paris by late July, when Nasser triggered the Suez Crisis by unilaterally nationalising the Suez Canal Company (owned by British and French interests). This joint staff was to play a major role in subsequent events. It provided the infrastructure for joint military moves against Egypt. As far as Israel was concerned, the fateful decision had been made in June 1956, with the signing of the Vermars agreement, and not following the outbreak of the Suez Crisis. Moreover, the mutual commitments arising from that agreement moved closer to implementation completely outside the context of the crisis, in which Israel, after all, was never directly involved.

The question of whether Israel would go to war against Egypt had depended, since June 1956, more on France than on Israel. Nevertheless, the policy Dayan had been seeking to implement since early 1955 now bore fruit. The necessary conditions for an Israeli-initiated war had been met: Israel received both arms and political support from a world Power, France.

France, Israel and Britain

During the early stages of its handling of the Suez Crisis, France refrained from involving Israel in its preparations for war against Egypt. Britain, France's partner in this prospective war, made it perfectly clear that collaboration with Israel was out of the question. Israel itself felt, during these early stages, that it had little to do with the Suez Crisis. But when a series of disagreements between France and Britain made their joint operation look doubtful, France invoked the Vermars agreement and asked Israel to join in a war initiative against Egypt. Ben-Gurion had his reservations – not so much about questions of principle, since those had already been settled, but about the modalities. The question was not "why", only "how".

For France, sorting out the Suez Canal problem was perceived as an aspect of the situation in Algeria. The French Army was already engaged in a war in North Africa and need only shift its forces from one place to another. Even French public opinion was primed for this. Britain, though, had a very different perspective. The British took the Suez Crisis at face value. The nationalisation of the Suez Canal raised their anxiety about losing their position in the Middle East to new heights. Involved were economic problems such as energy supply, and global problems such as the effort to curb the onslaught of world Communism. On both counts, there were many in Britain who felt Nasser represented a clear and imminent danger. To British Prime Minister Anthony Eden and some of his Cabinet colleagues, present-day Egypt bore the potential to trigger events, still fresh in their memory, of the kind which had brought about World War II.

British policy in the Middle East had sustained a series of humiliations in the early 1950s: the agreement Britain was forced to make with Egypt in 1954 for the withdrawal of British troops from the Suez Canal Zone (the withdrawal had been completed just before the nationalisation); the almost certain collapse of the anti-Soviet Baghdad Pact, mainly due to Egyptian opposition; the creation of the bloc of Non-Aligned Nations, in which Egypt was a major force; the failure of the Anglo-American Alpha and Omega plans, which sought to settle the Arab-Israeli conflict in a way that would be conducive to Western interests; and finally, the removal of Sir John Glubb as the commander of Jordan's Arab Legion, in March 1956, which was a powerful blow to Britain's position in Jordan and to its prestige throughout the region. It was this background that led Eden to conclude, upon the advent of the Suez Crisis, that there could be only one viable solution to the Suez problem in particular and the Nasser problem in general: a devastating war against Nasser's Egypt.

France, for all its military readiness, felt itself dependent on Britain in every aspect of a possible strike against Egypt. Politically, the French felt they needed Britain as a partner, as they could not on their own flaunt the will of the United States, which flatly rejected the Anglo-French idea of a military solution. There were also some concrete military problems: France, though it maintained forces in Algeria, had no bases near the prospective theatre of operations, but the British had bases on both Cyprus and Malta. Nor did the French have long-range bombers, which Britain had. This dependence meant that Eden's domestic problems were also French problems, and indirectly they involved Israel as well.

Eden found it difficult to convince his government, Parliament and British public opinion of the necessity of war against Egypt; and he had a still harder time in convincing the United States and the Canal user countries of the same. Initially, Britain paid lip service to the American approach, which called for a negotiated settlement – Eden believed that the only possible solution was a military one. Still, he needed a better excuse than the nationalisation of the Canal Company for a war that would be acceptable to public opinion, both domestic and international.

The French understood Eden's problems full well. Indeed, this was why they had invited Israel to become a partner: to provide Britain with an "acceptable" pretext for a war. At this juncture of British, French and Israeli interests, Israel was to assume the role of "aggressor" in a scenario which was largely a French creation. Israel would perpetrate a provocation near the Suez Canal, which the world would interpret as a "real act of war". Britain and France could then move into the Canal Zone as peacemakers, intending only to secure the Canal for the benefit of the international community.

Casus Belli

Ben-Gurion was uncomfortable with this scenario. Nevertheless, Britain's undertakings, coming on top of his desire to engage Egypt before it had time to absorb its new Czech-provided Soviet weaponry, persuaded him to join the collusion. Britain, at Israel's insistence, agreed not to honour its contractual commitment to come to Jordan's aid should Jordan come under Israeli attack as a result of actions it took. In return, Britain demanded and received from Israel both a pretext for war and a pledge not to attack Jordan without provocation. Israel was worried about British-inspired Iraqi troop movements into Jordan in order to prop up King Hussein's faltering regime. Israel also knew that Britain had a fully-developed plan for war against Israel (the Cordage Plan). Israel, then, had reasons to accept the French proposal.

Even in early October 1956, when a joint move with France was almost a certainty, the "British question" continued to disturb Ben-Gurion deeply. This anxiety was to persist throughout the war itself. In retrospect, it seems that this fact not only engendered the "pretext move" itself, it also determined its modalities. In an atmosphere of mutual suspicion, in which Israel was worried that it would be attacked by the British, and the British regretted that they could not make war on Egypt and Israel at the same time, France was able to get both countries to accept the "pretext idea", which meant, for Israel, to "begin the war from the end" (i.e., with an airdrop near the Canal instead of getting there across land). As for Ben-Gurion, he was in no position to renege on his commitment to the first significant ally Israel had had in its brief history – and not least because the French had stepped up their arms deliveries to Israel as soon as it expressed its willingness, even in principle, to take part in a joint campaign against Egypt.

Although, as we saw, elements in the Israeli leadership had reasons of their own for going to war with Egypt at this time, they were unable to persuade the government that they were sufficient for Israel itself to initiate a war. Throughout the 1950s, and especially in the wake of the Czech–Egyptian arms deal, Israel feared Egypt's military might and distrusted Nasser's intentions, felt obliged to remove the blockade from the Straits of Tiran, and thought that a change in its borders would be conducive to the emergence of a "new order" in the Middle East, in which it could survive peacefully. Yet all these motives were no more, or less, valid in the fall of 1956 than they had been a year before. None of them prescribed war on that particular Monday afternoon, 29 October 1956. It took both the "French connection" and the British threat to get Israel to act. The connection and the threat are what differentiated the fall of 1956 from the fall of 1955, as far as Israel was concerned. The time of war was determined in Paris and London, not in Jerusalem.

The Role of Britain and France

For the allies, Britain and France, the Sinai War was a failure. For Israel it was a military success, which could not have been achieved without French direct and British indirect support. Yet the Anglo-French débacle bore more of a political than a military character. Its root cause lay in London, where Prime Minister Eden was never able, throughout the crisis, to marshal broad support for a military move – not even by jettisoning the rules of the democratic game and deceiving his Cabinet, Parliament and the British people. (Ben-Gurion was no different in his deceptions, but in Israel the Prime Minister could rely on a feeling shared by the majority of the people that Israel was in imminent danger and was therefore justified in initiating war to forestall it.) Eden also deceived the United States, jeopardising Britain's "special relationship" with America and causing a rupture in NATO that was one of the more serious consequences of the Sinai War. Little wonder that Eden's political career came to an end shortly after the war – in fact, even before its outcome was finally resolved.

French responsibility for the military failure lay mainly in the fact that France subordinated its expeditionary force completely to British authority, leaving no room for its own independent action. French behaviour throughout the crisis was characterised by a strange combination of political and diplomatic activism, and military passivity.

Letting the British take the lead turned out to be a huge mistake; in fact, the whole allied operation took place without real plans. Despite three months of work, the joint (Anglo-French) planning staff found it impossible to formulate a plan of operations. Then came the political constraints (mainly, Israel's involvement), of which the planners were told nothing. Thus, Operation Musketeer was in large measure one vast improvisation. Its commanding officers were unclear, at best, about Israel's role. They could not understand why they were suddenly ordered to stop, 48 hours after their successful landing at the northern gateway to the Canal on November 7. As a matter of fact, Israeli commanders in the field also suffered from the same problem. One consequence of this strict policy of compartmentalisation which was decreed by the supreme political level was that military moves did not always reflect political intent.

To begin with, Israel sought a joint, overt, simultaneous operation with France. The French refused. They were willing to provide Israel with covert air and naval support, but no more. The operation against Egypt, they felt, should proceed in stages: an Israeli attack and France coming in as peacemaker. As it turned out, covert support sufficed for Israel. French assistance, particularly in terms of an "umbrella" to protect Israeli air space from enemy aircraft, was critical for the Israeli war effort. Israel could thus risk a daring gambit in the form of mobile warfare which spread its fighting forces and stretched its lines of communications across the vast (four times Israel's area) Sinai Peninsula. Any effective activity by the Egyptian Air Force at this stage could have disabled the IDF. France, though, provided Israel with the requisite "umbrella" from the very start of the war. Subsequently, Anglo-French air-raids completely neutralised the Egyptian Air Force, enabling the IDF to operate in Sinai with relative impunity. The Israel Air Force, relieved of the burden of protecting civilian population centres, could then concentrate its efforts on supporting the ground forces.

Still, it was not enough. The IDF soon found itself stretched thin over distances it was not used to, and had to rely heavily on the French for logistical supplies from the air, including arms and ammunition. Israel felt secure in the naval arena thanks to Anglo-French activity in the Mediterranean, the Gulf of Eilat and the Gulf of Suez. Moreover, Egypt's ground forces were not properly deployed to counter Israeli moves, first because of expectations of an attack on the Suez Canal Zone, and then in the wake of the attack itself.

Egypt

It is not certain whether Nasser intended to attack Israel in the summer or fall of 1956. Certainly his main problems lay in the Suez Canal Zone and not in Sinai. Prior to the Canal's nationalisation Egyptian Army deployment in Sinai was thinned out, significantly weakening its posture *vis-à-vis* Israel. The Israeli defence establishment was well aware of the Egyptian redeployment – indeed, it was this knowledge that allowed Dayan to propose at Sèvres the daring gambit of dropping a single battalion so far from the Israeli border.

During the war, the Egyptian Army offered, until the night of October 31, strong resistance where it maintained significant forces (particularly the Abu 'Agueila complex in central Sinai). As of November 1 – that is, once the allies launched their offensive – the Egyptian Army initiated a series of moves, which were only partially successful, to withdraw its forces in an orderly manner towards the Suez Canal Zone, in order to reinforce its deployment there. This was yet another important contribution to Israel's war effort by the Western allies. Thus, with the single exception of Abu 'Agueila, the IDF had to contend more with the difficult terrain and the "hourglass" of international pressures than with an actual enemy. This should not detract from the IDF's overall success, and more importantly, its impact at the time on Israeli morale and on its image in the Arab world and elsewhere. Still, Israel's military success should be placed in its more complex historical context.

The war came to an end on November 6, when Israel completed its conquests by seizing the two islands at the mouth of the Gulf of Eilat, Tiran and Sanafir, and Britain and France accepted the UN demand for a cease-fire. What happened next was a frantic race, in which Israel, Egypt, Britain and France each tried to turn the war's outcome to their advantage.

Withdrawal

The Israeli withdrawal from the territories of Sinai and the Gaza Strip it had occupied during the war was preceded by a general decline in the euphoria which prevailed in Israel during the war and immediately afterwards. Thus, on November 4, Colonel Ne'eman suggested to Dayan that Israel should affirm its religious attachment to the "Mountain of Moses" (Jabel Musa, as the Sinai Bedouin called it). Even the Prime Minister was swept up by the drama. On November 6, at a victory parade in Sharm el-Sheikh, Dayan read to the soldiers of the 9th Mechanised Brigade a letter from Ben-Gurion which spoke of "Israel's Third Kingdom". The next day Ben-Gurion repeated this in a statement to the Knesset, which reflected the heady sense of nascent empire in the country. But the downfall was swift and hard, and completely incomprehensible to anyone who was not privy to the legions of secrets which surrounded this war. Planning for withdrawal actually began on November 7, or 8, and morale began to plummet. It looked as if everything achieved in the war was about to be lost.

On November 6, Soviet Prime Minister Nikolai Bulganin sent threatening messages to Britain, France and Israel. The USSR, said Bulganin, would use force against Israel and its allies unless they abided by UN resolutions that called for an immediate cease-fire, followed by withdrawal from all territories occupied during the war. The message to Israel contained a half-veiled threat to use nuclear weapons. Apparently the severity of the message was not immediately absorbed by Israel's leaders – was there some sort of psychological mechanism at work? Whatever the reason, the impact of the Soviet note is not discernible in Ben-Gurion's letter to the 9th Brigade, which was written after its receipt (adding insult to injury, Bulganin's letter was hardly couched in normal diplomatic language). Still, a sensitive ear, and even more a retrospective one, can sense already in Ben-Gurion's address to the Knesset that the Prime Minister was, nevertheless, worried. In his statement the

Prime Minister announced that the armistice boundaries between Israel and Egypt were null and void, which could be construed to mean that Israel intended to hold on to at least some of the territories it had occupied. Henceforth, he added, Israel would no longer act obsequiously before "the mighty of this world". But he also took pains to make it clear that Israel had no intention of abandoning its membership in "the family of nations".

Within 24 hours of those words Abba Eban, Israel's UN representative, announced that Israel would abide by the General Assembly resolution and withdraw its forces from Sinai, provided of course that the security arrangements dictated in the same resolution were also implemented. Why did Ben-Gurion retract so fast? What was the hurry?

The answer lies in the West rather than the East. Western capitals were thrown into a panic by the Soviet threat. More importantly, from Israel's point of view, American pressure was stepped up. Washington was concerned that the USSR would try to use the crisis to expand its influence in the Middle East. The Americans therefore wanted a swift resolution of the crisis. And the pressure they brought to bear on Israel was unprecedented. As of November 8, Israeli withdrawal from the Sinai was only a question of time. All Israel could do was bargain: first on the scope of the withdrawal, looking for a way to keep possession of the Gaza Strip and the Sinai coast down to the Straits of Tiran, as agreed at Sèvres. Once it became clear that this was impossible, the Israeli government tried to make the withdrawal conditional upon the presence of UN rather than Egyptian forces in the Gaza Strip and along an otherwise demilitarised Sinai Peninsula, together with American guarantees for freedom of navigation in the Straits of Tiran. These conditions were granted.

Finally, a staged withdrawal was agreed upon. On 30 November 1956, one month after war broke out, troops were already being pulled back. On 15 January 1957, the IDF left El-'Arish. Israel tried, even this late, to bargain again for the Gaza Strip and the Straits, but to no avail. The IDF completed its withdrawal from the Gaza Strip on 6 March 1957. Finally, on March 8, the last forces were pulled out of Sharm el-Sheikh. Behind the withdrawing troops, IDF tractors ploughed up the roads, in a symbolic gesture of defiance.

The public mood was harsh in Israel during the winter of 1957, in stark contrast with the euphoria which had prevailed during and immediately after the war. Still, it was very different from the anxious mood of just one year earlier, when the government had asked the public to volunteer to dig trenches in border settlements, when school children gave their allowance for arms purchase, when everybody knew that "there will be war next summer" and was terrified at the prospect.

Ben-Gurion, Dayan, Peres

Lt.-General Moshe Dayan, Israel's Chief of Staff, was a central actor in each and every step along the road to war. In particular, one should note his contribution to the fateful meeting at Sèvres. His ability to translate Anglo-French ideas into operational military terms was decisive both in persuading the British finally to join in a tripartite effort and in allaying some of Ben-Gurion's concerns. The ideas presented by Dayan at Sèvres pleased all concerned: even more aggressive than anything the French dared propose, satisfactory to the British, fast enough for Israel.

This is not to say that Ben-Gurion was dragged into war kicking and screaming. Convincing him was not overly difficult, since he believed that war was inevitable in the long term and preferred to have Israel initiate rather than respond to it. He sought only an opportunity, the right combination of circumstances. Once Dayan and Peres were able to show him that this had been achieved, he was satisfied. Ben-Gurion's general approach, in fact, remained steady from the intensification of Egyptian-inspired terrorist attacks on Israel in March 1955, through the Sèvres conference in October 1956. Throughout, his attitude was a combination of willingness to go to war in principle, tempered by concern about a move which might leave Israel in an untenable position, militarily or politically. It is hardly imaginable that he would have gone to Paris for an academic discussion of ideas about war and peace. He was genuinely outraged by the "pretext" scenario, finding it difficult to swallow a pretence which cast Israel in the role of aggressor, while its partners would play the parts of unimpeachable peacemakers. However, once persuaded that a tripartite military collaboration would provide Israel with the security it needed in a war, and having been in favour of an initiated war to begin with, Ben-Gurion signed the Sèvres agreement.

Domestically, Ben-Gurion had no problems obtaining public acceptance for the decision. Both the political system and the public at large had long been prepared for such a move. Thus the formal Cabinet decision was made only one day in advance, on October 28, without significant opposition. After all, the groundwork had been laid since April 1955. The Cabinet was only partially aware of the factors which had made up the leadership's mind. The ministers knew about the collaboration with France and Britain, but were never briefed about the practical details. The IDF's most senior officers were in the same situation, or even more so. And the public at large was completely ignorant of the war's underpinnings.

Ben-Gurion, Dayan, Peres and a handful of aides did an impressive job in keeping the Sèvres agreement secret. Underlying their efforts in this regard were Anglo-French demands and the hope that Israel's aggressive role could be swept under the carpet. The cover story, an aggressive move aimed eastwards, was readily available for use. The "eastern front" problem was real and acute for Israel before the war, and the three leaders utilised it to deceive not only the country's enemies but everyone else as well, including the IDF itself. But beyond this, the intention was to seize any opportunity which might come along in order to sort out a series of very real problems along Israel's uncomfortable boundaries with Jordan and Syria, at least in such sensitive areas as Jerusalem or the eastern shore of the Sea of Galilee. The best deception is one founded on solid ground.

It has not been the purpose of this book to elucidate the professional military aspects of the war itself; such aspects are only dealt with in passing, when they touch upon the main themes. Generally speaking, though, it can be said that the Sinai war taught the IDF more about its shortcomings than about its strengths. Still, it took the IDF just one week to conquer most of the Sinai Peninsula.

Israel became involved in the Sinai War largely through the combination of Peres's political flair and Dayan's military daring. Both of them genuinely admired Ben-Gurion, but they also knew how to manipulate him in the direction they thought right, and nudge him when they felt that he wanted to act but dared not. Dayan and Peres completely acknowledged Ben-Gurion's authority, but unlike almost everyone else in Israel's political and military systems, they were not afraid of him. Their supreme confidence was an inspiration to the French officials and officers who were in contact with them during the preparations for the war and earlier.

From the time Dayan and Peres were appointed to their respective offices – on the same day, 6 December 1953 – relations between the Israeli and French defence establishments grew ever closer. The personal ties that were cultivated in France by the Chief of Staff and the Director-General of the Ministry of Defence, beginning in 1954, were instrumental in bringing about the alliance of June 1956, which in turn made possible the joint campaign against Egypt that October.

Did Dayan and Peres seek war at any cost? Probably the "red line" in this regard was, very clearly, the point at which Dayan's ability, with Peres's help, to persuade Ben-Gurion or manoeuvre him, ended. Ultimately, of course, everything depended on an explicit decision by the Prime Minister as to whether Israel should initiate a war. He had to be helped to make up his mind, but no one contemplated deciding for him.

The rest mattered little to Dayan. His disdain for the United States and the United Nations (reflecting both arrogance and ignorance, or at best naïveté), as well as for the military capabilities of the Arab states or the ability of his adversaries in Israel to stop him – this disdain brought him to the conclusion that Israel could initiate a war even without outside help. He believed, further, that no one could prevent Israel from reaping the full harvest of political and military advantages which such a war would certainly yield. For Dayan, the turn to France was intended primarily to allay Ben-Gurion's fears, since for the Chief of Staff the only real obstacle on the road to war was the Prime Minister's opposition. Even during the hostilities, what worried Dayan most during the crucial gap between the scheduled start of the allies' operation and its actual start was how Ben-Gurion would react. The apparent duplicity of Britain and France did not seem an insurmountable obstacle – but an explicit order by Ben-Gurion to withdraw the Israeli forces from Sinai would terminate the project.

At the personal level, each member of the triumvirate that led Israel into war in 1956 emerged much stronger in its aftermath. Ben-Gurion's status had suffered following his resignation in 1954, but was now restored. His domestic image was now that of a leader of international standing, capable of leading his country in an alliance with Great Powers. Israel's performance as an effective member of a coalition with world Powers impressed even those in Israel who objected to the campaign itself. It was Ben-Gurion who earned the credit for this. In 1955, his seemed to be near the end of his tether, but his party's impressive victory in the 1959 general elections, which kept him in power until 1963, was to a certain extent due to the impact of the Sinai War. Once the dust had settled and the war's results could be evaluated in a sober manner, public morale soared, particularly when it became clear that the borders were quiet. Israel began to perceive itself in a new way, and for that rewarded Ben-Gurion at the polls.

Moshe Dayan's career had been on the rise since 1949, but the Sinai War made him a recognised leader of national and indeed international renown. For the rest of his career, virtually until his death, his prestige was based on his most successful role: as Chief of Staff from December 1953 to January 1958. And the highlight of his tenure as head of the armed forces was the period leading up to and during the Sinai War.

Shimon Peres, despite his relative young age, established himself, following the war, as Ben-Gurion's closest confidant. He acquired the image of a manipulator who could devise and implement complex, sensitive moves domestically and internationally. His career, like Dayan's, gained considerable momentum from the war. Despite resistance from the Old Guard of Mapai (the ruling party), both Dayan and Peres consolidated their positions after the war. True, there was a brief cooling in their relations with Ben-Gurion immediately after the war, during the debate over withdrawal from Sinai, but both soon resumed their roles as the Prime Minister's chief aides. Already in the 1959 elections, both were placed on Mapai's list of candidates and became Knesset Members. From now on they were elected rather than appointed officials. In the government which Ben-Gurion formed after the elections, Dayan was Minister of Agriculture and Peres Deputy Minister of Defence.

The Short-Term and the Long-Term Results of the War

Some of Israel's war objectives were formulated in advance of the Sinai War, others as the fighting proceeded. Were these objectives, of either kind, achieved? Did the three leaders of Israel's war effort – Ben-Gurion, Dayan and Peres – have reason for satisfaction after the war? They had been looking for a war, and when it came it was fought under extraordinarily convenient circumstances. The military campaign was swift, and casualties were relatively small: 176 killed, one Israeli prisoner of war. The IDF crushed the Egyptian Army everywhere in Sinai and now controlled the entire peninsula, apart from a narrow 10-mile strip along the Suez Canal. On the other hand there was Israel's withdrawal from the Sinai – the opposite of victory. Israel moved out almost as fast as it had moved in.

A systematic evaluation of results against stated objectives serves little purpose. Some prior objectives were attained, others were not, while some results, even highly favourable from Israel's point of view, were not formulated as objectives before the war.

Israel's short-term objectives, before the war, were to strengthen its alliance with France, neutralise the British threat, see Nasser's regime in Egypt removed, and open the Straits of Tiran – "Israel's Suez". It should be pointed out that the elimination of terrorism from Egyptian-controlled territory, an obvious *casus belli*, was never set as a direct war objective. Of all these, what did Israel achieve? With the exception of Nasser's downfall, Israel emerged with everything it wanted. The alliance with France was tightened to the point that France helped Israel set up its nuclear reactor at Dimona in 1958. The British threat was totally removed; in fact, in the late 1950s Israel's relations with Britain reached new heights of cordiality, recalling the early days of the British Mandate in Palestine. Generally speaking, Israel's value as a strategic asset in the Middle East was at last recognised by the West. Although Israel's standing with the non-aligned nations was somewhat tarnished because of its collaboration with unreconstructed imperialism, it was able to develop close links with several countries in Asia, and subsequently with many in Africa. In addition, the willingness of Iran, Turkey and Ethiopia to respond, at least in part, to Ben-Gurion's efforts to set up an "alliance of peripheral states" (i.e., non-Arab) in the Middle East, in the late 1950s, was very much a result of Israel's display of strength in the Sinai War.

The Straits of Tiran were opened to Israeli navigation and remained open until May 1967. It will be recalled that Ben-Gurion and Dayan wanted a permanent Israeli presence along the eastern Sinai coast, to secure the sea lanes to and from Eilat. They were able to get this included in the Sèvres agreement, but it did not materialise. Still, Israel obtained guarantees for its freedom of navigation from the US and the UN (Dayan's disdain notwithstanding), and Eilat began its transformation from a wilderness outpost into a flourishing port and major tourist attraction.

Nasser and his regime were not removed. On the contrary, in the short term Nasser's personal prestige, within Egypt and outside it, was much enhanced. His political victory over the tripartite coalition, which immediately after the war was forced to relinquish all its material gains, was obvious. In retrospect, though, it can be argued that the Sinai War gave another push to the process that eventuated in Nasserism's final downfall. The growing animosity between Egypt and the West, the Soviet bear hug, the fervour with which Egypt prepared for the "next round" with Israel instead of addressing its acute social and economic problems – all these distanced Nasser's regime from the original objectives of the Free Officers. When they assumed power, in 1952, they had wanted to save Egypt for the Egyptians. But by the time of Nasser's death in 1970, Egypt was deeply mired in a host of domestic problems, many of them heightened by its crushing defeat by Israel in June 1967 – this time, a defeat without a subsequent political victory. Suez, then, was a significant landmark on the road down, for Nasser and his regime.

Israel, though, also had long-range objectives. To begin with, it sought to reduce the level of military threat and change conditions in the Middle East in its favour. The answer to the question of whether Israel achieved these aims is necessarily more complex. For a while, at least, the level of military threat did subside. The Sinai War ushered in what came to be known as the "quiet decade" of 1957–67, a lengthy period – in Israeli terms – without a major war. This second decade of Israeli statehood was a period of impressive achievements. The social and economic progress which had its inception in the previous decade was consolidated. Israel emerged as a modern democracy, adopting Western social and cultural patterns. The question of Israel's physical survival seemed to have been resolved, at least until the 1967 crisis broke out.

For the IDF, this period of calm was an unexpectedly lengthy opportunity to rebuild, train and prepare itself for the next war on the basis of lessons learned in the Sinai War. It was a time of continuous military build-up in Israel, aided first by the French and then, on a larger scale by the Americans. Reports, couched in ambiguous language, began to filter out that Israel might have nuclear capability as a result of its alliance with France. The ambiguity served both to deter Israel's Arab enemies and strengthen Israel's links with the US, which now considered it imperative to increase its influence *vis-à-vis* Israel and provide it with means that would make it unnecessary to resort to doomsday measures in a critical situation.

The tranquillity along Israel's border with Egypt, due (at least in part) to the presence of UN peacekeeping forces, reflected on the other borders, although these were never as calm as the Egyptian-Israeli one. It took until 1967 for Egypt to join in an all-Arab war effort against Israel, following years of gradual escalation between Israel and Syria over the allocation and use of water resources, and security problems along the Jordanian border. Egypt's lengthy reticence was almost certainly a direct result of Israel's military success (with its allies' help) in 1956; while the US and the UN became more involved in Middle Eastern affairs, Egypt contemplated its options very carefully before making a move against Israel.

At the same time, another point also bears consideration, a dynamic which Ben-Gurion had pointed out already in the early 1950s, namely, that the conclusion of each war is the first step towards the next one. Thus, from the present-day perspective, it is clear that the Sinai War greatly intensified Egyptian hostility towards Israel. In 1948, Egypt had gone to war against Israel very reluctantly. The results of that war, however, sowed in Egypt seeds of animosity towards Israel which had hitherto hardly existed. The Sinai War only augmented these. From 1956, Egypt had yet another reason to settle the score with Israel. Although some Israeli leaders felt that an Israeli victory was a necessary step towards peace (by proving that military force could not liquidate Israel), the Sinai War in fact made the next round almost inevitable.

From this perspective, it is also important to note that the Sinai War had no effect on Israel's geopolitical situation: Israel gained nothing from the war which could have afforded it a better strategic posture for the next clash. Still, even if the geostrategic aspect was unchanged, the IDF, as pointed out earlier, bettered itself quantitatively and qualitatively and gained useful combat experience in the Sinai War, all of which placed it in an improved position for the "third round". Research on this point is far from adequate, but it seems that the lessons of 1956 were internalised by the IDF in preparation for 1967. In this view, the Sinai War can be regarded as a very useful exercise.

Israeli historiography tends to belittle the import of the Sinai War. Nevertheless, it was through this war that Israel underwent a transformation from a state whose right to exist had rested on a moral foundation only, into a regional power whose interests must be taken into account in every calculation. Yet this depiction could also be carried too far. The war in general, and Dayan's flamboyance in particular, tended to create a feeling in Israel of an omnipotent Israel capable of vanquishing any foe in one fell swoop – almost a world power. Most scholars attribute this sentiment, which is still all too prevalent, to the results of the 1967 Six-Day War. The seeds, though, were planted in 1956. In 1949, Israel did not emerge from its War of Independence with the feeling of a "power high" as it did in the aftermath of the Sinai War seven years later. The disappointments of withdrawal soon faded, and what lingered was the sense of forcefulness and confidence produced by military and political achievements. Therefore, even though historiography tends to downplay the Sinai War as compared with other Israeli wars, larger in scope and in death toll, there is no doubt that the initiative which led to the war, the course of the war itself, and its aftermath constitute a highly significant landmark in the history of the State of Israel.

Chronology of Events of the Suez Crisis and the Sinai War

1955

Jan. 4 US, Britain and France call on Egypt to lift ban on passage of Israeli ships through Suez Canal.

Feb. 20 David Ben-Gurion, Israel's "founding father," returns to government Defence Minister after being voluntarily out of office since December 1953.

Feb. 25 Israeli murdered by infiltrators from Gaza Strip.

Feb. 28 Operation Gaza: Israeli forces attack Egyptian Army positions north of Gaza City.

Mar. 25 Israeli woman murdered during wedding celebration at Moshav Patish in southern Israel.

Mar. 26 For first time, Ben-Gurion and Israeli Chief of Staff Moshe Dayan put forward demand for Israeli-initiated war against Egypt.

Mar. 30 UN Security Council unanimously condemns Israel for Operation Gaza.

Apr. 5 Anthony Eden replaces Winston Churchill as Prime Minister of Britain.

Aug. 20–
Sep. 4 Israel-Egypt border heats up to brink of war.

Aug. 26 US Secretary of State John Foster Dulles announces Anglo-American "Plan Alpha" to resolve Arab-Israeli conflict.

Sep. 12 Egypt reimposes ban on passage of Israeli ships through Straits of Tiran.

Sep. 28 Egyptian President Gamal Abd el-Nasser announces arms deal of unprecedented scope with Czechoslovakia.

Oct. 23 Ben-Gurion orders preparation of offensive to capture Straits of Tiran.

Nov. 2 Ben-Gurion again Prime Minister.

Dec. 4 Israeli Cabinet decides time is not appropriate for war.

1956

Jan.–May Eve-of-war atmosphere in Israel, Egypt expected to attack in summer, mediation efforts by US (in secret) and UN.

Feb. 6 New socialist government in France with Guy Mollet as Prime Minister.

Mar. 2 Jordan's King Hussein dismisses John Glubb Pasha, British

	founder and commander of the (Jordanian) Arab Legion.
May 4	French Defense Minister Bourgès-Maunoury and director-general of Israel's Defence Ministry Shimon Peres agree on main points of Franco-Israeli alliance.
June 13	Last British soldier leaves Suez Canal Zone as part of October 1954 Anglo-Egyptian agreement.
June 17	Israeli Foreign Minister Moshe Sharett removed from office.
June 24–26	Franco-Israel alliance signed at Vermars Conference.
Early July	Joint Franco-Israeli HQ begins operations in Paris.
July 19	US informs Egypt that because of Nasser's refusal to reduce ties with USSR, Washington will not underwrite construction of Aswan High Dam on the Nile.
July 24	First French arms shipment as part of the new alliance reaches Israel clandestinely.
July 26	Suez Crisis erupts: Nasser announces nationalisation of Suez Canal in reaction to American refusal to finance Aswan Dam project.
July 27	Eden decides to attack Egypt.
July 31	British Joint Planning Conference briefs chiefs of forces on plan to invade Suez Canal Zone via Port Sa'id.
Aug. 1	Britain chooses "Musketeer" as codename for projected war.
Aug. 9	First meeting of joint Anglo-French planning team within Operation Musketeer framework.
Aug. 18–23	Canal Users Conference (first London Conference) held at American pressure.
Aug. 22	Anglo-French HQ for Musketeer set up under command of General Sir Charles Keightley.
Aug. 24	Eden approves first version of Musketeer, "Alexandria Plan".
Sep. 1	Israeli General Staff discusses operation of Armoured Corps in possible future war.
——	France asks Israel to begin military talks with view to possible Israeli participation in Operation Musketeer.
Sep. 7	Major General Meir 'Amit, head of Operations Branch, meets with French Army personnel involved in preparing Operation Musketeer.
Sep. 9–12	Menzies Commission, set up by Canal Users Conference, unsuccessful in mission to Cairo.
Sep. 12	Britain and France inform Security Council that Nasser's rejection of Menzies Commission jeopardizes peace and security.
Sep. 13	Eden declares establishment of Suez Canal Users Association.
Sep. 18	Bourgès-Maunoury and Peres reach preliminary agreement on Israel's participation in Anglo-French Operation Musketeer.
Sep. 26	British and French Prime Ministers and Foreign Ministers meet in Paris.
Sep. 9– *Oct. 11*	Series of sabotage raids, border incidents and Israeli reprisals along Jordanian border; Britain threatens to intervene.
Sep. 10	Eden approves new plan (Musketeer Revise), basically a return to conception that prevailed at the end of July.
Sep. 19–21	Second Canal Users Conference in London.
Sep. 30 –	

Oct. 1   St. Germain conference: Israel and France agree on Israel's place in planned war with Egypt.

Oct. 1   Revised Operation Musketeer becomes "Winter Plan", i.e., Musketeer with more protracted schedule to suit approaching winter conditions

Oct. 5   Dayan orders Israeli army (IDF) to prepare plan for war against Egypt; codename: "Operation Kadesh".

Oct. 14   Meeting at Chequers, official residence of British Prime Minister: French General Challe explains to Eden the "pretext idea" by which a staged Israeli attack near the Canal will provide the pretext for Britain and France to launch a joint offensive against Egypt

——   UN attempts to engineer compromise between Canal-user states and Egypt fail irrevocably.

Oct. 15   Meeting of British and French Prime Ministers and Foreign Ministers at Matignon Palace in Paris: agreement reached on the conspiracy.

Oct. 16   Ben-Gurion agrees to attend tripartite meeting.

——   IDF completes preparations for war against Egypt ("Kadesh 1").

Oct. 21–24 Sèvres Conference in Paris suburb: tripartite conspiracy worked out.

Oct. 21   French advance force arrives in Israel.

Oct. 24   Sèvres agreement signed.

——   Musketeer HQ gets go-ahead to begin moves towards war, though forces advancing into Mediterranean think they are part of military exercise codenamed "Boathook".

Oct. 25   Keightley informs commanders of the units that "Musketeer Revise" again in force; timetable in effect that day means Canal landing unfeasible before Nov. 5–6.

——   Mass military call-up begins in Israel.

Oct. 26   Israel revises war plan in light of Sèvres agreement: "Kadesh 2".

——   Eden ratifies Sèvres agreement.

Oct. 27–28 US President Eisenhower warns Ben-Gurion not to attack Jordan.

Oct. 29   Sinai War begins: Israeli paratroop battalion air-dropped in western Sinai to create impression of offensive against Suez Canal.

——   British, with American backing, try to bomb strategic targets in Syria: "Operation Straggle".

Oct. 30   Britain and France submit "ultimatum" to Israel and Egypt warning that if they do not withdraw, the two powers will intervene.

——   IDF enters eastern Sinai contrary to advance plan.

Oct. 31   Start of Anglo-French air operation against Suez Canal Zone.

Nov. 2   End of fighting in central and northern Sinai.

——   UN General Assembly decides on immediate cease-fire and withdrawal of IDF from Sinai.

Nov. 3   Encounter between Israeli planes and British destroyer in Straits of Tiran.

Nov. 4   French planes lift off from Israel for depth-bombing strikes in Egypt.

——   Israel agrees to cease-fire but retracts consent under Anglo-French pressure.

Nov. 5	IDF completes takeover of Sinai Pensinsula apart from Suez Canal.
———	Anglo-French invasion of Egypt begins, Port Sa'id and Port Fuad captured.
Nov. 6	Israel seizes islands of Tiran and Sanafir in Straits of Tiran.
———	Sinai War concludes: cease-fire under pressure of Superpowers, Anglo-French force stops around town of Kantara in northern Canal Zone.
Nov. 8	Israel states readiness in principle to withdraw from Sinai Peninsula.
Dec. 22	Anglo-French forces leave Egypt.

1957

Mar. 7	End of Suez Crisis: Israel concludes withdrawal from Sinai.

Notes

Details of published material are given in full in the Bibliography.

Abbreviations:

BGA   Ben-Gurion Archives, Ben-Gurion Heritage Institute, Kibbutz Sde Boker
BGD   Ben-Gurion's personal diary, kept at BGA
CoSBD   Chief of Staff's Bureau diary
PRO   Public Records Office, London
SA   Israel State Archives, Jerusalem
SCP   Supreme Command Post
SHAA   Service Historique de l'Armée de l'Air, Paris

Chapter 1: Israel on the Road to War

1   Israel Police, monthly reports: SA 2429/1–3, 2428/2, 2402/14–13.
2   Ya'ari 1975, pp. 20–1; Khouri 1985, p. 200; Sharett 1978C, pp. 837–8. On Nasser's contacts with Israel following Operation Gaza, see Bar-On 1988, ch. 7.
3   Dayan 1976, p. 142; BGD, 1 March 1955.
4   Dayan 1976.
5   Sharett 1978, vol. 3, p. 894.
6   BGD, 2 March 1955; weekly meetings files, nos 822 through 897, BGA.
7   Sharett 1978, vol. 3, pp. 816, 894.
8   Dayan 1976, p. 124.
9   Sharett 1978C, pp. 666, 669.
10 Dayan 1976, p. 125; Sharett 1978, vol. 2, pp. 591; Peres 1965, p. 11.
11 Teveth 1972, p. 413; Dayan 1976, p. 129.
12 Sharett 1978C, pp. 639; S. Peres, Night of Decision (unpublished manuscript, in my possession – M.G.), pp. 49–50.
13 Dayan 1976, pp. 122–3, 125; BGD, 20 August 1954; Ben-Gurion's discussions with Mapam leaders Chazan and Ya'ari, 7 August 1955: BGA, Meetings Protocols.
14 Evron 1989.
15 Y. Teko'a, "In the Armistice Commission and on Israel's Borders", memorandum by the Director for Armistice Affairs at the Israeli Foreign Ministry, 6 September 1955: SA 2454/7; Sharett 1978, vol. 3, pp. 1096–7.

16 Teko'a (note 15); Burns 1962, pp. 69–84.
17 Chief of Intelligence Col. Harkabi at General Staff meeting, 29 August 1955.
18 "Operation Elkayam: The Raid on the Khan Yunis Police Station and Outpost 132", internal report, IDF.
19 IDF, *Current Security Review, 1951–1956*; IDF, *Restrictions on the Movements of Foreign Elements*, 1956. Concerning the cease-fire negotiations, see Teko'a (note 15).
20 IDF, General Staff Branch/Operations, *Operational Instruction No. 2* and *Operational Instruction for 1 September 1955*; IDF, *Current Security Review, 1951–1956*.
21 Teko'a (note 15); Ya'ari 1975, pp. 20–2; Weekly Meeting, 5 September 1955, Minister of Defence Bureau files. Concerning order of combat in the south, see: IDF, General Staff Branch/Operations, *Operational Instruction No. 7*, 6 September 1955. Concerning lessons from the "near-war" with Egypt in early September 1955, see, for example: Israel Air Force, Commanding Officer's Bureau, "Summary of Lessons from Operation Tempo" 10 October 1955.
22 Sharett 1978, vol. 2, p. 332.

Chapter 2: The Egyptian–Czech Deal

1 On Egypt's arms deal with the USSR (through Czechoslovakia) see: Bar-On 1992, pp. 13–16; Kyle 1991, pp. 72–5.
2 Steigman 1990, p. 123; Bar-On 1991, pp. 12–13. According to Bar-On, of the 230 tanks involved 60 were Stalin IIIs. No further evidence for this was found elsewhere.
3 Israel Foreign Ministry, Information Dept., "News for Israeli Legations Overseas", 19 October 1955, which included a statement by the Prime Minister: SA 2446/10/b; Sharett 1978, vol. 4, p. 1182.
4 Ya'ari 1975, pp. 21–2; IDF, *IDF Operational Activities, 1955–1956*, 1957. The latter reference is based on debriefings made immediately following the various operations.
5 IDF, Operational Orders: Tzefa Hol, Shahar, Omer.
6 Sharett 1978, vol. 4, p. 1193.
7 IDF, Operational Orders Omer and Zohar, 15 November 1955. For the first Omer postponement, see: Dayan 1976, p. 165; for the second, see Dayan's comments at the weekly meeting, 22 December 1955: Minister of Defence Bureau files.
8 Weekly meeting, 8 November 1955: Minister of Defence Bureau files. Concerning civil defence reorganisation, see weekly meetings during November–December 1955.
9 Weekly meeting, 8 November 1955: Minister of Defence Bureau files; Ben-Gurion's letter to Galili, 30 November 1955: BGA-Correspondence. On the 22 December postponement, see: Dayan 1976, p. 169.
10 Concerning the Cabinet meeting, see: Dayan 1966, pp. 18–19. On Ben-Gurion's address to General Staff forum, see: Dayan 1976, p. 174. Comments to the same effect can also be found in a letter from Ben-Gurion to members of Mapai, 28 June 1956: BGA-Correspondence; 'Amit 1986, p. 2.
11 Ben-Gurion's continued support of the principle of preventive war is indicated, for example, in an exchange of notes with Galili in January and

March 1956. See BGA-General Chronological Documentation, 3 January, 6 March 1956. Bar-On notes without explanation the contradiction between the Cabinet's decision and the IDF's continued preparations: Bar-On 1990, p. 197.

12 Statement by the Chief of Staff, General Staff meeting, 26 October 1956; Ben-Gurion's comments at the weekly meeting, 1 December 1955; Ben-Gurion's letter to Kollek, 29 April 1956: SA 2448, Eliav's files.

13 See, for example, review by Chief of Intelligence Harkabi at General Staff meeting, 3 April 1956.

14 Author's interview with Harkabi, 24 August 1991.

15 Quoted from the original summation of the Sinai War and its background according to CoSBD kept by Lt.-Col. M. Bar-On: *Challenge and Conflict: Israel's Defence Campaigns in the Year 5717* [Hebrew calendar = 1956/7], 15 September, 1958. The original document exists in four typescript copies, one of which was made available to the author courtesy of Dr Bar-On. The original diary was later converted (with significant deletions) into a book: Bar-On 1991, p. 15.

16 Sharett 1978, vol. 5, p. 1327.

17 Concerning Egyptian Army deployment in the Sinai, see: Harkabi at General Staff meeting, 3 April 1956; Bendman 1978, pp. 944–7.

18 It should be pointed out that this discussion concerns the official announcement of the deal, rather than its actual conclusion. Concerning Israel's relations with the USSR, see statements to the Knesset by Ben-Gurion and Sharett, 2 January 1956. The former is quoted in Ben-Gurion 1971, pp. 225–36, the latter in SA 2446/10/b. On the idea of seeking arms from the USSR, see also: Sharett 1978, vol. 5, p. 1324.

19 See exchange of notes between Ben-Gurion and Galili, 2 March 1956: BGA-General Chronological Documentation.

20 Weekly meetings, 17 November, 1 December 1955. Sharett shared Ben-Gurion's views on this point; see his statement to the Knesset, note 18 above.

21 Weekly meeting, 1 December 1955.

22 Weekly meetings, 8, 17 November, 1 December 1955; Bar-On 1988, pp. 25–6.

23 Sharett's statement to the Knesset, note 18 above. On Plan Alpha, see: Shamir 1989. See also Ben-Gurion's comments on the role played by the USA and France, weekly meeting, 17 November 1955.

24 Peres described his unusual methods of securing arms sources for Israel in his unpublished journal, Night of Decision; he also expressed there his views on Ben-Gurion's priorities. See also Peres's discussion with senior members of his Ministry, 17 November, 28 December 1955.

25 Ben-Gurion's statement at weekly meeting, 1 December 1955; Evron 1986, p. 33. Although Evron's account seems slightly exaggerated, it does reflect Ben-Gurion's intentions.

26 Tzur 1972, pp. 271–2, 286.

27 Ben-Gurion's letter to Peres in Paris, 22 April 1956: BGA-Correspondence.

28 Statements to the Knesset by Ben-Gurion, 22 April 1956, and by Sharett, 23 April 1956; Ben-Gurion at weekly meeting, 8 December 1955.

29 Ben-Gurion's letter to Mapai members, 28 June 1956: BGA-Correspondence.

Chapter 3: The Israeli Deal

1 Addresses by the Chief of Staff and the Director-General of the Defence Ministry at a conference of senior officers, 8 February 1956.

2 Concerning the Jackson mission, as well as other mediation missions, see the "Anderson File" prepared at the Foreign Ministry prior to the arrival of the US President's representative: "Talks and Contacts Regarding Possible Settlement between Israel and Egypt, 1949–1955", written by Pinhas Eliav, 16 January 1956: SA 2454/2; see also detailed discussion in Kyle 1991.

3 For a description of the internal situation in France and French motives, see: Horne 1977, ch. 7; see also Peres, Night of Decision. For the French perspective, see the memoirs of Christian Pineau, then French Foreign Minister: Pineau 1976. The French perspective on the Suez Crisis is elaborated in ch. 4.

4 Dayan's comments in discussions on arms procurements at General Staff meetings, 23 January and 26 February 1956; Peres, Night of Decision.

5 Tzur 1968, pp. 269–73.

6 On the Vermars conference, see: Bar-On 1958, pp. 429–30; Dayan 1976, pp. 200–18; see also Bar-On 1991, pp. 153–9. For the political background to the conference, see: Bar-On 1988, ch. 10 (Bar-On was present at the conference). See also the author's interview with Harkabi, 24 August 1991.

7 Weekly meeting, 27 June 1956.

8 Bar-On 1958, pp. 431–59; Dayan 1976, p. 206.

9 Bar-On 1958, pp. 434–6; quoting Dayan verbatim, with slight modifications.

10 *Ibid.*, p. 436.

11 *Ibid.*, p. 438. On Operation Straggle against Syria, see: Gorst and Lucas, 1989. Concerning American fears about a possible *coup* in Syria, see, for example: FRUS XVI, p. 165.

12 Bar-On 1958, pp. 438–9.

13 *Ibid.*, p. 439.

14 Cable from Chief of Intelligence to Zore'a in Paris, 6 July 1956: in Bar-On 1958, p. 440.

15 Cable from Mission in Paris to Chief of Intelligence, in: *ibid.*, pp. 440–1.

16 *Ibid.*

17 *Ibid.*, pp. 441–2.

18 *Ibid.*

19 Report by Ne'eman to the Chief of Staff, 20 July, 1956: in *ibid.*, pp. 450–2.

20 *Ibid.*

21 *Ibid.*, p. 458.

22 *Ibid.*, pp. 443–8.

23 *Ibid.*, p. 446.

24 *Ibid.*, p. 449.

25 Ya'ari 1975, pp. 27–31. Ya'ari relates the story of the assassination of Col. Mustafa Hafez, Chief of Egyptian Intelligence in the Gaza Strip, in July 1956. For a different source: Argaman 1990, pp. 15–30.

26 Bar-On 1958, p. 447.

27 *Ibid.*, p. 448.

28 Report by Chief of Intelligence, Col. Y. Harkabi, from the Vermars conference, p. 429.

29 Bar-On 1958, p. 430; Ben-Gurion's letter to Mapai members, 28 June 1956: BGA-Correspondence.
30 Dayan 1976, p. 207.
31 Bar-On 1958, p. 436; General Staff meeting, 19 July 1956.

Chapter 4: The Suez Crisis

1 Concerning the legal aspects of the Canal's nationalisation, see for example: Kyle 1991, pp. 138–43. For the memorandum by the legal advisor to the British Foreign Office, see letter from Kirkpatrick to Fitzmorris, 31 October 1956: PRO FO800/747.
2 On the Conference of Canal Users and the Menzies mission, see: Thomas 1967, chs 10–12.
3 BGD, 3 August 1956.
4 Horne 1979, pp. 8–9 (page references are to the 1989 Hebrew translation).
5 *Ibid.*, pp. 29–30.
6 Neff 1981, p. 161.
7 Horne 1979, pp. 155–6.
8 Tzur 1968, p. 100.
9 See Horne 1979, p. 162; Neff 1981, pp. 161–2. Bourges-Maunoury's address is quoted by Bar-On 1988, p. 156.
10 Horne 1979, p. 155–6, 166; Bar-On 1988, p. 159.
11 Bar-On 1958; Tzur 1968, pp. 230–1.
12 Tzur 1968, pp. 244–5.
13 *Ibid.*, pp. 247, 257–8.
14 Martin 1990, pp. 54–5.
15 This is based on conclusions reached by Vaisse, a French historian who studied the Suez Crisis, and on Beaufre's testimony: Vaisse 1989, pp. 137, 337; Beaufre 1969, p. 23.
16 Martin 1990, pp. 54–9.
17 See, for example, testimony by Adam Watson, who in 1956 was Head of the Africa Department at the British Foreign Office, in charge of Algerian affairs: Watson 1990, pp. 341–46.
18 Chanderli is quoted in: Horne 1979, pp. 132–3.
19 Neff 1981, pp. 161–2.
20 Report by Israeli Military Attaché in Paris, Col. Nishri, to the Chief of Staff, 13 May 1955. Gen. Guillaumat was interviewed by Sylvia Crosbie: Crosbie 1974, p. 46.
21 Neff 1981, pp. 160–2.
22 This view is supported by Crosbie (1974, p. 46).
23 Concerning the way this debate was viewed by the Chief of Staff's bureau, see: Bar-On 1991, pp. 140–3. For the Ministry of Defence view, see: Peres, Night of Decision.
24 Author's interview with Harkabi, 24 August 1991.
25 See chapter 3.
26 Peres to Minister of Defence, "Report on My Visit to Europe".
27 Tzur 1968, pp. 255–6.
28 On the lead-up to the Vermars conference, the conference itself, and the French-Israeli convergence of interests against the background of the Algerian war, see: Bar-On 1991, pp. 144–54. On France's military difficulties in dealing with the rebels in Algeria, see: Horne 1979.

29 This view appears in Horne, 1979, pp. 166–9. It is no coincidence that in the French Air Force Archive (SHAA) at Vincense, for example, documents relating to the Sinai War are subject to the same restrictions that apply to the war in Algeria. According to the Head of the Historical Service at French Air Force HQ, Gen. Robineau (interview with the author, 16 April 1991), this material will become available to the general public together with the material on the Algerian war.

30 Louis 1989, pp. 43–71.

31 *Ibid.*, pp. 55–9.

32 *Ibid.*, pp. 60–3.

33 *Ibid.*, pp. 46–7.

34 *Ibid.*, pp. 66–7.

35 *Ibid.*, pp. 62–3, 66.

36 Kyle 1989, pp. 103–4.

37 Louis 1989, p. 48.

38 Kyle 1989, pp. 105–9. Kyle quotes a memorandum from Shuckburgh to Foreign Minister Macmillan dated 23 September 1955. See also: Shuckburgh 1986, p. 281.

39 See, for example, the description of the Suez Crisis by Minister of State at the Foreign Office Anthony Nutting, who during the entire crisis was in strong opposition to Eden: Nutting 1967, pp. 17–18. For a more sympathetic description of Eden's role in the crisis, see: James 1986; Bellof 1989, pp. 319.

40 Carlton 1988, pp. 18–19, 63–4.

41 Concerning the centrality of the "spirit of Munich" in Eden's perception, shared by some members of his government and party, see: Eden to Eisenhower, 10 January 1956: PRO, PREM11/1170/183005; Bellof 1989, pp. 328–30. This attitude, which saw Nasser as a new Hitler, was also prevalent in France: Crosbie 1974, pp. 18–19.

42 Louis 1989, p. 47. Concerning Eden's attitude towards Israel, see, for example: Eden to Secretary of State for Foreign Affairs (Nutting), 26 July 1956: AP 20/21/159.

43 For a thorough analysis of the Eden-Nasser relationship, and their relevance to the Suez Crisis, see: Kyle 1991, pp. 39–61.

44 See: Nutting 1967, pp. 28–35. On Nasser, see: Heikal 1972, pp. 84–7. On the impact of the crisis atmosphere in which Eden found himself, see also: Lamb 1987, pp. 183–97.

45 Louise 1989, p. 47.

46 Kyle 1991, pp. 39–61.

Chapter 5: Someone Else's Problem: The Israeli Perspective

1 Weekly meeting, 9 August 1956. Quoted from a discussion about training 17-year-old youths to form a reserve force for deployment in border settlements in a war.

2 Ben-Gurion to US Ambassador Lawson, 4 July 1956; Ben-Gurion to French Ambassador Gilbert, 6 July 1956: BGA-Correspondence. See also Tzur 1972, p. 273.

3 See, for example, a general discussion of Israel's defence problems at a General Staff meeting held at the Prime Minister's Office in Jerusalem, 19 July 1956.

4 Weekly meeting, 23 July 1956.
5 General Staff meeting, 19 July 1956.
6 Weekly meeting, 23 July 1956.
7 Dayan 1976, p. 210; General Staff meeting, 19 July 1956.
8 Hence it is obvious why most published memoirs by contemporaries make no mention of discussions of an Israeli-initiated war before the outbreak of the Suez Crisis, or even afterward. This was a well-kept secret until access was granted to archives recently. See: Dayan 1976, p. 210; BGD, 14 August 1956; weekly meeting, attended also by Foreign Minister Meir, 17 August 1956; Tzur 1972, pp. 270–2.
9 BGD, 30 July 1956; Dayan 1976, p. 221.
10 BGD, 19 August 1956; weekly meeting, 31 August 1956.
11 Alterman's verse is included in the *Knesset Record*, 15 October 1956: Statement by the Prime Minister, vol. XXI, nos 1–21, pp. 57–65.
12 Prof. Dan Laor made available to the author material from his study of the Ben-Gurion-Alterman relationship, against the background of preparations for the Sinai War. See also: Dayan 1976, p. 217; Bar-Zohar 1987C, pp. 1201–3; BGD, 30 July, 3 August 1956; Steigman 1990, pp. 144–6.
13 Dayan 1976, pp. 219–20; BGD, 3 August 1956.
14 Peres 1972, pp. 155–6; Bar-Zohar 1987C, p. 1210.
15 Bar-On 1958, pp. 429–59. When Col. Uzi Narkiss arrived in Paris as Military Attaché in 1959, he found that the intelligence collaboration (Zagit) file had not been changed since June 1956: author's interview with Narkiss, 24 September 1990. See also: Dayan 1976, p. 218; BGD, 2 August 1956; Bar-On 1991, p. 183; Steigman 1990, p. 166.
16 Dayan 1976, p. 220; BGD, 2 August 1956; Bar-On 1991, p. 183–5.
17 Bar-Zohar 1987, vol. 3,, pp. 1210–11.
18 BGD, 5, 6, 13 August 1956.
19 BGD, 5 August 1956.
20 Dayan 1976, pp. 218–19.
21 BGD, 9 August 1956. Concerning American U-2 flights over Israel, see: Brugioni 1992, pp. 33–5.
22 BGD, 10, 14, 19, 22 August 1956; Dayan 1976, pp. 220–1.
23 Steigman 1986, pp. 69–71.
24 BGD, 15 August 1956.
25 Cable from Israel's UN legation (Abba Eban) to the Foreign Ministry, 30 August 1956: SA 2450/3; exchange of cables between the Israeli embassy in Washington and the Foreign Ministry, 21, 26 August 1956, *ibid*.
26 Bar-On 1958, p. 530; this is the only source on this matter. It is not mentioned elsewhere, including Bar-On 1991, which, as noted (note 15 to ch. 2), is an edited version of the original.
27 *Ibid.*, p. 531.
28 Taken down by Chief of Staff's aide Bar-On: *ibid.*
29 Chief of Staff to the Military Attaché in Paris, 26 August 1956: *ibid.*, p. 532.
30 Cable from Col. Nishri to Col. Ne'eman, 25 August 1956: *ibid.*
31 Dayan to Ne'eman: *ibid.*, p. 533.
32 Ne'eman to Dayan, 29 August 1956: *ibid.*
33 Dayan to Ne'eman: *ibid.*

Chapter 6: *Vive la France et Israel*

1   Dayan to Laskov (his second-in-command), 28 June 1956; Ne'eman 1987, pp. 30–1. Ne'eman's article is filled with inaccuracies, but nevertheless important, since he was at the nexus of Israeli-French military collaboration at the time. See the author's interview with Ne'eman, 11 January 1990.

2   BGD, 2 August 1956; Bar-On 1991, pp. 183–5.

3   Nahmias to Peres, 31 August 1956, quoted in: Bar-On 1991, pp. 189–90. Dayan (1966, p. 24) noted only that "a cable has arrived from the [Military] Attaché in Paris".

4   Bar-On 1991, p. 189; Ne'eman's report following 'Amit's meeting with Barjot, quoted *ibid.*, pp. 190–1. See also: Dayan 1976, p. 223; Dayan 1966, p. 24.

5   Dayan 1976, p. 223.

6   *Ibid.*; author's interview with 'Amit, 18 December 1990; Peres's cable to Nahmias, quoted in: Bar-On 1991, p. 190.

7   Dayan's instructions to 'Amit quoted in: Bar-On 1991, p. 190.

8   Bar-On 1991, p. 190–1; Ne'eman 1987, p. 32.

9   Cable from Peres to Ben-Gurion, 18 September 1956, quoted in: Bar-On 1991, p. 193.

10   *Ibid.* Evron (1986, pp. 65–6), who relied on Peres's diaries, gives a similar description. Bar-Zohar (1987C, p. 1214) claims – without citing any supporting reference – that Bourgès-Maunoury sent his "birthday cable" a few days before his meeting with Peres.

11   On Israeli-French negotiations on nuclear energy during the 1950s, see: Aharonson 1992, pp. 141–65.

12   *Ibid.*; Bar-On 1991, pp. 194–5.

13   Bar-On 1991, pp. 195; Peres 1970, pp. 158–9.

14   BGD, 25 September 1956.

15   BGD, 25, 26, 28 September 1956; Dayan 1976, pp. 230–3.

16   Evron 1986, p. 172; author's interview with Peres, 12 November 1990.

17   Dayan 1976, pp. 231–2; BGD, 25–27 September 1956.

18   BGD, 27 September 1956; Dayan 1976, pp. 231–2; CoSBD, 27, 28 September 1956; Bar-On 1988, p. 192.

19   Bar-On, article in the daily *Ma'ariv*, 5, 8 June 1973; CoSBD, 28, 29 September 1956.

20   CoSBD, 30 September 1956. On British demands not to involve the French Foreign Ministry in the war preparations, see: Minutes of Staff Conference held at Chequers on Saturday, 11 August 1956: PRO, PREM11/1099.

21   On Pineau's statement in the first morning's meeting at St. Germain, see: CoSBD, 30 September 1956; Tzur 1968, pp. 288–9; Lucas 1991, p. 214. Dayan's impressions can be found in: Dayan 1976, p. 235.

22   Medzini 1990, p. 243.

23   *Ibid.*; author's interview with Peres, 12 November 1990.

24   Bar-On (note 19, above).

25   Dayan 1976, pp. 235–6; Peres 1970, pp. 161–3; CoSBD, 30 September 1956. Concerning the on-going disagreement between the US and France over Algeria, see: Horne 1979, pp. 254–8, 439, 488.

26   CoSBD, 30 September 1956.

27   *Ibid.*

28   *Ibid.*

29 *Ibid.*
30 *Ibid.*
31 *Ibid.*
32 *Ibid.*
33 *Ibid.* See discussion of the Sèvres conference, below.
34 *Ibid.*; Bar-On (note 19, above).
35 CoSBD, 30 September 1956; Sidon report for September–October 1956.
36 Enclosed with the St. Germain conference protocol in CoSBD.
37 CoSBD, 30 September 1956.
38 CoSBD, 1 October 1956.
39 Dayan 1976, pp. 237–8.
40 CoSBD, 1 October 1956; Dayan 1976, pp. 237–9.
41 Dayan 1976, pp. 240–2.
42 Concerning this timetable, see: Dayan 1976, p. 240.
43 This is the logical conclusion that emerges from the series of discussions among Dayan, Peres and Ben-Gurion, between their return from St. Germain and their departure for Sèvres.
44 Peres, Night of Decision, pp. 49–52. All major studies of the Suez Crisis and the Sinai War regard the Sèvres conference as the politically decisive milestone on the road to the tripartite move. See, for example: Bar-On 1988, ch. 13; Bar-Zohar 1987C, Part II, ch. 6; Kyle 1991, ch. 17; Lamb 1987, ch. 11; and Lucas 1991, ch. 21. Lucas tends to stress, more than the others, the period between early October and the Sèvres conference, in which Eden, Lloyd, Mollet and Pineau reached a secret understanding. On the other hand, Medzini (1990, p. 243) argues that the St. Germain conference had no significant results – a groundless claim.
45 Other writers have not made an explicit connection between political hesitations and developments in early October and the mission of the French delegation. See, for example, Bar-On 1988, pp. 215–19; Bar-Zohar 1987C, pp. 1223–4; Evron 1986, pp. 77–80.
46 CoSBD, 30 September 1956; Bar-On 1988, p. 221. Concerning Pineau's attitude, see, for example: Paris to Foreign Ministry, 26 September 1956: PRO, PREM11/1102.
47 BGD, 3 October 1956; CoSBD, 3 October 1956; Medzini 1990, p. 243.
48 BGD, 3 October 1956; Dayan 1976, pp. 242–3; CoSBD, 3 October 1956. For a summation of discussions between the Prime Minister and the French delegation, see: CoSBD, 10 October 1956.
49 BGD, 3 October 1956.
50 BGD, 4 October 1956; notes from the meeting taken by the Prime Minister's political secretary are attached to CoSBD, 4 October 1956; Dayan 1976, p. 224. On arms shipments, see: BGD, 8–9, 15 October 1956.
51 Concerning Israel's fear of Britain, see Ben-Gurion at an internal consultation of the Israeli delegation at Sèvres: CoSBD, 23 October 1956. On France's position: Kyle 1991, p. 260; author's interview with Peres, 12 November 1991; international developments during 4 October through 21 October are thoroughly detailed by: Lucas 1991, chs 17–21.
52 Peres, Night of Decision.
53 CoSBD, 3 October 1956. Ben-Gurion's further points to the Chief of Staff's instructions: CoSBD, 14 October 1956
54 Cable from Lt.-Col. Gazit to the Chief of Staff, 13 October 1956: attached to CoSBD, of the same day.

55 Ben-Gurion's political statement in *Knesset Record*, vol. XXI, 169th meeting, 15 October 1956, pp. 58–60.

56 On French-Israeli military co-operation before the Suez Crisis, see chapter 3. For France's independent efforts to learn about the IDF, see, for example: *Forces Armées Isrealiennes*, Etat-Major des Forces Armées, 25 August 1956: SHAA, C2317.

57 A detailed account of the IDF's efforts to impress the delegation with its capabilities can be found in the memoirs of Col. Uzi Narkiss, then Assistant Chief of General Staff Branch, who "ran the show" for the Frenchmen: Narkiss 1991, ch. 4, "The French Are Coming". On discussions with Gen. Ely and his staff, the visit of the "Milk and Honey" delegation to Israel and its members' impressions, see: CoSBD, 30 September, 1 October 1956; Bar-On 1991, pp. 207–20.

58 Bar-On 1991, p. 218; Tzavta Report 1956; CoSBD (Ben-Gurion's discussion with Challe and his men on 3 October, with Mangin on 4 October 1956).

59 *Ibid.*, p. 219.

60 French military analysis is included in: "Fiche sur le Plan Israélien", L'Etat-Major du General Beaufre, Paris, 12 October 1956. This is a staff paper prepared by the HQ of the French ground task force for Operation Musketeer under Gen. Beaufre, who was in charge of planning for Israel's involvement in the operation. Courtesy of Gen. Delmas, President of the French Society for Military History, provided during an interview in Paris, 17 April 1991. Dayan's statement at the St. Germain conference is included in CoSBD, 1 October, 1956. Statements by Tolkovsky and Lahat, Tolkovsky 1957. Ben-Gurion's statement at the opening session of the Sèvres conference in CoSBD, 22 October 1956.

61 CoSBD, 23 October 1956.

62 "Fiche sur le plan Israélien" (note 60); Liaison Officer in Paris to the Chief of Intelligence, 13 October 1956, included in CoSBD, 22 October 1956. At this stage, cables such as this one, for the Chief of Staff, were routed through this channel.

63 *Ibid.*

64 Ben-Gurion's further points to the Chief of Staff's instructions: CoSBD, 14 October 1956; Chief of Staff to Liaison Officer in Paris, 15 October 1956: CoSBD.

65 Tzur to the Foreign Ministry, 5 September 1956: SA 2450/3. Concerning French Army preparations for war during August through October 1956, see: Bar-On 1991, p. 237; Beaufre 1969, pp. 26–74. Beaufre's patently apologetic memoir nevertheless reflects sentiments within the senior field echelons of the French Army about the decisions made by HQ in Paris and moves made by the two partners, Britain and Israel.

66 Tolkovsky 1957; Bar-On 1991, pp. 237–8.

67 BGD, 11, 15 October 1956 (recording Harkabi's reports from New York); author's interview with Harkabi, 24 August 1991.

68 Kyle 1991, pp. 296–7; Nutting 1967, pp. 90–4.

69 Bar-On 1991, pp. 237–8; CoSBD, 14 October 1956.

70 On the meeting at Chequers, see: Nutting 1967, p. 92.

71 Ben-Gurion entered his instructions to 'Amit in his diary, 18 October 1956; see also Bar-On 1991, pp. 238, and further details in CoSBD, 14–15 October 1956.

72 BGD, 18 August 1956. CoSBD, 14–18 October 1956; author's interview with

'Amit, 18 December 1990.

73　For Macmillan's ideas about collaboration with Israel, see: Horne 1988, pp. 408–10.

74　Cable from Nahmias in Paris, quoted in: BGD, 18 August 1956; 'Amit's report to Ben-Gurion, *ibid.*; Bar-On 1991, p. 240.

75　BGD, *ibid.*; Bar-On 1991, *ibid.*.

76　BGD, *ibid.*; 'Amit's reports on his discussions in Paris, CoSBD, 18 October, 1956; author's interview with 'Amit, 18 December 1990. On military discussions in Paris in early October, between 'Amit and Gen. Gajins, see also: Bar-On 1988, pp. 70–2.

77　BGD, 18 October 1956.

Chapter 7:　A Reluctant Coalition

1　Egypt Committee first meeting, 27 July 1956: PRO, PREM11/1098.

2　On Monckton's position, see, for example, his statement in the Cabinet on 11 September 1956: PRO, CAB128, CM (56) 64.

3　According to Egypt Committee minutes, kept in: PRO, PREM11/1098. For Nasser's evaluations of the prospects for war prior to the Suez Crisis, see: Heikal 1972, pp. 90–1.

4　Eden's private secretary to Churchill's private secretary, 17 October 1956: AP 14/14/47. Churchill gave Eden full support throughout the crisis.

5　Egypt Committee meeting, 2 August 1956: PRO, PREM11/1098; Kyle 1991, pp. 176, 206.

6　Kyle 1991, pp. 176,206; Horne 1988, pp. 408–14.

7　On Eden's and Gaitskell's positions, see: Kyle 1991, pp. 170–3, 247.

8　Eden to Nutting, 29 July 1956: AP 20/21/162; Guildhall address: Carlton 1988, pp. 59–60.

9　Kyle 1991, p. 178; Eden to Holland, 23 October 1956: AP 20/21/182; Eden's report to Cabinet, 14 August 1956: PRO, PREM11/1099.

10　Macmillan to Eden, 26 August 1956 (reached Eden the next day): PRO, PREM11/1135.

11　Peres, Night of Decision, pp. 55–7; CoSBD, 18, 21 October 1956.

12　Peres, Night of Decision, pp. 55–6; CoSBD, 21 October 1956.

13　Lucas 1991, pp. 93–5 ; Heikal 1972, pp. 85–6 ; Eden 1960 p. 389.

14　Eden 1960, pp. 390–2; Shuckburgh 1986, p. 343; Lucas 1991, p. 96.

15　Eden 1960, pp. 391–5.

16　Lucas 1991, pp. 98–103.

17　Lucas 1991, pp. 99, 228–9; Chiefs of Staff 94th meeting, 18 September 1956: PRO DEFE4/90; Kyle 1991, p. 264.

18　BGD, 27–28 September 1956. See also Ben-Gurion's statement at the General Staff meeting, 19 July 1956.

19　BGD, 1 October 1956. On the same meeting, see also Lawson's messages to the State Department in: FRUS, V. XVI, E.N No 289, p. 622.

20　See: "In Conclusion of the Iraqi Affair", CoSBD, 13–14 October 1956; BGD, 9 October 1956.

21　Lucas 1991, pp. 229–36; Lucas's interview with the author, Birmingham, 3 December 1991; COS 12th meeting, 26 January 1956: PRO DEFE4/82.

22　Kyle 1991, p. 92.

23　*Ibid.*; BGD, 23–24 September 1956.

24　CoSBD, 19 October. 1956; COS 97 meeting, 9 October 1956: PRO,

DEFE4/90.
25 COS 98 meeting, 10 October 1956: PRO, DFFE4/91.
26 Eden's promises to the French are quoted in: Lucas 1991, pp. 239–40.
27 Bar-On 1991, p. 243.
28 Peres, Night of Decision, pp. 53–4; CoSBD, 16 October 1956; Bar-On 1991, p. 243.
29 CoSBD, 16 October 1956; Bar-On 1991, p. 242; BGD, 16 October 1956. See also: Challe 1968, p. 26; Evron 1986, pp. 87–8.
30 Ben-Gurion's cable to Nahmias and Peres's reaction in: Bar-On 1991, p. 242.
31 Concerning the cables exchanged between Ben-Gurion and Mollet, see: Peres, Night of Decision, pp. 52; Bar-On 1991, pp. 244–6.
32 CoSBD, 17 October 1956.
33 CoSBD, 18 October 1956; Bar-On 1991, pp. 244–6.
34 CoSBD, 18 October 1956.
35 On Dayan's and Peres's morning talks with Challe and Mangin, see: CoSBD, 21 October 1956
36 BGD, 22 October 1956; Dayan 1976, pp. 233–46, 254–5; Bar-On 1988, pp. 227, 236 (quoting CoSBD, of which he was in charge); Bar-Zohar 1978c, pp. 1247, 1232.
37 BGD, 22 October 1956 (delayed entry); CoSBD, 21 October 1956.
38 CoSBD, 22 October 1956; BGD, *ibid.*
39 CoSBD, *ibid.*
40 CoSBD, *ibid.*, first session at Sèvres.
41 Bar-On 1991, p. 258; Thorpe 1989, pp. 236–7.
42 On Lloyd's objections after his return on 16 October from New York, where he had reached an understanding with Egyptian Foreign Minister Fawzi, see: Thorpe 1989, p. 231. Israeli resentment of Lloyd, the "ex-slavemaster", comes clearly through in Bar-On's description of his meeting with him in: Bar-On 1991, pp. 258–61, as well as CoSBD, 23–24 October 1956. See also: Thorpe 1989., pp. 238–9; author's interview with Kyle, London, 6 December 1991. On Pineau's visit to New York, see: BGD, 22 October 1956.
43 BGD, 23 October 1956; CoSBD, 23 October 1956, and "Anecdotes from the Sèvres Conference", 24 October 1956.
44 CoSBD, 24 October 1956
45 *Ibid.*; BGD, 22, 25 October 1956; Bar-On 1991, pp. 276. The original Sèvres agreement cannot be found. The British and French copies must have been destroyed. A photocopy of the Israeli copy is kept in the Archives of the Ben-Gurion Heritage Institute at Sde Boker. At the time, Ben-Gurion did not allow Dayan and Bar-On to copy the agreement into their diaries. See also Kyle 1991, p. 566.
46 Eden's letter to Mollet was copied (in English) into BGD, 26 October 1956. On Eden and the Cordage affair, see: Kyle 1991, pp. 309, 310, 341–2.

Chapter 8: Decision at Sèvres

1 CoSBD, 24 October 1956: "Something about the Old Man's position at the Sèvres talks".
2 BGD, 15–24 October 1956; CoSBD of the same dates; Peres, Night of Decision, pp. 57–88; Dayan 1976, pp. 58–66.
3 CoSBD, 22 October 1956.
4 Peres, Night of Decision, pp. 57–88. On Eden's position, see: Nutting 1967,

pp. 97–9.

5 Mission in Paris to Chief of Intelligence, 13 October 1956, included in CoSBD, 22 October 1956; CoS's reply, 14 October 1956, *ibid.*

6 CoSBD, 22 October 1956.

7 *Ibid.*

8 *Ibid.*

9 *Ibid.*; Peres, Night of Decision, p. 60.

10 CoSBD, 22 October 1956; Peres, Night of Decision, pp. 64–5.

11 *Ibid.*

12 Concerning the Air Force's preparedness on the eve of war, see Tolkovsky 1957. For Dayan's views on possible air raids on Israeli population centres, see his discussion with Ben-Gurion quoted in: CoSBD, 17 October 1956.

13 Bar-On 1991, pp. 258–60; BGD, 22 October 1956.

14 Bar-On 1991, pp. 260–1; Thorpe 1989, p. 94.

15 CoSBD, 22–23 October 1956; Peres, Night of Decision, pp. 69–70.

16 CoSBD, 23 October 1956, "Meeting of the Military Level".

17 *Ibid.*; Peres, Night of Decision, p. 70.

18 CoSBD, 23 October 1956, "Meeting of the Military Level".

19 CoSBD, 23 October 1956, "Afternoon Session at Sèvres"; Peres describes in great detail Ben-Gurion's outrage at Challe's proposal in: Night of Decision, pp. 73–4; Bar-On's minutes in CoSBD, however, do not support this description.

20 CoSBD, 23 October 1956, "Afternoon Session at Sèvres".

21 CoSBD, 23 October 1956.

22 CoSBD, 23 October 1956, Dayan's meeting with the French team (including Dayan's note to Bar-On); briefing to the Israeli military mission in Paris, *ibid.*; meeting of the Israeli team, *ibid.*, 24 October 1956; Peres, Night of Decision, p. 64.

23 CoSBD, 24 October 1956, meeting of the Israeli team; BGD, 24 October 1956.

24 CoSBD, 24 October 1956, "Afternoon Session at Sèvres".

25 CoSBD, 24 October 1956, "Final Session with the British and the French at Sèvres". Final revision of the Sèvres agreement (see note 45, ch. 8); it is not clear who, if anyone, signed the French version on behalf of Israel).

26 Concerning the timetable for the Winter Plan, see order of Combined Allied HQ signed by Stockwell, Barnett and Richmond dated 12 October 1956, in: PRO, ADM 205/138. This timetable is also included in Stockwell's report: Stockwell Papers, LHCMA, p. 36. See also: Combined Allied Operational Instruction, Operation Musketeer, Winter Plan, 12 October 1956: PRO, ADM205/138/183251.

27 Correspondence between Admiralty and Ministry of Aviation during October 1956 on preparations for the Winter Plan: PRO ADM 205/118; Stockwell's report (note 26). Concerning the feeling that this plan was no longer realistic, see memorandum by the Air Chief Marshal to the Chairman of the Chiefs of Staff: Boyle to Dickson, 16 October 1956: PRO, AIR8/2084/1888.

28 Stockwell papers, LHCMA, pp. 37–8.

29 *Ibid.*

30 Keightley to Force Commanders, 25 October 1956: PRO, ADM/ 205/119/183149.

31 Stockwell papers, LHCMA.

Chapter 9: In the Forefront of the Hottest Battle

1   See: Sheffy 1990, pp. 7–56; Hewedy 1989, pp. 167–70; CoSBD, 31 October 1956.
2   Immediately after the war, the IDF prepared a report at the request of the Prime Minister, which included a review of the forces which took part in operations in the Sinai Peninsula and the Gaza Strip: "Answers to the Prime Minister's Questions", 6 November 1956.
3   IDF, Intelligence Branch, "The Egyptian Army in Sinai".
4   On the military uselessness of the Israeli gambit at the Mitla Pass, see, for example: Bar-On 1988, p. 242. Concerning the linkage between the "Mitla move" and the Straits of Tiran and the Suez Canal, see Dayan's discussion with Ben-Gurion on 31 October, regarding possible withdrawal of the paratroopers in view of the delay in allied operations: CoSBD, 31 October 1956. On Britain and Jordan, see: "SCP Review", documentation by the IDF's History Department, 30 October at 7 p.m., and draft files for that report.
5   Eban 1978, p. 201.
6   For Egypt's reaction to the Israeli gambit, see: intelligence evaluation included in "SCP Review", 30 October 1956; Hewedy 1989, p. 169.
7   SCP to Southern Command and Air Force Operations, 29 October 1956 at 10 a.m.; CoSBD, 29 October 1956; Dayan 1966, p. 72.
8   "Review of the SCP", 30 October 1956; Tzavta Report; Steigman 1986, pp. 94, 111.
9   CoSBD, 31 October 1956. Concerning the delay of Anglo-French campaign, see the next chapter.
10   CoSBD, 31 October 1956; "Review of the SCP", 31 October 1956; Bar-On 1991, p. 307.
11   CoSBD, 31 October 1956. Dayan explained why he would not meet with Ben-Gurion in a closed session with 'Amit and Harkabi at SCP late on Tuesday, 30 October: CoSBD, 30 October 1956.
12   CoSBD, 31 October 1956.
13   Developments within the allies up to the start of the air campaign are described in chapter 11.
14   CoSBD, 2 November 1956.
15   SCP, "Diary of Operations"; SCP current meetings, 1 November 1956; Tolkovsky 1957.

Chapter 10: A Partnership in War: Israel and France

1   Tolkovsky 1957; 'Amit 1986, p. 3.
2   CoSBD, 31 October 1956: Ne'eman's report to Dayan from Cyprus; "Minutes of a Meeting with the French Held on 1 November 1956", CoSBD.
3   CoSBD, 29 October 1956; cable from Britain's Ambassador in Israel to the Foreign Office in London: Nicholls to Foreign Office, No. 567, 29 November 1956: PRO, FO371/121782; minutes of a session of the Israel Society for Military History devoted to Operation Kadesh [the Sinai War] on 29 October 1981, in the author's possession.
4   Dayan's instructions to Ne'eman are quoted in CoSBD, 30 October 1956.
5   Ne'eman's report to Dayan, CoSBD, 31 October 1956.
6   *Ibid.*

7   Ne'eman 1986, p. 36; CoSBD, 2–6 November 1956; Tolkovsky 1957.
8   Tzavta Report, Air Force Archives, file no. 15.
9   Tolkovsky 1957; Tzavta Report, 1956; "Events at the SCP with Gavish".
10 Tolkovsky 1957; Tzavta Report, 1956; author's interview with Gen. (then Lt.-Col.) Souvier, Paris, 18 April 1991.
11 CoSBD, 29 October 1956; internal report of the French Navy (not for circulation at the time): Masson 1966, pp. 118, 120.
12 CoSBD, 29 October 1956; Masson 1966, p. 120.
13 CoSBD, 29 October 1956.
14 Masson 1966, pp. 120–1.
15 CoSBD, 1 November 1956; Masson 1966, p. 121.
16 CoSBD, 29 October 1956; Masson 1966.
17 CoSBD, 2 November 1956; "Diary of Operations"; Navy HQ to SCP: General Staff Branch, "War Diary", 1 November 1956, 4:35 p.m.
18 Navy HQ, "Report on Contact with *Ibrahim el-Awwal*", 12 November 1956; Tolkovsky 1957; Steigman 1986, pp. 157–61.
19 Masson 1966, p. 118.
20 *Ibid.*, p. 119. On the US Sixth Fleet during the Suez Crisis, see: Kyle 1991, pp. 411–13.
22 Dayan 1976, p. 284. Concerning rivalry within the IDF about the Egyptian destroyer, see Navy HQ report (note 18 above); see also: Steigman 1986, pp. 157–61; Masson 1966, pp. 118–19.
23 CoSBD, 29 October 1956; Beaufre 1969, pp. 64, 74, 79–80.
24 Ne'eman's report to Dayan from Cyprus, CoSBD, 31 October 1956.
25 CoSBD, 2 November 1956.
26 As Ben-Gurion made no diary entries while he was ill, this is based on CoSBD, with obvious limitations.
27 CoSBD, 2–3 November 1956.
28 CoSBD, 3 November 1956; for a general description of the situation in the French Army at the time, see: Rapport sur l'operation d'Egypt, Force A, Juillet–Décembre 1956: SHAA C2307.
29 General Staff Branch, "War Diary", operative order "Advance to the Canal and Deployment", *ibid.*; "Events at the SCP with Gavish"; CoSBD, 3 November 1956.
30 Final report by Barnett, 27 November 1956: PRO, ADM116/6133.
31 CoSBD, 3 November 1956; Dayan 1966, pp. 142–4. Discussion of the entire affair (possible French-Israeli collaboration at the Canal) can be found in: Bar-On 1991, pp. 318–20.

Chapter 11: A Partnership in War – Israel and Britain

1   CoSBD, 30 October 1956.
2   CoSBD, 31 October 1956.
3   CoSBD, 31 October 1956; "Minutes of a Meeting with the French Held on 1 November 1956."
4   Author's interview with Kyle, 10 December 1991. See also: Kyle 1991, p. 372.
5   Report of Bomber Wing, Cyprus, on Operation Musketeer: PRO AIR20/9967.
6   Compartmentalisation was not a problem for Israel only. See correspondence between Keightley and the military in London: Chiefs of Staff to

Keightley, 30 October 1956: PR0, AIR8/1490; Keightley to Chiefs of Staff, 30 October 1956: PR0, AIR8/2111.

7   *Ibid.*; Report of Bomber Wing, Cyprus, on Operation "Musketeer": PRO AIR20/9967; Kyle 1991, pp. 372–5.
8   *Ibid.*, p. 374.
9   CoSBD, 31 October 1956.
10 *Ibid.*
11 *Ibid.*; Kyle 1991, pp. 373.
12 CoSBD, 31 October–1 November 1956; Intelligence Branch, "The Egyptian Army in the Sinai", 1957 reconstruction.
13 CoSBD, 4 November 1956.
14 *Ibid.* Concerning international developments, see report by Ambassador Eban, "The Political Campaign in the UN and the US following the Sinai Operation, October 1956–March 1957", Washington, June 1957, in BGA. See also: Bar-On 1991, pp. 321–5; Bar-On 1988, pp. 257–61.
15 CoSBD, 4 November 1956.
16 Kyle 1991, pp. 238–40.
17 Correspondence between Nicholls in Tel Aviv and Logan in London and final report by Ross, head of Levant Department at the Foreign Office: PRO, FO371/121696, 3 November 1956; background material for Foreign Office responses to questions in Parliament: PRO, FO371/121706.
18 See, for example, military intelligence about the enemy: PRO, AIR20/9677, 30 October 1956.
19 CoSBD, 2 November 1956; report by Chief of Naval Intelligence to the Admiralty, 30 October 1956: PRO, ADM/205/19. On this subject, see also a paper by the head of History Branch, French Air Force: Robineau 1986, pp. 44–6; and author's interview with Robineau, Paris, 16 April 1991.
20 CoSBD, 28–29 October 1956.
21 Bar-On 1991, p. 320; Barnett's final report (note 30, ch. 10).; Tzavta Report, 1956.
22 Daily report by the Musketeer aerial task force HQ, 4 November 1956: PRO, AIR20/9675; Tolkovsky 1957; author's interview with Gen. (then Lt.-Col.) Souvier, Paris, 18 April 1991.
23 "Southern Command Announcements", 31 October, 6:30 p.m.; "Southern Command War Diary"; "Review of the SCP".
24 "General staff Branch War Diary". Discussion of 9th Brigade at the SCP on 31 October 7:25 p.m.: "SCP Review".
25 SCP current events report; SCP Diary.
26 SCP current events report, 1 November 1956, 3 p.m.
27 *Ibid.*
28 Southern Command Intelligence to SCP: SCP Diary; SCP current events report, 2 November 1956, 0:55 a.m.
29 SCP discussion on 4 November 1956: CoSBD, 5 November 1956.
30 SCP current events report, 4 November 1956, noon; SCP discussion on 4 November 1956, 7 p.m.; CoSBD, 3 November 1956.
31 "General staff Branch War Diary"; report of 9th Brigade commander, quoted from "SCP Review".
32 Steigman 1990, pp. 281–2; Steigman 1986, pp. 182–4; daily reports by AFHQ, 3 November 1956.
33 CoSBD, 4 November 1956. On Toreador, see: Operation Toreador: PRO, ADM116/6103, vol. VII in a 10-volume report by the Royal Navy; Masson

1966, pp. 121–4. See also: CoSBD, 30 October 1956; Dayan 1976, p. 307.
34 "SCP Review".
35 SCP current events report; CoSBD, 4 November 1956.
36 Report to the Admiralty and Commander, Mediterranean Theatre: PRO, ADM205/141, 6 November 1956.
37 Tolkovsky 1957.

Bibliography

Primary sources include archival material, other documentation and oral testimonies (interviews). The secondary material includes research studies, journalistic accounts and memoirs. In the Notes, secondary sources contain author's name and year of publication; full publication details appear in the Bibliography.

Primary Material

1 Ben-Gurion Archive at Sde Boker (BGA), containing:
 Ben-Gurion's persona diary (BGD), 1949–1956; Correspondence; Ben-Gurion's speeches and addresses; Minutes of meetings; general chronological documentation; subject files; archives of Yehuda Arazi (who handled the publication of Ben-Gurion's writings); Oral Documentation Division.

2 The State of Israel Archives (SA). Divisions:
 43 – Prime Minister's Office.
 44 – Information Administration.
 45 – Broadcasting Authority (announcements, news and contemporary interviews).
 55 – Government Press Office (formerly: Press Information Office).
 60 – The Knesset.
 68 – Foreign Ministry, Archive of Leo Kohn (political secretary).
 72/2 – Archive of Teddy Kollek (Director-General of the Prime Minister's Office).
 78 – Cabinet and Cabinet Commitees Secretariat.
 93 – Foreign Ministry, overseas legations (Paris, London, Washington, D.C., and Moscow).
 101 – IDF Command in the Gaza Strip, 1956–7.
 103 – Archive of Golda Meir (Foreign Minister as of June 1956).
 130 – Foreign Ministry, Bureaus of the Minister and the Director-General.

3 IDF and Defence Establishment archives.
4 IDF History Department archive.
5 Israel Air Force History Branch archive.
6 Public Records Office (PRO), London. Divisions:
 CAB – Cabinet;
 PREM – Prime Minister's Bureau;

FO371 – Foreign Office, general;
FO800 – Foreign Office, personal;
DEFI – Ministry of Defence;
WO – War Office;
ADM – Admiralty;
AIR – Ministry of Aviation.

7   Imperial War Museum (IWM) archives, London: personal material of soldiers and officers who took part in Operation Musketeer; raw materials collected for an unpublished study of the British Army in the Middle East after World War II.

8   The Liddel Hart Centre for Military Archives, King's College, University of London (LHCMA):
Stockwell Papers 7, 8, 9.

9   The Anthony Eden (Lord Avon) Archive, Birmingham University, UK:
Avon Papers (AP) 14, 19, 20, 21.

10 Service Historique de l'Armée de l'Air (SHAA). Divisions:
E, G – Operation 750 (military collaboration with Israel);
C – Operation 700 (Musketeer).
11 Archives of Israeli newspapers.

12 Author's interviews (rank when relevant, and position at the time of the Sinai War):
Major General Meir 'Amit: Chief of General Staff Branch.
Lt.-Colonel Mordechai Bar-On: Head of Chief of Staff's bureau.
Mr. Moshe Carmel: Minister of Transport.
Lt.-Colonel Yeshayahu Gavish: Head of Operations Division, General Staff Branch.
Colonel Yehoshafat Harkabi: Chief of Intelligence.
Mr. Keith Kyle: *The Economist*'s Washington correspondent.
Colonel Uzi Narkiss: Deputy Chief of General Staff Branch.
Lt.-Colonel Yuval Ne'eman, Deputy Chief of Intelligence.
Mr. Shimon Peres: Director-General, Ministry of Defence.
Col. Paul Souviat, CO French Squadron at Ramat David and Chief of Operations, French mission in Israel.
Major General Dan Tolkovsky: CO, Israel Air Force.
Colonel Yehuda Wallach: CO 38 Division.
Lt.-Colonel Rehav'am Ze'evi: Chief of Staff, Southern Command.

Secondary Material

Acheson, D. *Present at the Creation*, New York, 1969.
Aharonson, S. "New Light on the 'Shelter in Time of Need' Doctrine", *'Iyunim* [Hebrew], vol. 2, 1992, pp. 141–65.
Alon, Y. *Curtain of Sand* [Hebrew], Tel Aviv, 1959.
——. *Connected Vessels* [Hebrew], Tel Aviv, 1980.
Alterman, N. *The Seventh Column* [Hebrew], vol. 2, Tel Aviv, 1981.
'Amit, M. "The Sinai Campaign – The IDF's First Test as a Regular Army", *Ma'arachot* [Hebrew], 306–7, 1986, pp. 2–4.

Argaman, Y. *It Was Top Secret*, Tel Aviv, 1990.

Argov, A. excerpts from his diary in: *In Memoriam* [Hebrew], published by friends, 1959.

Avineri, S. *The Zionist Idea: Its Various Shades* [Hebrew], Tel Aviv, 1980.

Ayalon, A. "The War of Independence, Operation Kadesh, the Six-Day War – Points of Similarity", *Ma'arachot* [Hebrew], 192, July 1968.

Azeau, H. *Le Piege de Suez*, Paris, 1964.

Baer, I. *Israel's Security: Yesterday, Today, Tomorrow* [Hebrew], Tel Aviv, 1966.

Bar, M. *Red Lines in Israel's Deterrence Strategy* [Hebrew], Tel Aviv, 1990.

Bar-On, A. *Untold Stories* [Hebrew], Tel Aviv, 1981.

——. *Challenge and Conflict: Israel's Defensive Campaign in 1956* [Hebrew], IDF, Chief of Staff's Bureau, 15 September, 1958.

——. *Challenge and Conflict* [Hebrew], Ben-Gurion Heritage Institute, Sde Boker, 1991 (abridgement of the 1958 material).

——. *Israel's Defence and Foreign Policies, 1955–57* [Hebrew], doctoral thesis presented to the Department of International Relations, Hebrew University of Jerusalem, December 1988.

——. "The Sinai Campaign – Objectives and Expectations", *Zemanim* [Hebrew], 24, 1978, pp. 94–104.

——. "*Status Quo* Before or After the Fact? Comments on Israel's Defence Policy, 1965–67", *'Iyunim* [Hebrew], 5, 1995, pp. 65–111.

——. "With Golda Meir and Moshe Dayan at St. Germain", *Ma'ariv* [Hebrew], 5, 8 June, 1973.

——. "The Czech–Egyptian Deal – A Question of Dating", *Ma'arachot* [Hebrew], 306–307, December 1986, January 1987, pp. 38–42.

——. *The Gates of Gaza* [Hebrew], Tel Aviv, 1992.

Bar-Zohar, M. *Ben Gurion* [Hebrew], Tel Aviv, vol. II, 1978; vol. III, 1978.

——. *Bridge Across the Mediterranean: Israeli-French Relations, 1947–1963* [Hebrew], Tel Aviv, 1964.

Barjot, P. "Reflexion sur les Operation de Suez 1956", *Revue de Defense National*, 22, 1966.

Barker, E.G. *Seven Days to Suez* [Hebrew trans.], Tel Aviv, 1966.

Battesti, M. "Les Ambiguites de Suez", *Revue Historique Des Armées*, L'affaire de Suez, 30 Ans Apres, 4, 1986, pp. 3–14.

Beaufre, A. *The Suez Expedition 1956*, London, 1969.

Bellof, L. "The Crisis and Its Consequences for the British Conservative Party", in: R. Louis and R. Owen (eds), *Suez 1956: The Crisis and its Consequences*, Oxford, 1989, pp. 319–34.

Ben-Gurion, D. *Uniqueness and Destiny, Writings on Israel's Defence* [Hebrew], Tel Aviv, 1971.

——. *Foreign Policy* [Hebrew], Tel Aviv, 1955.

——. *The Renewed State of Israel* [Hebrew], Tel Aviv, 1969.

——. *The Sinai Campaign, Collected Speeches* [Hebrew], Tel Aviv, 1964.

——. *Army and Security* [Hebrew], Tel Aviv, 1956.

Ben-Moshe, T. "Liddel Hart and the IDF – A Reappraisal", *State, Government and International Relations* [Hebrew], 15, 1980, pp. 40–56.

Bendman, Y. "Egypt's Armed Forces in the Kadesh [Sinai] Campaign" [Hebrew], unpublished, courtesy of the author.

——. "The Egyptian Army in the Sinai Campaign", in: I. Troen and M. Shemesh (eds), *The Suez-Sinai Crisis 1956, Retrospective and Reappraisal*, London, 1994, pp. 65–97.

Berar, S. *As a Stormy Day* [Hebrew], Tel Aviv, 1957.

Bialer, U. "David Ben-Gurion and Moshe Sharett: The Development of Two Political-Security Orientations in Israeli Society", *State and Government* [Hebrew], 1971, pp. 70–84.

——. *Between East and West: Israel's Foreign Policy Orientation 1948–1956*, Cambridge, 1990.

Bondi, R. *Felix-Pinhas Rosen and His Times* [Hebrew], Tel Aviv, 1990.

Borenstein (Oren), M. *From Revolution to Crisis: Egypt-Israel Relations, 1952–1956*, Princeton, 1989.

Bowie, R. "Eisenhower, Dulles, and the Suez Crisis", in: I. Troen and M. Shemesh (eds), *The Suez-Sinai Crisis 1956, Retrospective and Reappraisal*, London, 1994, pp. 189–214.

Brecher, M. *Decisions in Israel's Foreign Policy*, Yale, 1975.

——. *The Foreign Policy System of Israel*, Oxford, 1972 .

——. "Operation Sinai", in: B. Neuberger (ed.), *Diplomacy Under the Shadow of Conflict* [Hebrew], Tel Aviv, 1984, p. 244.

Brendon, P. *Ike, The Life and Times of Dwight D. Eisenhower*, London, 1987.

Bromberger, S. and Bromberger, M. *Secrets of the Campaign against Egypt* [Hebrew trans.], Tel Aviv, 1957.

Brugioni, D.A. *Eyeball to Eyeball*, New York, 1991.

Burns, E.M. *Between Arab and Israeli*, London, 1962.

Butler, D. and Butler, G. *British Political Facts 1900–1985*, London, 1988.

Butler, R. *The Art of the Possible*, London, 1971.

Cabot-Lodge, H. *As It Was*, New York, 1976.

Cairnshaw (ed.), E. *Khrushchov Reminisces* [Hebrew trans.], Tel Aviv, 1971.

Calvocoresy, P. *Suez: Ten Years After*, London, 1967.

Campbell, J. *Defence of the Middle East*, New York, 1960.

——. "The Soviet Union, the United States, and the Twin Crises of Hungary and Suez", in: R. Louis and R. Owen (eds), *Suez 1956: The Crisis and its Consequences*, Oxford, 1989, pp. 233–53.

Carlton, D. *Britian and the Suez Crisis*, London, 1988.

Carmoy, G.D. *The Foreign Policy of France 1944–1968*, Chicago, 1970.

Challe, M. *Notre Revolte*, Paris, 1968.

Cohen, A. and Lavi, Z. *The Sky Is Not the Limit* [Hebrew], Tel Aviv, 1990.

Crook, P. *Came the Dawn*, Tunbridge Wells, 1989.

Crosbie, S.K. *A Tacit Alliance, France and Israel from Suez to the Six Day War*, Princeton, 1974.

Dayan, M. "Israel's Border and Security Problems", *Foreign Affairs*, vol. 33, no. 2, 1955.

——. *Milestones* [Hebrew], Tel Aviv and Jerusalem, 1976.

——. *Sinai Campaign Diary* [Hebrew], Tel Aviv, 1966.

——. "Sinai – 10 Years Later", *Ma'arachot* [Hebrew], 306–307, 1986, pp. 26–7, 62–3.

——. "Military Actions in Peacetime", *Davar* [Hebrew], 4 September, 1955.

Eban, A. *Word to the Nations: Collected Speeches* [Hebrew], Tel Aviv, 1959.

——. *Chapters in a Life* [Hebrew], Tel Aviv, 1978.

A. Eden, *Full Circle*, London, 1960.

Eisenhower, Dwight D. *The White House Years: Mandate for Change, 1953–1956*, New York, 1963.

——. *The White House Years: Mandate for Peace, 1956–1961*, New York, 1965.

Elath, E. *Through the Fog of Days* [Hebrew], Jerusalem, 1986.

Erez, Y. *Talks with Moshe Dayan* [Hebrew], Tel Aviv, 1981.

Erez, Y. and Kfir, A. (eds), *Military and Defence (1948–1968)*, in: *The IDF and Its Strength* [Hebrew], a series, Tel Aviv, 1982.

Eshed, H. *Who Gave the Order?* [Hebrew], Jerusalem, 1979.

——. *A One-Man Institution* [Hebrew], Tel Aviv, 1988.

Evron, Y. *A New Look at Suez 56* [Hebrew], Tel Aviv, 1986.

Eytan, W. *Between Israel and the Nations of the World* [Hebrew], Tel Aviv, 1958.

Facon, P. "Dayane de l'air et l'affaire de Suez", *Revue Historique des Armées*, 4, 1986, pp. 30–40.

Farmbecher, W. "Revelations of a Consultant to the Egyptian Army", *Cyclon* [Hebrew], 76, pp. 3–12 and 77, pp. 3–14, 1957.

Fawzi, M. *Suez 1956, An Egyptian Perspective*, London, 1986.

Feinberg, N. *The Arab-Israeli Conflict in the Light of International Law* [Hebrew], Jerusalem, 1970.

Ferrel, H. (ed.), *The Eisenhower Diaries*, New York, 1981.

Foreign Relations of the United States (FRUS), vol. VI, *Suez Crisis*, US G.P.O., Washington, D.C., 1990.

Fullick, R. and Powell, G. *Suez: The Double War*, London, 1979.

Gafner, B. *Sinai Album* [Hebrew], Tel Aviv, 1957.

Galili, I. *To and From: Letters* [Hebrew], Tel Aviv, 1990.

Gaujac, P. *Suez 1956*, Paris, 1986.

Gawrych, G. *Key to Sinai: The Battle for Abu Agueila 1956 and 1967 Arab-Israeli Wars*, U.S Army Staff College, 1990.

Gelber, Y. *Nucleus for a Regular Hebrew Army* [Hebrew], Jerusalem, 1986.

——. *Volunteerism and Its Role in Zionist Policy, 1939–1942* [Hebrew], Jerusalem, 1979.

Gorst, A. and Lucas, S. "The Other Collusion: Operation Straggle and Anglo-American Intervention in Syria", 1955–1956", *Intelligence and National Security*, 3, 4, 1989, pp. 576–95.

Gillard, F. interviews General Sir H. Stockwell, "Suez, Success or Disaster?", *The Listener*, BBC, 4 November, 1976, pp. 562–3.

Golani, M. *Zion in Zionism* [Hebrew], Tel Aviv, 1992.

——. *Black Arrow: Operation Gaza and Israel's Policy of Retaliation during the 1950s* [Hebrew], Haifa and Tel Aviv, 1994.

Gur, M. "Khan Yunis – A Company in Raid", *Ma'arachot* [Hebrew], 176, 1966, pp. 9–14.

Guvrin, Y. "Soviet Moves against the Establishment of Military Alliances in the Middle East, 1951–1956", *State, Government and International Relations* [Hebrew], 28–29. 1989, pp. 19–38.

Habbas, B. *A Nameless Movement* [Hebrew], Tel Aviv, 1964.

Harkabi, Y. *War and Strategy* [Hebrew], Tel Aviv, 1990.

——. *Israel's Position in the Israeli-Arab Conflict* [Hebrew], Tel Aviv, 1986.

——. *The Arabs' Position in the Israeli-Arab Conflict* [Hebrew], Tel Aviv, 1967.

Heikal, H. *The Cairo Documents*, London, 1972.

——. *Cutting the Lion's Tail*, London, 1986.

——. *The Sphinx and the Commissar* [Hebrew trans.], Tel Aviv, 1981.

Henriks, R. *100 Hours to Suez* [Hebrew], Jerusalem, 1957.

Herzog, Y. *A People That Dwells Alone* [Hebrew], Tel Aviv, 1975.

Hewedy, A. "Nasser and the Crisis of 1956", in: R. Louis and R. Owen (eds), *Suez 1956: The Crisis and Its Consequences*, Oxford, 1989, pp. 161–72.

Higgins, R. *United Nations Peacekeeping 1947–1967, Documents and Commentary*,

Oxford, 1969.

Horne, A. *Macmillan*, London, 1988.

——. *A Savage War of Peace* [Hebrew trans.], Tel Aviv, 1989.

Horowitz, Dan "Permanent and Changeable in Israel's Defence Conception", *Policy Guideline Publications* [Hebrew], 4, Jerusalem, 1982.

——. "Israel's Conception of National Security (1948–1972)" [Hebrew], in: B. Neuberger (ed.), *Diplomacy Under the Shadow of Conflict* [Hebrew], Tel Aviv, 1984, pp. 104–48.

Horowitz, David *Envoy of a Nascent State* [Hebrew], Tel Aviv and Jerusalem, 1951.

Jackson, R. *Suez 1956: Operation Musketeer*, London, 1980.

Keightley, C. *Operation in Egypt*, Supplement to the *London Gazette*, 10 september 1957.

Klein, M. "Egypt's Inter-Bloc Policy, 1955–1965", *State, Government, and International Relations* [Hebrew], 26, 1987, pp. 57–92.

Knesset Record, Jerusalem, vols xx–xxi.

Kyle, K. "The Gulf War: the Lessons of Suez", *The World Today*, vol. 47, no. 12, 1992, pp. 216–19.

——. *Suez*, London, 1991.

——. *The Suez Conflict: Thirty Years After*, London, 1988.

Lacouture, J. *Nasser and His Successors* [Hebrew trans.], Tel Aviv, 1972.

Lamb, R. *The Failure of the Eden Government*, London, 1987.

Levite, A. *Israel's Military Doctrine: Defensive and Offensive* [Hebrew], Tel Aviv, 1988.

Levkowitz, Z. *The Development of the Quartermaster's Branch and the IDF Logistic System, 1949–1966* [Hebrew], Tel Aviv, 1988.

Liddel Hart, B.H. *The Strategy of Indirect Approach* [Hebrew trans.], Tel Aviv, 1980.

Lloyd, S. *Suez 1956 – A Personal Account*, London, 1978.

Lorch, N. *In the Clasp of Powers* [Hebrew], Tel Aviv, 1990.

Louis, R. "The Tragedy of the Anglo-Egyptian Settlement of 1954", in: R. Louis and R. Owen (eds), *Suez 1956: The Crisis and Its Consequences*, Oxford, 1989, pp. 43–72.

Louis, R. and Owen, R. (eds), *Suez 1956: The Crisis and Its Consequences*, Oxford, 1989.

Lucas, W.S. *Divided We Stand: Britain, the US and the Suez Crisis*, London, 1991.

Martin, A. "Military and Political Contradictions of the Suez Affair: A French Prespective", in: I. Troen and M. Shemesh (eds), *The Suez-Sinai Crisis 1956, retrospective and Reappraisal*, London, 1990, pp. 54–9.

Masson, M. *La Crise de Suez*, Vincennes, 1966.

Masson, P. "Origines et Bilan d'une defaite, *Revue Historique des Armées*, 4, 1986, pp. 51–58.

Medzini, M. *The Proud Jewess: Golda Meir and the Vision of Israel* [Hebrew], Jerusalem, 1990.

Medzini, M. (compiler) and Gabza-Brawerman, N. (ed.), *Collected Documents in the History of the Nation* [Hebrew], Tel Aviv, 1981.

Meir, G. *My Life* [Hebrew], Tel Aviv, 1975.

Minutes of the Knesset, Jerusalem, vols xx–xxi.

Monroe, E. *Britain's Moment in the Middle East*, London, 1981.

Naor, M. *Laskov* [Hebrew], Tel Aviv, 1988.

Narkiss, U. *Jerusalem's Soldier* [Hebrew], Tel Aviv, 1991.

Nasser, G. "The Suez Campaign", *The Egyption Gazette*, 6 December, 1956.
——.*The Philosophy of the Revolution* [Hebrew trans.], Tel Aviv, 1961.
Ne'eman, Y. "Contacts with the French and British During the Sinai Campaign", *Ma'arachot* [Hebrew], 306–7, 1986, pp. 28–37.
Neff, D. *Warriors at Suez: Eisenhower Takes America into the Middle East*, New York, 1981.
Neuberger, B. (ed.), *Diplomacy under the Shadow of Conflict* [Hebrew], Tel Aviv, 1984.
Nutting, A. *No End of a Lesson: The Story of Suez*, London, 1967.
Pa'il, M. "The Indirect Approach Is Better", *Ma'arachot Shirion* [Hebrew], 1973.
——"IDF Attacks on Abu Agueila in Three Wars", *Ma'arachot* [Hebrew], 306–7, 1986, pp. 43–63.
Peres, S. "The Road to Sèvres: Franco-Israeli Strategic Co-operation", in: I. Troen and M. Shemesh (eds), *The Suez-Sinai Crisis 1956, Retrospective and Reappraisal*, London, 1990, pp. 140–9.
——. "Current Security and National Defence", *Niv HaKvutza* [Hebrew], 1954.
——"Conciliation Is No Security", *Niv HaKvutza* [Hebrew], 1955.
——. *David's Sling* [Hebrew], Jerusalem, 1970.
——. *The Next Stage* [Hebrew], Tel Aviv, 1965.
——. Night of Decision (unpublished manuscript, in the possession of the author).
Pineau, C. *1956–Suez*, Paris, 1976.
Ra'anan, U. *The USSR Arms and the Third World*, Cambridge, Mass., 1969.
Raphael, G. *In the Councils of Nations* [Hebrew], Jerusalem, 1982.
Reingold, A. *The Trek to Sharm el Sheikh* [Hebrew], Tel Aviv, 1966.
Robineau, L. "Les Porte-a-faux de L'affaire de Suez", *Revue Historique des Armées*, 4, 1986, pp. 41–50.
Robinson, B.J. *John Foster Dulles: A Biography*, New York, 1957. C. Ryan, *A Bridge Too Far* [Hebrew trans.], Tel Aviv, 1979.
Safran, N. *The Arab-Israeli Conflict, 1948–1967* [Hebrew], Jerusalem, 1969.
Sellers, J.A. "Military Lessons: The British Perspective", in: I. Troen and M. Shemesh (eds), *The Suez-Sinai Crisis 1956, Retrospective and Reappraisal*, London, 1990, pp. 17–53.
Shalev, A. *Co-operation under the Shadow of Confontation* [Hebrew], Tel Aviv, 1989.
Shamir, S. "The Collapse of Project Alpha", in: R. Louis and R. Owen (eds), *Suez 1956: The Crisis and Its Consequences*, Oxford, 1989, pp. 73–102.
Sharett, M. *Personal Diary* [Hebrew], 8 vols, Tel Aviv, 1978.
——. *Political Diary* [Hebrew], vol. 2, Tel Aviv, 1971.
Sharon, A. *Warrior*, New York, 1989.
Shavit, M. *Six Behind Enemy Lines* [Hebrew], Tel Aviv, 1969.
Sheffer, G. "Sharett, Ben-Gurion and an Israeli-Initiated War in 1956", *State, Government, and International Relations* [Hebrew], 27, 1988, pp. 1–27.
Sheffy, Y. "Unconcern at Dawn, Surprise at Sunset: Egyptian Intelligence Appreciation Before the Sinai Campaign", *Intelligence and National Security*, vol. 5, no. 3, July 1990, pp. 7–56.
Shuckburgh, E. *Descent to Suez: Diaries, 1951–1956*, London, 1986.
Steigman, Y. "The Cancellation of the Air Offensive against Egyptian Air Bases in Operation Kadesh", *Ma'arachot* [Hebrew], 306–7, 1986, pp. 12–17.
——. *Operation Kadesh: The Air Force During the Years 1950–1956* [Hebrew], Tel Aviv, 1986.
——. *From the War of Independence to Kadesh: The Air Force from 1949–1956*

[Hebrew], Tel Aviv, 1990.

——. "The Beginnings of the Air Force's Helicopter Branch, 1948–1956", *Cathedra* [Hebrew], 53, 1989, pp. 131–48.

Stephens, R. *Nasser: A Political Biography*, London, 1971.

Stockwell, H. "Suez from the Inside", *Sunday Telegraph*, 30 October 1966.

Syrkin, M. (ed.), *Golda Meir Speaks Out*, London, 1973.

The Suez Canal Conference, London 2–24 Aug 1956, HMSO, CMND 9853.

Tal, D. Israel's Reaction to Infiltrations into Its Territory from Jordan and Egypt, 1949–1956 [Hebrew], M.A. thesis, School of History, Tel Aviv University, April 1990.

Tal, I. "Offensive and Defensive in Israel's Military Campaigns", *Ma'arachot* [Hebrew], 311, 1988, pp. 4–7.

——. "The Theory of National Security: Background and Dynamics", *Ma'arachot* [Hebrew], 253, 1974, pp. 2–9.

Tehan, B. *The Sinai Campaign* [Hebrew], Tel Aviv, 1958.

Teveth, S. *The IDF's Campaign in the Sinai* [Hebrew], Jerusalem and Tel Aviv, 1957.

——. *Moshe Dayan* [Hebrew], Jerusalem and Tel Aviv, 1971.

Thorpe, D.R. *Selwyn Lloyd*, London, 1989.

Tolkovsky, D. *Operation Kadesh: The Air Force's Final Report* [Hebrew], November 1957.

Troen, I. and Shemesh, M. (eds), *The Suez-Sinai Crisis 1956, Retrospective and Reappaisal*, London, 1990.

——. (eds), *Operation Sinai and the Suez Campaign, 1956: A Reappraisal* [Hebrew], Sde Boker, 1994.

Tzavta Report [Hebrew], written by Col. N. Eldar, Israeli liaison officer with French Air Force mission in Israel, November 1956.

Tzur, Y. *Paris Diary* [Hebrew], Tel Aviv, 1968.

UN General Assembly and Security Council Official Records, 1955–1957.

US Foreign Policy: Middle East, US Information Service, Basic Documents, Tel Aviv Embassy, 1950–1973.

Vaisse, M. "France and the Suez Crisis", in: R. Louis and R. Owen (eds), *Suez 1956: The Crisis and Its Consequences*, Oxford, 1989, pp. 131–44.

——. "Post-Suez France", in: R. Louis and R. Owen (eds), *Suez 1956: The Crisis and Its Consequences*, Oxford, 1989, pp. 335–40.

Wallach, Y. *The Carta Atlas of Israel's History: The Early Years* [Hebrew], Jerusalem, 1978.

Weitz, Y. *The Man Who Was Assassinated Twice* [Hebrew], Jerusalem, 1995.

Ya'ari, E. *Egypt and the Fedayeen, 1953–56* [Hebrew], Givat Haviva, 1975.

Yakobowitz, M. (ed.), *"Gulliver", A Man and a Warrior* [Hebrew], Tel Aviv, n.d.

Yaniv, A. *Deterrence Without the Bomb*, Toronto, 1987.

Index